SO-AEW-735

PENGUIN BOOKS

The Saturday Night Special

A native of Georgia, Robert Sherrill was edu-
cated at the University of Texas, where he
later taught English. He has worked for a
number of newspapers, including the Miami
Herâld, the Austin *American-Statesman,* and
the freewheeling *Texas Observer,* of which he
was associate editor. More recently he has
been Washington Correspondent for *The
Nation.* In addition to *The Saturday Night
Special* he is the author of *The Accidental
President,* an irreverent biography of Lyndon
Johnson; *The Drugstore Liberal,* a study of
Hubert Humphrey; *Gothic Politics in the Deep
South; Military Justice Is to Justice as Military
Music Is to Music;* and an unorthodox text-
book entitled *Why They Call It Politics: A
Guide to America's Government.*

Books by Robert Sherrill

Robert Sherrill

The Saturday Night Special and Other Guns

with Which Americans Won the West,
Protected Bootleg Franchises,
Slew Wildlife, Robbed Countless Banks,
Shot Husbands Purposely and by Mistake,
and Killed Presidents—Together with
the Debate over Continuing Same

Illustrated by Julio Fernandez

Penguin Books

Penguin Books Inc, 72 Fifth Avenue,
New York, New York 10011, U.S.A.
Penguin Books Inc, 7110 Ambassador Road,
Baltimore, Maryland 21207, U.S.A.
Penguin Books Ltd, Harmondsworth,
Middlesex, England
Penguin Books Australia Ltd, Ringwood,
Victoria, Australia
Penguin Books Canada Limited, 41 Steelcase Road West,
Markham, Ontario, Canada L3R 1B4
Penguin Books (N.Z.) Ltd, 182–190 Wairau Road,
Auckland 10, New Zealand

First published by Charterhouse, New York, 1973
Published by Penguin Books, 1975

The poem by E. E. Cummings quoted on page 8 is taken
from *Complete Poems 1913–62*, copyright © 1968 by
Marion Morehouse Cummings, and reprinted by permission
of Harcourt Brace Jovanovich, Inc.

The poem by Archibald MacLeish quoted on page 290 is
taken from *Collected Poems 1917–1952*, copyright © 1952 by
Archibald MacLeish, and reprinted by permission of
Houghton Mifflin Company.

To Harvey Shapiro

As we drift outward
The tribal gods wave farewell.

A Prefatory Note

First, a word of warning. Thumbing through a Library of Congress bibliography on gun controls recently, I was flabbergasted to find that, because of assignments from *The Nation* and *The New York Times Magazine*, I had written nearly as much on the subject as anybody around. I hope no one is misled by this quantity. I freely confess right at the outset that everything I have written on the subject of guns and gun controls in the past has been the fruit of well-rooted dilettantism—the same tree, by the way, that dropped this fruit as well. That's a cautionary, pro-consumer statement, not an apology. Next to the war in Vietnam, our political assassinations and urban thuggery have done more to keep us on an unhappy edge than anything else this generation; so violence and the instruments of violence are something that everyone is obliged to think about and come to some ad-hoc conclusions about, which is what I have done in this book—and it is all that I have done. By my opening disclaimer I simply mean that whatever I know about guns has been borrowed from more profound students of the subject and whatever opinions I have on gun controls, being based largely on emotion, fluctuate from day to day and are not very reliable. But what the hell.

If one prefers to read something briefer that covers the subject just about as well, I recommend a portion of the transcript of the broadcast made by Andrew West, a Mutual Broadcasting System correspondent who, witnessing the assassination of Robert Kennedy at close hand, said about that pistol what could be wisely applied to all firearms: "He has fired the shot. . . . He still has the gun, the gun is pointed at me right at this moment. I hope they can get the gun out of his hand. *Be very careful. Get the gun. . . . Get the gun. . . . Get the gun. . . . Stay away from the gun. . . . Stay away from the gun. . . .*"

My very special thanks to Dan Schwarz, Lewis Bergman, Harvey Shapiro, Carey McWilliams, and Ned Chilton for magazine and newspaper assignments that helped my research. Members of the staff of the Senate Juvenile Delinquency Subcommittee as it was made up under the late Senator Thomas Dodd were very helpful, and members of the staff as organized by the present chairman, Senator Birch Bayh, were not at all helpful. Several executives in the gun industry were unusually candid, and the best thanks I can give them is not to mention them by name; I give the same kind of appreciative non-notice to the several NRA officials who somehow escaped the paranoid secretiveness that afflicts that organization generally. It was virtually impossible to get information from the Treasury's Bureau of Alcohol, Tobacco, and Firearms, but one bright exception was Paul H. Westenberger, firearms enforcement officer, who not only answered all my questions with generous expertise but even took me to the Treasury Department's gun range and directed me through an afternoon of firing a variety of Saturday Night Specials. I should add that long before I had ended my study I began to realize that the reason many in the NRA and in the Treasury Department avoided being questioned was not—as I had first thought—solely because they were trying to protect a special interest, but because they were grossly ignorant of the intricacies of the gun world and *could* not answer me. The depth of stupidity that exists in Washington behind the impressive titles is sometimes almost beyond belief.

Congressional aides William Broydrick and Brady Williamson helped force the Library of Congress to divulge some of its secrets to me. My debt to other newsmen and writers, such as Dan Strawn, Homer Ayres, C. C. Tashi, Horace Naismith, and Harry Hartley, is wide and deep and probably not fairly suggested by the number of citations I have within the text; the bibliography lists some to whom I am especially beholden. Richard Kluger was constructively obnoxious, as a vengeful God makes all good editors, I suppose. And of course Mary Sherrill, as always, prevented the book from being any more jerrybuilt than it is: quite a chore for her, since she detests everything about guns.

R.S.
Washington, D.C.
April 1973

Contents

There is a tragic element in the life of every day that is far more real, far more penetrating, far more akin to the true self that is in us, than is the tragedy that lies in great adventure. . . .

—MAETERLINCK

The Saturday Night Special

THE PERFECT
FATHER'S DAY GIFT

"It's all over for the Indians just like it is for the gunfighter," lamented that grand drunken gunslinger Kid Shelleen. " 'Cept they didn't give us no reservation or teach us how to weave rugs. Yeah, it's all over in Dodge. Tombstone too. Cheyenne, Deadwood, all gone. All dead and gone. Pow! Why, the last time I come through Tombstone the biggest excitement there was about the roller-skatin' rink they'd laid out over the O.K. Corral."

If many Americans seem to share Kid's nostalgia, they can be forgiven. Nostalgia is reserved for landmark events that occurred

3

recently enough that the current generation can identify with them, and if Americans feel—as their periodic celebrations of the event would indicate—that they were present at the birth of the gun, they aren't far wrong. Perhaps the most remarkable thing about guns is that, although their basic principle of operation has been known and utilized for at least five hundred years, the gun as a symbol of *efficient* deadliness is a relatively recent phenomenon.*

The musket of Shakespeare's time could not reach an enemy thoughtless enough to stand farther than eighty or ninety yards away. Pirates who stuffed their waistbands with half a dozen single-shot flintlock pistols may have presented a fearsome sight, but all those pistols combined produced no more firepower with far less mobility than is possessed today by an apprentice sidewalk pirate with one five-dollar .22-caliber junk gun. In 1557 Hernando de Soto wrote sullenly that "before a Christian can make a single shot an Indian will discharge three or four arrows and he seldom misses his object." Though guns had improved considerably, the white invader heading west two centuries later found himself at much the same disadvantage. Benjamin Franklin is said to have advised our military leaders at the outset of the Revolution that they should equip the troops with bows and arrows rather than guns—and the generals listened respectfully.

Two full lifetimes would encompass the inventions of the

* It may be that some cosmic thumb was held on the scale to keep gun-design progress down, in balance with medical progress, which was slow indeed. Back in the days when European armies were trying to kill each other with bullets that wouldn't travel the length of a football field, serious physicians were using a gunshot balm concocted from two boiled puppies, whose flesh was then mixed with a pound of boiled earthworms, plus white wine, brandy—and prayer. By the seventeenth century medical knowledge had progressed to the point that when a patient who had been shot in the head was brought to one of the famous physicians of the day, he located the fracture by the sound caused through striking the skull with a cane. Gunshot wounds in the eighteenth century were commonly treated indirectly—which, considering everything, was probably best—with purgative salts and blue pills. For more of this esoterica, see Dr. Theodor Billroth, *Historical Studies on the Nature and Treatment of Gunshot Wounds From the Fifteenth Century to the Present Time* (New Haven: Nathan Smith Medical Club, 1933).

revolver, the repeating rifle, the metallic cartridge, smokeless powder, pump action, bolt action, self-loading, and most of the other firearm perfections that have helped establish the American way of life and have sanctified the names Colt, Winchester, Sharps, Remington, Smith & Wesson, Gatling, Deringer, Thompson, Browning, and Savage. Are any names left out that should be included? Every man to his own faith.

To say that these weapons have helped establish the American way of life is actually too modest a judgment: they are a *part* of America's life, and we respond to and with guns in a very American way. Could any response be more American than that of the two New York youths who shot and killed a storekeeper because they had asked for apple pie and he had offered them Danish pastry instead? Or the husband who shot and killed his wife for being thoughtless enough to run out of gas on the way home? Or the jivey New York youth who shot the discothèque manager who wouldn't sell him a ticket? Or the Maryland host who decided to restore gaiety to his party by shooting the guest who refused to stop arguing with his own wife? Or the Ohio engineer who got tired of hearing the bomb-loaded B-52s flying over his home near Wright-Patterson Air Force Base and used one of his three high-powered rifles to puncture the planes that came near? Or the two motorists in Maryland who ended their little traffic dispute with a pistol and a shotgun, one shot in the leg, the other in the chest; or the New York woman who killed one and wounded two in a gunfight over a parking space; or the Virginia woman who, claiming she was run off the road by another motorist, climbed out of her car with a .38 pistol in hand and dispatched the driver who had irritated her—one year after her husband had been arrested for shooting another motorist in a highway dispute? Shootouts between drivers is becoming so commonplace that someday we will be able to look upon them nonchalantly as a kind of annual twenty-one-thousand-gun salute to the auto industry. And what more beautiful American family scene than this, coming to us via the *Charleston Gazette*: A twenty-three-year-old West Virginia man painstakingly shows his two-year-old son how to hold the .22-caliber pistol and how to pull the trigger—"Now, son, pull!"—and "deputies reported Mrs. V—— as saying she heard the crack of the pistol and turned around to find her husband had been shot." Well, yes, dead in fact. The little rascal. What speaks more eloquently of rootless America than the Californian who expressed his irritation toward his Glendale landlady by shooting her with a six-foot-long German antitank weapon? Seeing a parked motorist discard a crumpled cigaret package on his front lawn, a Washington, D. C., suburbanite picked up the rifle he always kept handy at the front door and shot him dead. What other nation's environmental movement could inspire such zeal?

Where but in this marvelous showplace of capitalism would a political assassin plan to say with wry gladiatorial intimacy, as Arthur Bremer tells us he planned to remark to George Wallace after filling him with .38 slugs, "A penny for your thoughts"? Where but in this sprawling land, filled with wonderful, recalcitrant misfits who fled other countries seeking the wide-open spaces of anarchy, would you find twenty thousand state and local gun-control laws that are mostly ignored with impunity? Where but in America, with its reverence for education, would a college youth who shotgunned to death a newsboy, without cause, be punished only by being required to write a theme on "The Reverence of Life" and to serve a summer jail term that would end in time to allow him to start the fall semester? Indeed, we hold education so dear that we are ready to fight for it from a very early age; at least that is one interpretation that can be put on the recent shakedown of Baltimore students that yielded one hundred twenty-five handguns, and the casual and incomplete shakedown in Los Angeles schools that yielded forty guns in one month alone. (Yes, the L.A. kids are not afraid to use them, as was proved at the homecoming parade at Jefferson High School that left five students, including the homecoming princess, wounded.) "RICHMOND, VA. (AP)—A 17-year-old boy was killed and a 14-year-old girl wounded early today when caught in the crossfire of a gun battle between two youths in a corridor of a Richmond high school." In one month San Francisco high schools expelled four students, three of them girls, for carrying guns. Armed patrols for school hallways is a growth industry. In some of the livelier school jurisdictions, teachers and principals consider a handgun to be as much a part of their equipment as nineteenth-century teachers considered the hickory stick.

Where else among the major nations of the world (and even most banana republics) does justice come equipped not only with scales but with pistols as well? In a recent survey of the judicial environment, *Newsweek* found "quite a few" judges "packing guns themselves" and others hiring armed bodyguards or protecting themselves from armed attacks by putting up armor-plated or bulletproof shields around their benches.

And in what other national legislature would it seem quite natural for an eighty-seven-year-old politician (ex-sheriff turned U.S. Senator, Carl Hayden) to shuffle into a hearing on gun controls, grab a .45 Colt exhibit from the witness table, yell "Who shall I shoot?!" and start waving it around the room, pointing it first at one of his colleagues and then another (while they tried to pretend they were ducking merely as part of the gag). Our state legislators come just as well equipped and just as naturally inclined to the dramatic, as was seen in the Georgia legislature during a debate on the proper punishment for rapists when one lawmaker whipped out a pistol, waved it around the crowded chamber before coming to focus on one of his colleagues and shrieking "I could kill him!" (He didn't.)

Given the prevailing atmosphere, nobody in Washington seemed to think it very queer that Secretary of Labor Peter Brennan got deputized as a U.S. marshal so that the pearl-handled revolver that had been his constant companion for years when he was living in New York could be legally carried into any state, or that it was odd for him to hire five armed guards (costing the taxpayer $60,000) to protect his office. After all, a bureaucrat can't be too careful.

Only an American President would—as Richard Nixon on the day he announced his opposition to new controls on the sale of handguns—call for federal legislation to provide $50,000 to the family of any policeman slain in the line of duty (about six hundred having been slain, by handguns, during the past decade).

We have flattered ourselves in pretending that the gun-control debate in this country is based on philosophical differences. We like to think that we hang on to our guns and buy more, and then more, because of our "frontier heritage" or because, as one Texas historian wrote for a government publication, "a boy still becomes a man, usually on his birthday or at Christmas, when his father gives him a gun [and] in his gun ownership he is following a tradition that goes back to John Smith and Jamestown and has persisted ever since." Or we like to talk about how, by God, nobody's going to come into our homes and rape our wives. Such convictions do have a profound influence on the debate, of course, but they are not the biggest obstacle to establishing reasonable gun controls. The individual emotions wrapped up in gun-ownership could be dissipated. Plinking at tin cans can get extremely boring. Waiting for the burglar who never arrives will ultimately make any man feel foolish. Owning a gun just because Daddy owned one is not the most persuasive argument in an increasingly sophisticated society. Arming for bear in a city that supports only rats and mice would strike most people as nonsensical. The tradition that was made at Jamestown can be unmade, in time, in New York City.

But none of these changes will happen—none can happen—because of one insurmountable hurdle: the money in guns and ammunition and all the concomitant services and auxiliary equipment.

> (for man is enslaved by a dread dizziz
> and the sooner it's over the sooner to biz
> don't ask me what it's pliz)*

* From E. E. Cummings, "XII," in *One by One* (New York: Harcourt, Brace, 1944).

The firearms economy is almost impossible to escape. Even the most conscientious reformers occasionally trip over one of its insidious roots. In the same issue of *The New York Times Magazine* that carried an article deploring the existence of the inexpensive handgun called the Saturday Night Special there was, oops, a two-page Sabena airlines advertisement detailing "Seven reasons to start your trip in beautiful Belgium," Reason Number 2 being ". . . firearms. All beautiful bargains"—which is to say, transatlantic Saturday Night Specials.

It's a very big business, big enough to prevent the rest of us from coming to terms with each other. Gun owners spend an estimated $2 billion a year, at the minimum, on this business— quite enough money to keep Congress and all state legislatures apprised of the desires of the gun and ammunition manufacturers, retail gun dealers, sports-clothes manufacturers, gun-magazine publishers, antique-gun dealers, hunting-resort owners, and "conservation" groups who get a kickback from ammunition sales. At bottom, it isn't tradition but trade that controls this issue.

There's a bright side to it. The trade does have a lilt. Madison Avenue responds with all its heart: a military surplus submachine gun offered for sale as "The Perfect Father's Day Gift"; an imported Persian Mauser Carbine peddled with a wink and the guarantee, "The Shah himself test-fired each gun"; a Beretta automatic pistol recommended to suburbanites of Peoria and Pasadena as "the choice of soldiers of fortune everywhere." In the good old pre-1968 Gun Control Act days, when only money stood between the citizen and his own private war, perhaps the acme of advertising was reached by the Service Armament Co., of Ridgefield, New Jersey: "U.S. 60mm Morter [*sic*] complete with bipod and base plate etc. An ideal item for your den or front lawn. Can be easily packed into trunk of any automobile. This is the perfect tool for 'getting even' with those neighbors you don't like. Perfect for demolishing houses or for back yard plinking on Sunday afternoon."

Since we already have many millions of guns on hand, it isn't always easy to figure out what to do with the 5 million new guns that come off the proud U.S. assembly lines each year for civilian consumption, but somehow we do make a place for them. We find them very useful, tucked into the night-table drawer for security (though it is said by such spoilsports as the National Commission on the Causes and Prevention of Violence that householders succeed in shooting home robbers less than 2 percent of the time and home burglars less than .2 percent of the time)* or tucked into the belt (the famous sawed-off "belly gun," which is accurate for no more than two feet, but, after all, most tavern brawls are decided on playing fields no broader than that). We use them to conclude dreary marriages with much more passion than the marriages ever knew in their most romantic moments; the Houston real estate executive who pumped twenty-four bullets into his wife was giving her more attention than she was accustomed to receiving.

Even the swells among us have learned that firepower is the only sure route to peace of mind. *New York Times* writer Eric Pace caught this mood vividly when he told of how people were responding to the stickups and violence in one area of New York City:

> It was a fine summer's day, and the two garment district executives were carefully decked out for their noonday stroll along Eighth Avenue. S. Irene Johns, the honorary president of the American Woman Buyers Club, wore a pastel frock and a big-rimmed sailor hat. Edward A. O'Donnell, a restauranteur who is active in neighborhood affairs, chose a mod suit and a .38-caliber Colt Cobra revolver with a blued steel finish. With them on their promenade was Martin Newman, a coat manufacturer who had selected a classic singlebreasted suit and a .38-caliber Colt Detective Special revolver. . . . Around the corner on West 40th Street, Leonard Weiss, a garage

---

* The best explanation of the difference between a home robbery and a home burglary was given recently by a Los Angeles lawyer who caught a thief in her home with his pockets full of her jewelry. "So far," she told him, "this is only a burglary. If you point or use that gun, it's a robbery." Thoroughly confused, he fled. Robbery carries a harsher sentence.

owner, said . . . 'There's hardly a night goes by that we don't have a mugging around here. It's hard to get men to work late at night. They're scared and I don't blame them.' Mr. Weiss is a casual dresser, but he carries a .38-caliber Smith & Wesson Chief revolver with a stainless steel finish.*

And, to mention the most important of the many other uses of the firearm in America, the gun of course provides the prime requisite for our most profitable industry: crime. To be sure, white-collar crime does not depend on it, but in a democracy it is fitting that a trade be open to the lowest as well as to the highest, and without the gun the underprivileged would be cut out of much crime that now profits it. As an inmate of the Joliet penitentiary, a former stickup artist, explained with impressive simplicity to a visiting reporter, "With a gun in your hand, it's a little bit more easier to control the situation, no matter grocery store, bank, or what it is. I mean, you can't go in with a broomstick and secure any authority for an armed robbery."

Unfortunately, there are always some people who become too greedy or somehow excessive in their gun-ownership; this is a fault that can be found across the sanguine spectrum, from policemen to gangsters. Albert Lee Nussbaum, the bank robber of the early 1960s, was certainly showing conspicuous consumption when he was caught with several submachine guns, seventeen revolvers, an automatic carbine rifle, an antitank gun, two dozen hand grenades, four bulletproof vests, and several thousand rounds of ammunition. Consider, too, the excesses of those folk heroes, Wild Bill Hickok, Jesse James, and John Dillinger. Hickok walked the streets of Abilene as the city's law enforcement officer with an ostentatious show of armaments: a pair of six-guns on his hips, strapped down in the gunfighter's style, a pair of .41 derringers in his side pockets, and either a shotgun or a repeating rifle cradled in the crook of his arm. Not to mention the Bowie knife in his belt.

When Jesse James was called to his reward at the age of

---

* *The New York Times*, July 30, 1972.

thirty-four years, six months, and twenty-eight days, he left a widow and a personal arsenal of one .45-caliber Colt, one .45-caliber Smith & Wesson, one .44-caliber derringer pistol, one Winchester rifle, and one double-barreled shotgun, make unknown. That made him almost as much a menace as the modern cop. When author Garry Wills poked inside a Philadelphia police stakeout car, he found as *standard* equipment: one Thompson submachine gun, three rifles, two shotguns, 1305 rounds of ammunition, not to mention an assortment of bulletproof vests, riot shields, riot clubs—and, of course, the officers' regulation handguns.

Though Dillinger's personal firearms were usually mixed in with his gang's armaments and therefore there was no way to be certain about them, authorities believe they included a Thompson submachine gun, a machine pistol, a 1917 Colt .45 revolver, a Colt .380 automatic, a Colt government .45 automatic, and a converted Winchester rifle-machine gun with silencer. Apparently this was standard equipment for the times, for Will Irwin, a chronicler of gangsterdom, told the readers of *Liberty* magazine in 1935 that

> the armament of the well dressed bank robber includes two .45 automatic pistols, a little .25 "rod" as a reserve in case the police begin to search him, a sawed-off shotgun, an automatic rifle and a submachine gun. To this they have been adding of late the murderous European-made twenty-shot automatic pistols—the weapon which killed the King of Yugoslavia and the Foreign Minister of France. Here again the police have staggered along at a disadvantage. The average town constable or country sheriff has no weapons except revolvers and automatics.*

Well, let's not worry about town constables and country sheriffs who could uphold the law no better with a Gatling gun than they could with a crossbow. What is worrisome is that there does sometimes get to be an imbalance in the distribution of guns in America.

---

* "Our New Civil War," *Liberty*, Jan. 12, 1935.

Some contend that peaceful citizens are at the mercy of gun abusers because there are so many guns available and because it is so easy to obtain a weapon if one is not immediately available. Where there is a will, there is a weapon. Just how many guns are floating around the country is anybody's guess; "experts" have appeared before Congressional committees in recent years to estimate everything up to 200 million guns, or about one per person for the entire population. The National Commission on the Causes and Prevention of Violence guessed 90 million in 1969. It's a guessing game that depends very much on the mood: shortly after John Kennedy's assassination a writer for *The Reporter* magazine got carried away and estimated one *billion* guns in America.

In any event, there are apparently enough firearms to keep things rather lively. About twenty thousand Americans are killed with guns (homicide, suicide, accident) each year. The firearms homicide rate in the United States is reportedly thirty-five times higher than the rate in Germany or in England. In 1970 three people were killed with handguns in Tokyo, while in New York City, which is not as large as Tokyo, five hundred persons were shot to death. In a typical year guns will be used to commit 120,000 robberies. All of this is regrettable, of course, but if one puts morality aside for the moment, much can be said for the superiority of firearms for certain missions. Two barrels of 00 buckshot in the mouth—which would guarantee the removal of the entire back of the head, as well as much of the ceiling—comprise a much quicker and more humane method for suicide than, say, a bottle of rat poison. Guns are obviously the most efficient method for assassination: no American President has ever been stabbed or clubbed to death. Rifles, of course, are de rigueur for firing the twenty-one-gun salute at Presidential funerals; they might be put to more appropriate service, perhaps, if the salute entailed shooting the late Chief Executive's twenty-one worst advisers in a graveside ceremony— something like burying a fallen Indian chief's horse and dog with him. And although many people still prefer the knife, guns are at least an equally sound way for letting off steam. When New York

City, irritated by the heat wave, set a new murder record (fifty-seven) for a one-week period, July 16–22, 1972, it was found that while the traditionalists used knives for twenty-six of the jobs, the modernists used guns to account for twenty-four (and then, of course, there are always those who insist on something exotic: an eighteen-month-old baby was thrown out of a window, and another of the victims was set on fire).

Partly because of such spirited outbursts among the citizenry, some opinion-shapers have sought sharp restrictions on the availability of guns. The U.S. Conference of Mayors in 1972, following the recommendations of Mayors Richard J. Daley and Roman S. Gribbs—from two of the most bulletmarked cities in America, Chicago and Detroit—urged national legislation against the manufacture, importation, sale, and private possession of handguns. The chiefs of police of several large cities—though certainly not all large cities—have joined the mayors and a majority of the National Commission on Reform of Federal Criminal Laws in demanding a total prohibition on the ownership of handguns. The only exceptions to the proposed ban would be military personnel, policemen, and sportsmen's clubs.

The likelihood of this ban ever being put into effect does not appear to be strong, to say the least. When Senator Philip Hart of Michigan gave the Senate an opportunity to approve just such a ban on August 8, 1972, his colleagues rebuffed the proposal by a majority that would have made the old bones of Hickok rattle in glee: 83 to 7. And when Massachusetts Senator Edward M. Kennedy proposed a few minutes later that the Senate at least pass a law that would enable the government to find out who has the guns, by requiring that all firearms—rifles and shotguns as well as handguns—be registered, and that no one be permitted to own a gun without a federal permit, the greatest deliberative body in the world said "No, no" almost as firmly: 78 to 11. It was, after all, an election year, and the owners of those 200 million guns might not appreciate being put to the trouble of registering.

The fever of reform comes only in spurts in this country, and cools swiftly. In 1971 the National League of Cities, an organization representing fifteen thousand municipalities, advocated federal laws prohibiting interstate sale of all firearms to individuals and mandating a minimum ten-year sentence for the use of a firearm in any federal, state, or local crime. But the very next year it withdrew this advocacy and by a lopsided margin voted down a substitute resolution calling for national legislation to prohibit the manufacture, importation, sale, and private possession of handguns—in short, the Hart bill. Apparently the smaller cities, which predominate in this organization, had lost sympathy with the gun problems of their big brothers.

But whether these defeats in municipal organizations and in the U.S. Congress—not the first defeats of this kind and certainly not likely to prove the last—were intolerable for the future of civilization is highly debatable.

For my part, I am not against guns; in fact, I am quite fond of a certain type of gun—the fondness growing out of early experiences.

The only well-known gunman who ever lived in my hometown, Sweetwater, Texas, was Bat Masterson. He didn't stay long but he did stay long enough to get into a gunfight with a soldier over a dancehall girl—the outcome being a dead soldier, a dead dancehall girl, and a wounded Masterson. This was one of the few times Masterson's aim was good enough to kill an opponent. He was actually a rotten shot, which is probably why he preferred to hit people over the head with a billiard cue when subduing them in his occasional role as a "peace" officer.

I feel a real affinity for Masterson because I was always a rotten shot too. My first gun was a single-shot .22 rifle which I inherited from my brother when he went off to sea. I took it up as a way to kill boredom more than anything else. Young people are not likely to be bored, no matter where they live, but life in Sweetwater was a little too dreary at times to permit youth's natural enthusiasm to prevail, so I used the .22 as a handy way to while away some of the dull, dry, windblown West Texas days, roaming the scrubbled fields at the outskirts of town to hunt rabbits. A single-shot .22 is certainly not the best weapon for hunting rabbits unless the hunter is far more accurate than I was. If I ever hit one, I don't remember it. I do remember spending one whole afternoon shooting at a waterbird sitting in the middle of a small lake; I never came close enough to ruffle its feathers.

My graduation to an Army-issue rifle came when I joined the Sweetwater National Guard, a show of patriotism that was motivated entirely by money. I was several years too young to sign up legally, but I was big for my age and in those Depression days one didn't mind telling any lie to get the one dollar we were paid per drill.

My next encounter with a gun, this time at the wrong end, came two years later. Working as a copyboy at the *Fort Worth Press* for ten dollars a week, a typically generous salary for the Scripps-Howard newspaper chain, I lived alone in a flophouse near the railroad yards. Returning home one night rather late, I was accosted by several young men who wanted my money, which, though they didn't know it, amounted at the moment to one twenty-five-cent piece. When I fought back, I discovered that the youth standing behind me not only had a pistol but was busy pulling the trigger, trying to make it fire. At about the third click of the hammer, I started running. A few hours later the young men were captured in an attempted holdup of an all-night grocery store, and the police found my would-be assassin still packing the little handgun containing five bullets—duds, as I had already learned—all showing hammer marks.

I was one bullet luckier than Wild Bill Hickok, who, at the age of thirty-nine, while playing cards in Saloon Number Ten on the main street of Deadwood, Dakota Territory, was shot by Jack McCall, a drifter. The instrument was a Colt. That one bullet was sufficient to blow a hole in the back of Hickok's head large enough to hide a playing card in; the bullet went its merry way through his head, out the front, tearing off his cheek, and thence to the left forearm of one Captain Massey, a riverboat pilot, who was holding a hand in the card game. Massey's arm was broken by the bullet. Wild Bill's hand contained a pair of aces and a pair of eights, a combination which has ever since been known as "the dead man's hand"—signifying bad luck, as indeed it had every right to signify, for it was later discovered that that particular bullet was the only one in McCall's gun that wasn't a dud.

There is no reason to detail more of this recollected trivia, for the only point that I wish to make is that I too have found the use of guns from time to time to be an instructive adventure, from which I concluded at a rather early age that the very best kinds of guns are those that can kill neither rabbits nor birds nor copyboys. And ammunition that will not go off is the very best kind, as President Andrew Jackson also discovered when confronted by an assassin with two guns, *both,* as it turned out, loaded with duds.

Indeed, I would be delighted if the capabilities of the gun had never developed beyond those of the pleasant military shooting irons whose effect or noneffect was described by W. W. Greener in his classic, *The Gun and Its Development*:

> At the battle of Salamanca only 8,000 men were put *hors de combat,* although 3,500,000 cartridges were fired, not including the 6,000 cannon balls (besides which there were cavalry charges and hand-to-hand engagements), so that it is estimated that only one musket-ball in 437 took effect. . . . In 1859 Colonel Wilford stated in a lecture at the United States Institution that during a single engagement in the Caffre War 80,000 cartridges were fired and only 25 of the enemy fell! In the Crimean War the French fired away 25,000,000 cartridges, and certainly did not hit 25,000 men, and the [London] *Times*, about the same period says, 'We believe the calculation used to be one bullet in 250 carried death; and that estimate is probably not far from the truth.' In 1838 a series of experiments were undertaken by the officers of the Royal Engineers to ascertain the real properties of the Service musket, with the result that they instructed the soldier to aim 130 feet above a man at 600 yards if they wished to hit him! *

---

* (Longman, Rees, Orme, Brown, Green and Longman, ninth edition, 1910). Reprinted by Bonanza Books.

But my favorite quality of gun (inaccurate) and my favorite quality of marksmanship (same) are not the qualities most admired by such American corporations as DuPont (owners of Remington) or Olin Corp. (owners of Winchester-Western) or by the American public generally, and in fact we are moving farther and farther from my ideals all the time. Perhaps the right solution is in the opposite direction: instead of less firepower, more. I keep an open mind to such suggestions.

Recently one of our more profound writers, Art Buchwald, suggested that the balance of terror that has worked so well in foreign affairs should be tried at home. "Unless everyone in America owns a handgun there will never be peace in this country"—a goal which was altogether reasonable, for "no country in the world offers its citizens a greater choice of guns than the United States." Buchwald notes:

> There are snub-nosed guns that can fit in a woman's handbag, semi-automatics that fire eight slugs at a time, .38s that can hit someone at 50 feet, .45s that can make holes as large as a fist, and very light .22s that a six-year-old can fire.
> We are blessed because anyone in America can have the gun of his choice at a price he can afford. For those who are on relief and unemployed the government could supply surplus weapons from the armed forces at the same time they give out food stamps and unemployment checks.
> There is absolutely no reason why everyone in this country could not be armed by 1973.*

Why not arm everyone? It's the only proposal that was not seriously made during the Great Gun-Control Debate in Congress during the last decade, and considering the categorical bilge, historical cant, bogus piety, and flimsy sociology that accompanied· most other suggestions, it would seem to be at least a refreshing alternative.

It has been the most remarkable Congressional debate of

* *Washington Post*, May 23, 1972.

modern time. On no other recent legislative question has so much passion been spent, with so little effect. Drawing its heat and its momentum from a singular series of assassinations and riots crowding into the years from 1963 to 1972, the debate over who should be allowed to buy guns, and how, has taken us almost nowhere. There are probably 50 million more guns loose in the land today than there were on the day President Kennedy was assassinated in 1963—an event which most people thought would bring about rigorous gun controls almost immediately. And although there were a few restrictions put on the sale of guns by legislation passed in 1968—the first gun-control law passed by Congress in thirty years—generally speaking, the traffic in guns is no more restrained for either criminals or law-abiding citizens than it has ever been.

DEPARTMENT OF GOOD RIDDANCE

The movement to control guns and to crack down on the gunrunners has whipped those on the "reform" side into such a lather that they often forget to look on the bright side of homicide.

Although America's record of gun abuse is much more excessive than that of any other modern nation, there does seem to be a built-in ceiling to our bloodthirstiness—a ceiling that, in fact, for many years did not go up nearly as fast as the growth of the general population. Given the fact that we *are* gun nuts, there is still reason to boast that we are not visibly—using the number of dried bloodspots on the pavement as our measurement—getting much nuttier.

The United States is said to be the greatest gun-toting nation in the world. It has the reputation of there being more murders committed in its boundaries annually than in all the countries of Europe combined, and most of those crimes are committed with guns. It is said that there is one murder committed in this country every forty minutes, and over nine thousand each year. . . . Seemingly, the pistol is one of the most popular playthings in America today.

From the preceding passage we can infer that things are getting no worse, if no better. The comment was made *not* in 1973 but in 1929 by the New York State Crime Commission.* The annual number of murders in the United States, though the population has nearly doubled, was until 1968 still about the same as forty-three years ago.

Not that any of our "official" statistics are accurate: our leaders came late and grudgingly to count the civilian dead and wounded. The New York State Crime Commission used "It is said" before the murder count to indicate its awareness that the statistic was a guess. The official guessing today is not much better.

The National Center for Health Statistics ran its first nation-wide count of firearm homicides, suicides, and accidents in 1933. It found there were 7,863 gun slayings, 7,798 gun suicides, and 3,026 accidental gun deaths. At that time there were about 123 million people in this country. Two years later the number in every category dropped—to 6,506 slayings, 6,830 suicides, and 2,854 accidental deaths—and except for the number of suicides, which in 1956 rose above the 1933 level and has continued to rise ever since, gun deaths remained below the 1933 level until 1967, even though there were about 75 million more people living in the United States, their lives were more hectic and conducive to violence, and many more guns were available. Indeed, in 1951 and in 1955, when the population was roughly 25 percent greater than in 1933, there were only half as many reported homicides (3,898 in 1951; 3,807 in 1955). The same dropoff was noticed in the war years 1943 and 1944, when so many Americans with a yen to kill somebody could

---

* Baumes Crime Commission, 1929 Annual Report. Quoted in Report by the New York State Commission of Investigation Concerning Pistol Licensing Laws and Procedures in New York State, 1967, p. 7.

do so legally on other soil and did not feel the need to take out their pique on fellow citizens. There were only 3,444 homicides in 1943 and 3,449 in 1944—which also suggests that in times when violence is in the air and life is held to be cheaper than normal, the mood does not necessarily translate itself into mayhem.

Having indulged in that flurry of mild optimism about our sanity, one must add that between 1966 and 1967 there was a startling increase in homicides—an increase of more than 20 percent—from 6,855 to 8,332 (with suicides rising slightly to 10,550 and accidents rising to 2,896); and the number of gun slayings in 1968 was about 35 percent higher than in 1966—up to 9,425 (suicides up to 10,911, and accidents down to 2,394).

With its usual dinosaurian nimbleness, the National Center has been unable to produce a compilation more recent than 1968, so we must switch to FBI figures. They show about 11,500 gun homicides for 1971, a jump of a bit more than 20 percent over the Center's 1968 figures. So it appears that the pile of gun bodies that began in 1966 to move higher for the first time in forty years will continue to do so.

The slogan that FDR liked to apply to economics in the 1930s—that all we had to fear was fear itself—could also have been said at that time about America's gun habits, and it would have applied until the mid-1960s. But at that point, the statistics tell us, something uglier began to happen. Unfortunately, they don't tell us why. Assuming there are 200 million guns in America today, there must have been nearly that many—give or take 25 or 30 million— at the time the trend started sharply up. It seems unlikely that the fractional difference in quantity could have triggered what happened. The National Commission on the Causes and Prevention of Violence says 10 million firearms on the average were added to our civilian stockpile during each of the first five decades of this century (again, this is just their conservative guess), but that an estimated 30 million came into civilian hands between 1958 and 1968. The 1960s saw a doubling of the sales of rifles and shotguns and a quadrupling of the sales of handguns. Between 1966 and

1971 handgun murders jumped 87 percent. Doubtless there's some connection between the rise in crime and the increase in gun sales, but there is no way to know to what extent the teetering mound of new arms causes crime and to what extent it is simply there as a defensive response. After any serious riot gun sales are said to jump fourfold in that locale.

In any event, even granting that there is a direct relationship between the booming gun market and the booming undertaker business, some of it might be best seen *not* starkly as crime and violence but as a natural physical and psychological response. Perhaps, like the experimental rats that respond to overcrowded conditions by ad-hoc cannibalism, urban-packed Americans have simply decided it is time to help accelerate the natural thinning-out process. Or perhaps, taking a page from Claude Bernard's medical notebook, we can assume that while guns, like germs, are about us in ample numbers to effect a wipeout at all times, their plague-scale deadliness must await some disturbance in society's *milieu intérieur*.

Anyway, before laying too much weight by the annual number of gun homicides, we should, in this already overpopulated world, fairly ask ourselves if the typical victim of gunfire cannot be spared.

In many of our larger cities, for example, there are promising wars going on now between the oldtimey underworld, of which "Whitey" was for long kingpin, and the growing and already powerful web of black underworld bosses. What Nicholas Gage once wrote about Mafia attitudes—"The only effective means for change is the gun"—applies equally to the transfer of control along racial lines in our blackened urban centers.

The fighting is especially hard and bitter over domination of the drug market. Detroit authorities estimate that probably one out of every six or seven murders there is connected with the competition of forces in the drug trade, catering to an estimated forty thousand addicts in that city alone. "War" is no exaggeration at all. Police recently found seventeen pistols and twenty-seven rifles and shotguns in one "dope dispensary" and they know there are hundreds of underworld drug houses equally armed all over the city. The price for an assassination in Detroit is reportedly $200—a mere trifle to the dozens of successful drug dealers. Detroit crime, especially in the sprawling black sections of the city, is obviously out of control and police have all but given up. In those conditions, even a hundred gun deaths from underworld feuding is a very great social leap forward.

Much the same situation exists in Gary, Indiana. The long-established mobsters whose ethnic ties go back to Chicago are being challenged by a coalition of ambitious black street gangs who call themselves, with mimicry typical of social climbers, "The Family." The old underworld gangs were employing blacks to do their drug pushing for them, but The Family apparently felt that since 54 percent of Gary's population is black, the drug pushing management should be more heavily integrated. Instead of going to EEOC for help, however, The Family simply pushed in to take over by force. The mob struck back. Within a few days twenty-two bullet-perforated bodies were strewn about the alleys, streets, and sidewalks of Gary. Expressing the usual city hall sorrow over such litter, Mayor Richard G. Hatcher said that "local police simply can't do it all by themselves"—that is, control the drug traffic. Quite true; the warring hoodlums were doing what his police were incapable of doing: controlling one another. Twenty-two murders is a very good beginning.

In a similar dispute over how they were going to cut up the drug market at three housing projects, St. Louis hoodlums wounded at least three dozen of one another and killed at least six, mostly via guns, in 1972 alone. And along the Mexican border, where our Customs officers are showing their usual inability to stop anything but a crippled wetback, help has come in the form of an underworld war between a dozen Mexican gangs in and around Nuevo Laredo as they fight for control of the drug export business; in the past two years, they have killed off a hundred of one another.

In mid-1973 the dope war had spread to San Antonio, where Fred Gomez Carrasco, better known as Don Ramon, wiped out half a dozen pushers who had tried to muscle in on his business;

earlier, on the other side of the border he had by his own count taken care of forty-eight competitors, arguing his position with a .38 in one hand and a .45 in the other. Narcotics agents were doing all they could to stay out of his way and be grateful, for, as one of them put it, "You might say he hasn't killed anybody we couldn't do without."

It may be foolish to shape our hopes around the possibility that a well-armed underworld will thin itself out; but defended only by an impotent and immoral police, one begins to entertain desperately silly ideas. On the other hand, perhaps the hope is not entirely silly. In eight major gang wars over the past half century, the Mafia's strength has been so diluted that reportedly it is having to import a new generation from the old country to supply fresh fiber for its heart and thicken its blood. When the Mafia first moved into Chicago by removing the Irish gang leader Dion O'Banion with two bullets in his chest, two through his throat, another in his face, and a sixth in his brain, it launched a Chicago gang war that took nearly five hundred lives. What an abundant harvest of crooks—a gift that all the courts and police of Chicago could not give the citizenry in a hundred years.

No other weapon could have handled the Mafia wars, not rocks or crossbows or brass knuckles. The assassins of Don Salvatore Maranzano tried to put him away with knives, simply to avoid noise, but after stabbing him six times without total success, they ultimately had to get out their revolvers to finish the job. To the fine guncraftsmen of New England we must pay homage for many of the other scores: Guiseppe (Joe the Boss) Masseria, six shots in the back; Albert Anastasia, blown out of a barber chair by five gunmen's concert of bullets; Joe Colombo, superannuated by three shots in the back of the head; Joe Gallo, his birthday dinner interrupted permanently by three bullets, two in the chest, one in the throat—on and on, an almost endless list of worthy deaths, sometimes so many there was no listing them except in mass-grave fashion: sixty dead in the Castellammarese War, forty dead in that twenty-four-hour period immortalized as the "Night of the Sicilian

Vespers"; a dozen in the Gallo-Profaci War; a dozen in the Bonanno War; ten in the Colombo-Gallo War. It was something the police would not do; we had to depend on our godfathers to work on themselves, and for that purpose they fortunately were not bothered by gun-control laws—of the thirty-five New York State residents attending the notorious Apalachin crime convention, twelve held legal New York State pistol permits.

Moving to a pettier, but more pervasive, level of organized crime—the street gang—we once again find that self-destruction is one of society's principal sources of hope. Indeed, the brightest side of youth's violence is that they practice so much of it on one another. One must also credit the young gangsters with a high degree of ingenuity in devising ways to kill their colleagues. To hear the Deputy Commissioner in Charge of Youth Development for the New York Police Department itemize the weapons collected from street gangs is like listening to a *March of Time* documentary of the advances of military man since medieval times: "This [he is demonstrating] is a slung shot, a round brass ball, approximately an inch or an inch and a half in diameter, which resulted in a fractured skull. This is another slung shot, a sixteen-ounce sinker bound to a wire. This is a garrison belt studded with nuts and bolts. Hit somebody with that and you can make jelly of their scalp. Here's another ingenious weapon, an industrial conveyor belt, leather, into which are mounted thousands of razor-sharp, tiny blades. You can literally skin somebody with that. Then we have the crude zip gun, using adhesive tape to mount a radio aerial on a block of wood: the aerial is the gun barrel, a door latch is the firing pin. A little more sophisticated is this double-barreled zip gun. I have even seen one which was swivel-barreled."

A swivel-barreled zip gun. By God, who says our young men are lazy or dull! They have also done marvelous things with the innocent starter pistol, built to use only blanks and so harmless it can legally be sent through the mail. With deftness they have made it lethal by several means. Most ingenious of all, the young mobster can bore a small hole in the barrel, cover the gas port with a piece of chewing gum to compress the gas emitted by the firing of the blank shell, and place a phonograph needle or a small sliver of steel inside the gun to serve as ammunition. BB pellets work very well. Police say the pressure exerted in this way is quite ample to drive the homespun missile deep into a telephone directory—or a man's skull.

Still, though such devices are clever and though they served our lads very well in the comparatively primitive 1950s and early 1960s, such guns would not be adequate to do the job demanded today. Like developing nations that buy arms from the Pentagon in an effort to rise above the banana republic level, our slum youths are buying higher status too. Are they to be congratulated? "There is scarcely a gang in the Bronx that cannot muster a factory-made piece for every member—at the very least, a .22 caliber pistol, but quite often heavier stuff: .32s, .38s, and .45s, shotguns, rifles and—I have seen them myself—even machine guns, grenades, and gelignite, an explosive," Gene Weingarten writes in *New York* magazine, with the additional progress report that the older gangs, such as the Black Panthers, are helping the young gangs to destroy themselves by peddling guns and ammunition to them.

To be sure, the youngsters are not making as efficient use of this equipment as one might hope. Martin Tolchin of *The New York Times* says the South Bronx gangs claim a membership of ninety-five hundred, mostly Puerto Rican waifs, and in 1972 they knocked off no more than a couple dozen of one another. Black leaders like to pretend that the ultimate source of all Negro problems is the profit motive burning in the bosom of Whitey— "Blacks are killing their brothers and sisters in the service of the white men who control the narcotics traffic in this country," complained Gary's Mayor Hatcher, neatly ignoring the facts—but more and more it is the profiteering black gunrunners on whom we must depend to depopulate the slums, as in Philadelphia, where in the last four years there have been more than a hundred and eighty-six recorded gun deaths among the estimated seven thousand teen-age street gang members, 90 percent of whom are black.

Gathering the news from city to city, we see that it comes to only a small inroad, to be sure, but if the easy availability of the handgun to the young gangster can rid us of even a few hundred a year across this bright land, perhaps we should be grateful to the gun market's availability to the Reapers, the Ching-a-ling Nomads, the Young Sinners, the Javelins, the Black Assassins, and all their cousins.

It may be difficult to find a bright side to all this, but there seem to be flashes in the gloom. For one thing, you can thank the gat for giving the slum kid a chance to achieve status. So say some sociologists. The gat is the great elevator, or the great leveler, depending on your perspective. Writing in *The Annals of the American Academy of Political and Social Science* on "Some Social Functions of Violence," Professor Lewis Coser observes:

> In the area of Violence . . . the vaunted equal opportunity, which had been experienced as a sham and a lure everywhere else, turns out to be effective. In the wilderness of cities, just as in the wilderness of the frontier, the gun becomes an effective equalizer. Within the status structure of the gang, through a true transvaluation of middle-class values, success in defense of the "turf" brings deference and "rep" which are unavailable anywhere else. Here the successful exercise of violence is a road to achievement.*

Did it give some satisfaction to Anthony Cammareri, age twenty-two, to realize, in that last flash of thought, that by being shot with a .22-caliber Saturday Night Special and killed at his bachelor party (once in the back, once in the face, once in the leg), he had at least given some "rep" to his twenty-four-year-old assailant, whose reason for seeking "rep" was, as he later explained to police, that Anthony had "looked at me wrong"? Was the same generous sociological response to be found in the hearts of those six people who were shot by the nineteen-year-old boy in Elizabeth, New Jersey, when he toured the city just taking potshots with his

* Vol. 364 (March 1966), p. 10.

.22-caliber rifle? True, *they* didn't fare so well—in fact one died on the spot—but at least the young gunman was gaining status.

To the white middle class it may seem barbaric to concede that some killers or would-be killers gain inwardly from the services of a gun, but other voices speak from darker rooms. "The practice of carrying arms," said ex-slave Frederick Douglass in the last century, "would be a good one for the colored people to adopt, as it would give them a sense of their own manhood." It is a theory that blacks today seem to be responding to with increasing enthusiasm. About the harassment that her son, Mark Essex, had suffered at the hands of white men and his reason for killing nine and wounding nine in New Orleans, Mrs. Essex told newsmen, "You know, you just keep on putting a little snow on top of snow and pretty soon it's going to break. Jimmy wanted to be a man." Gunplay must have had something of the same significance to the four young blacks who seized John & Al's Sports, Inc., store in Brooklyn in January 1973 and engaged police in a forty-eight-hour battle, for in one of the gunfight's lulls they allegedly told a Muslim minister, "This is the end, this is glory, we'll go out in a hail of bullets." The use of the gun in such circumstances is the saddest use of all, because it is the most understandable: *machismo* means never, never again having to say you're sorry.

It is almost impossible for the white middle class to feel the freshness of this elation. From our remote position we know only that the use of the gun on the street is very often unaesthetic and bothersome in the extreme. And such irritations have evoked a feeling to which we are not yet willing to confess: it is the impulse that points to an *Untermensch*, judged not by genes but by impact on white-middle-class society—a logic that is already expressed in our hearts, though not on newspaper obituary pages, under the standing head *Good Riddance*. At a Methadone maintenance center in Washington recently, one hophead cut into the waiting line where he didn't belong, another patient challenged him, the first pulled a gun and shot his challenger between the eyes. Tomorrow society must assume the guilt that goes with allowing such conditions to exist, but today perhaps it can be forgiven if it simply is content that the Methadone line is one person shorter.

Several years ago the Senate Juvenile Deliquency Subcommittee staff put together a "gun murder profile" by using the Washington, D.C., biographies of a hundred and twenty-five defendants. The profile of the killer was this: he had been piling up a criminal record for ten years prior to his most recent charge of murder (some had already faced the same charge); 62 percent of the gun murderers had previously been arrested for crimes of violence; on an average he had been arrested 2.4 times for serious crimes. As for the victims and the occasion, 81 percent of the murderers chose their wives or friends or relatives to kill, and in 88 percent of the cases killed them during a lovers' quarrel or a drunken brawl. Furthermore, the subcommittee staff found that "in a nationwide survey of 120 major cities, the results tabulated thus far are consistent with the findings in the District of Columbia."

None of which comes as a surprise at all: it has been known for years that most murders are the ultimate expression of an already long-established chumminess between lowlifes. The only surprising thing about such revelations is that our opinion-shapers still pretend to care about what happens to such people, pretend to argue earnestly that in losing the friends and family of such men we are losing something we cannot muddle along without rather comfortably. It is more reasonable to suppose that the man who is shot while sharing a bottle or the woman who is shot while sharing the bed of somebody who has a ten-year record of felonies and has been convicted of at least two violent crimes is a comrade who has also likely shared the police blotter with him on numerous occasions.

The experts claim that this profile is beginning to change; they say that stranger homicides have increased 25 percent in some urban areas during the last five years. But the preponderance of killing is still between family members or friends.

And if the riddance is not always exactly good, it is very often tolerable.

News item: A mother is arguing with her nineteen-year-old son about his car. The son starts throwing bricks and stones at his mother. The mother gets out her .22-caliber German RG-23 revolver and fires several shots at him. He ducks, but his fourteen-year-old brother runs in front of him and catches a fatal slug in the neck. That is a family tragedy, but to what extent is it society's tragedy?

News item: A twenty-year-old Pittsburgh youth buys a twelve-dollar gun, loads it with .22-caliber bullets. Then he tries to take the bullets out of the gun, finds they are stuck, tries to expel one of the cartridges by striking it with a hatchet. The bullet hits him in the head. A personal tragedy, of course, but is it society's tragedy?

News item: A cop shoots and kills a sixteen-year-old bicycle thief, admittedly rather heavy going for such an insignificant crime; but as it turns out the victim is not a modern Huck Finn but an ageless being, neither young nor old, who has already racked up a record ranging from drugs to assault. The boy has been dealt a personal injustice, but how much has society lost in losing him?

For a final All-American vignette, let us turn to the city that provides so many perfect ones, Gun City, Detroit: Harvey and Tyrone have just finished an evening of revelry at Harvey's home. Tyrone leaves. A moment later Harvey looks out the window and sees Tyrone down the block, under the street lamp, being pushed around by four men. Harvey assumes his friend is being mugged, gets out his ever-ready .30-caliber carbine and begins blasting. By the time he runs out of bullets and pauses to reload, the four strangers are lying on the sidewalk, two dead, two seriously wounded. Meanwhile, Tyrone, desperate to interrupt the deadly fire, whips out a pistol and shoots Harvey in the chest. It turns out the bodies on the sidewalk belong to Tyrone's cousin and three brothers. They had just been horsing around with him as they had been doing since they were all kids together down South. Is it callous to say that Detroit, as well as mankind, can probably survive such family tragedies and that, considering the readiness with which they whipped out carbine and pistol, it is just as well they polished each other off before they had a chance to turn their guns on people outside their circle on some other occasion?

The members of any society are responsible to one another to some extent. "Human beings," as John Stuart Mill put it, "owe to each other help to distinguish the better from the worse, and encouragement to choose the former and avoid the latter. . . . But neither one person, nor any number of persons, is warranted in saying to another human creature of ripe years, that he shall not do with his life for his own benefit what he chooses to do with it."

To the extent that society fails to teach the ignorant to differentiate between good conduct and bad, and fails to provide the means to live accordingly—and to the extent that that withholding of instruction and opportunity leads to violence—society has failed, and part of the resulting tragedy is society's to bear. But the tragedy of the "creature of ripe years" who picks the wrong friends or the wrong spouse and gets shot for his error, that is not a tragedy society should share. We are all stupid at times, needless to say—though few of us are stupid enough to try to unload a gun with a hatchet—but that's the individual's problem, not society's, just as it is the individual's problem when he decides to use a gun to commit suicide. The fourteen-year-old who was accidentally shot by his mother did not, of course, choose that mother and, as things turned out, doubtless would have preferred another; he has our sympathy. Fate, if not society, let him down. But in his case we can at least comfort ourselves with the question, Is it likely that any issue of that family would have come to much? Indeed, this could be asked of most gun victims, and I suspect many of us *do* ask the question, though silently, not wanting to be rebuked for candor. An objective study of news stories on shootings for a year would likely persuade you that not more than one out of ten gun homicides is a real tragedy: the loss of a worthwhile innocent. The others are middle-class trash, or lower-class luckless, or—the great majority—that special hard-faced gang whom most Americans, black and white, would probably like to see consigned to a genuine ghetto, meaning segregated physically in one section of the city where, with any luck and enough armament, they could be expected to finish one another off—perhaps even to kill with some imagination and flair, as somebody did the thirty-seven-year-old drug pusher in the South Bronx who wound up with six bullet holes in his chest, in the shape of a cross. Albert Seedman, former Chief of Detectives of the New York Police Department and as nice a guy as the cops are likely to produce, once observed, "The same passions in these poor people are in everyone. Take away our white-collar jobs, our bank accounts, our expense accounts, our stable families, our nice homes, our air conditioners; add in some drugs and booze for solace, and we might kill somebody on a Saturday night too." Certainly. But meanwhile, we don't, and they do, which, the humanitarian hypothesis aside, seems to be what counts.

My favorite military man, Capt. John G. Bourke, in his rigorously honest *An Apache Campaign in the Sierra Madre*, told of one Judge Charlie Meyers of Tucson:

> . . . a terror to evil-doers and an upright, conscientious administrator of justice, although he knew scarcely any law. Being afraid of assassination, he kept in his house after dark. One night in response to a terrible knocking, he roused, raised the little shutter from a hole he had cut in his front door, and demanded to know who is there.
> "Me, Judge."
> "And who are you, mine frent?"
> "Judge, I want to give myself up. I've just killed a man."
> "Vot you keel him for?"
> "He called me a liar en I—"
> "Vare you keel him?"
> "Down in George Foster's Quartz Rock Gambling Saloon" [a notorious deadfall in Tucson].
> "Vary goot, mine frent, dot's all right," said the Judge

soothingly. "Dot's all right. Go now unt keel unudder von."
Then he turned back to bed.*

Dialect stories and frontier humor aren't much in favor these
days, which is probably just as well. But the Judge's notion of
justice and his balanced indifference to the loss of trash surely must
ring a responsive chord in the hearts of all whose neighborhoods
and cities of every era have had their Quartz Rock Gambling
Saloons and all that goes with them.

KIND HEARTS AND BAYONETS

When some of the preceding section was read in manu-
script by Richard Kluger, the fellow who happens to be the
proprietor of the house publishing this book, he took exception to
my "arch" tone, as he put it, and suspecting that I wasn't really
trying to be humorous, damned me in a long memo that I believe
can, in part, be inserted here with value because it is the typical
liberal response to another person's effort to adjust amicably to
sticky fate:

> Some of these data, offered rather straightforwardly and not
> readily detectable as tongue-in-cheek, register with me as
> highly anti-anti-gun. You work hard here to trivialize the gun
> toll. Do you *mean* that? I don't believe that—or let's say I
> don't *want* to believe that. First, a thousand tragic deaths is a
> lot of deaths, and if it all came down just to that, I'd say that's
> a lot of unnecessary killing and in no way defensible. Second,
> you take a remarkably elitist/reactionary-sounding position
> on the remaining 9,000+ gun deaths, saying in effect (and
> indeed quite specifically) Good Riddance to this human
> trash. . . .
> Unless you think there is not a jot of chance for improving

---

* Introduction by J. Frank Dobie (Scribner's, 1958), p. 12.

American society and its inequities, what you're doing here is reinforcing the school that holds that there will always be human dross among us and there's nothing we can do to prevent it or lower its potential for waywardness. If you can laugh it off, as you sort of do here by saying repeatedly that their self-slaughter may be a blessing in disguise, you're just tossing in the towel on America. You do that several places in the book, and when you recite our history with, say, gun control efforts, you have made something of a case for hopelessness.

But in this chapter . . . you leave yourself way open to the readers who are less susceptible to irony who will take you at face value and say, "Now wait a minute, Sherrill—I don't want these lowlifes and trash armed to the teeth because someday soon they're gonna stop shooting each other and come after me." In effect, your chapter here cops out . . . on the connection between the prevalence of guns in America and the crime rate; to say that most of the fatal crimes involve the trash among us is not only unhumane in the extreme; it overlooks the price that all of us pay in money, anxiety, hostility, etc. for allowing this rate of crime to fester.

Yes, there is that to consider, if one wishes to; but to weep over most of the gun deaths that result from what kind hearts like Kluger call "festering" crime is to waste one's tears on the wrong thing. Most murders occur in shabby neighborhoods; of the 690 murders in Detroit in 1971, for example, 575 occurred in the black slums. Going out to discover the cause, *Newsweek* correspondent Vern E. Smith was given a number of obvious answers by experts in the obvious, one answer being, "It's a kind of by-product of ghetto life. If you never achieve what you think you're capable of achieving, you have a tendency to get angry quick. . . . I think there's a lot of self-hate involved, too. It's hitting at a mirror—at somebody who is just as bad off as you are." * A Detroit psychologist added to the obvious: "Living in a frustrating, stress-inducing environment like a ghetto every day of your life

* *Newsweek*, January 1, 1973.

makes many people walking powder kegs." Correspondent Smith comments that the Detroit homicide rate has doubled since the riots of 1967 and so has the number of pistols; but he is too savvy to conclude that the former's principal cause is the latter. If Detroit—and the nation—wants to let thousands of its citizens live like stray dogs, it has to expect some of them to go mad. Then when they kill other stray dogs, it is rather silly to sigh and say their teeth were to blame; it is even sillier to pretend that we are sorry a few are killed when we do nothing to salvage the rest. Affluent Americans care not one whit what happens to their trashier neighbors, and it is hypocritical, at best, to suggest that we are improving their lives by depriving them of their guns. What Thomas Henry Huxley said of the world in general can certainly be said of Americans in particular—we are neither wise nor just but we make up for all our folly and injustice by "being damnably sentimental."

And being motivated by sentimentality rather than by humanity, it may be that America will, instead of cleaning up its slums, decide one day to confiscate *all* civilian guns—which is the only step that will prevent the deaths that Kluger and his sort lament. A wipeout would necessarily include at some point a mandatory death penalty for anybody who tried to evade the national gun-confiscation program. When that time comes I suggest that, just to demonstrate that guns aren't necessary, the executions of the holdouts be done by garroting. Moreover, the executions could be imbued with the kind of patriotic commercialism that always lifts the spirits of America. In the South, for instance, the executions could be performed by the reigning Maid of Cotton using a Fruit of the Loom cord. If we cannot live sanely, let us at least live bizarrely.

OUR LOVABLE DESPERADOES

The appetite for gun bravado being what it is in this country, there was never enough of the real thing to keep the public satisfied, so the manufacture and concoction of bogus courage became one of the biggest industries on The Frontier, and the remnants of this production line still litter the landscape or have been pasted together and gilded and sold by Hollywood. The impact of these myths has been concentrated with special intensity over only a few generations. The grandparents of a person of forty were young when the floodtide of gun hokum began. Every true American can recite the names of our frontier *lares*.

Calamity Jane, best remembered out of Hollywood in the figure of Jean Arthur, unquestionably leads the list of Old West legendary women, supposedly a crack shot, scout for the Army, pony express rider, etc. Gallant legend also, of course, portrays her as a beauty. Cruel accuracy tells another tale: her real name was Martha Jane Canary; her mother, Charlotte Canary, ran a brothel with the quaint name "The Bird Cage," in which Calamity Jane apprenticed. In her hands a gun would have been more of a threat to an innocent customer than to an enemy; for that matter, all men were her friends. Bruce Nelson, an historian specializing in her haunts, assures us that "her services to the Army were in a quite different capacity from that mentioned" in her autobiography. "Citizens of Deadwood who knew Jane well describe her as a common harlot—and one of such coarse and forbidding appearance as to frighten away all save the tipsiest miners."

Belle Starr (Myra Belle Shirley) epitomized the Frontier Woman, gracious but with a will of iron, and loyal to Her Man. She is immortalized in a movie bearing her name in which Gene Tierney plays the heroine. To the *National Police Gazette* (the *Playboy* of its time) she was "the Bandit Queen, more amorous than Antony's mistress, more relentless than Pharaoh's daughter, and braver than Joan of Arc." Legend made her quite handy with both six-gun and rifle. Something of that mystique must have hung over Ms. Starr during her lifetime, like cheap incense, for when she died (or rather, when she was shot down from behind by her own son using a charge of buckshot to knock her off her horse and a charge of turkeyshot to finish her), her admirers buried her with a handsome Colt in her right hand, the revolver that had been given to her years before by her first lover, Cole Younger. But, alas, the real Belle Starr was a whore who slept with every saddle bum and gunslinger who passed by, for which we might forgive her, but she was ugly besides. She dropped two bastards—a boy who grew up to be her incestuous lover and murderer and who was himself killed in a tavern brawl, and a girl who worked as a whore until she got enough money and community support to become a madam. Belle's talents were not with a gun.

For absolutely no reason relating to sanity, we made a folk hero of Jesse James (would you believe Tyrone Power? The murderous brother, Frank James, was played by Henry Fonda), whose career as a gunman, stripped of as much fantasy as possible, comes down to nothing more admirable than the leadership of a gang* that in fifteen years held up at least eleven banks, seven trains, three stagecoaches, and one county fair for a total take of nearly a quarter-million dollars. En route to that sum sixteen men were killed. If we are sappy about Jesse from this distance in time, the nice people who were his contemporaries were no less enamored of his gunplay. Jesse and Frank James seemed almost mascots to some important politicians and much of the press. On September 26, 1872, when Jesse and two sidekicks robbed the Kansas City fair of something less than a thousand dollars, after shooting a small girl in the leg (bad marksmanship: they had meant to hit the ticket-seller), the *Kansas City Times* described the robbery as "so diabolically daring and so utterly in contempt of fear that we are bound to admire it and revere its perpetrators. . . . It was as though three bandits had come to us from storied Odenwald, with the halo of medieval chivalry upon their garments, and shown us how the things were done that poets sing of. Nowhere else in the United States or in the civilized world, probably, could this thing have been done." † On his death the *Kansas City Journal* wailed "Goodbye, Jesse!"

---

* A nice bunch of fellows like Cole Younger, who is said to have shot fifteen federal prisoners during the Civil War just to test a Winchester rifle. Younger was as tough as he was wicked. In his lifetime he had been wounded by bullets twenty-six times and at the time of his death his body was still carrying seventeen of them.

† Quoted by Joe Frantz in his excellent essay, "The Frontier Tradition: An Invitation to Violence," in Graham and Gurr, eds., *Violence in America: A Staff Report to the National Commission on the Causes and Prevention of Violence* (U.S. Government Printing Office, 1969). Examples of the press's asinine attitude toward outlaws and gangsters are, of course, legion. Harry Tracy was the most murderous member of the famous Western gang known as The Wild Bunch. Escaping a posse's ambush on one occasion, he got off half a dozen fast shots in semidarkness, killing three lawmen. The *World* called it "magnificent marksmanship."

Of Billy the Kid, or the romanticized concept of Billy the Kid, Hollywood has made no fewer than twenty-one movies, in each of which the hero is represented by actors as handsome as the most recent to do the service, Paul Newman, which is indeed ironic considering the fact that the most accurate description of the real Billy was given by Peter Lyon in *The Wild, Wild West*: ". . . a slight, short, buck-toothed, narrow-shouldered youth whose slouch adds to his unwholesome appearance. He looks like a cretin, but this may be deceptive. . . ." * Billy usually killed from ambush; his only recorded face-to-face gun murder was of an unarmed man.

Hollywood's best-known Wild Bill Hickok was Gary Cooper, quite a contrast to the original, whose hair (as seen in most of the old photos) was long and greasy and whose face was marked by close-set eyes and a heavy-lipped puckered mouth that looked as if it had come from the womb sucking a green persimmon; for good reason Hickok kept it hidden as best he could under a drooping mustache.

The Wild Bill legend—typically American in its quantity of hokum—began at Rock Creek, Nebraska, where he and his claque claimed he wiped out singlehandedly the "McCanles Gang" of nine "desperadoes, horse-thieves, murderers, regular cutthroats" (as *Harper's Monthly* reported), using six-gun, rifle, and Bowie knife, while receiving eleven bullets in his own body. More temperate and accurate biographers, such as Richard O'Connor, say that while hiding behind a calico curtain in a trading post, Hickok gunned down Dave McCanles (a sodden bully who undoubtedly deserved the ambush), and that the other members of the "gang" consisted of McCanles' twelve-year-old son, a young cousin, and a young employee who blundered into the fray. The son didn't do anything but cradle his dying father in his arms. The other two young men, caught by surprise in the gunfire and wounded, ran away; for this insolence one was hacked to death with a hoe and the other,

* (Funk and Wagnalls, 1969), p. 143.

unarmed, was killed by a shotgun blast. Both murders were done by Hickok's friends, not by Wild Bill himself. Hickok's conquering of the "McCanles Gang" has sometimes been referred to as "the greatest one-man gunfight in history." *

A typical report of Hickok in later years came from Abilene, Kansas, where he was hired in 1871 to enforce the law. Some say he spent most of his nights sleeping with the whores in the section of Abilene called "Devil's Half Acre," and some critics complained that he spent the rest of his time protecting professional gamblers, madams, and saloonkeepers from irate and dissatisfied customers who thought they had been cheated—as indeed they probably had.

With the westward expansion under our belts and digested and the last of the "Lower 48," Arizona, admitted to the Union in 1912, Americans could no longer look to the frontier for sanctification of the gun. Something new was needed, and something new was found amid the post-World War ennui and the Depression doldrums of the 1930s as we again reveled in our strange national preoccupation with low-grade gunmen. The Hole in the Rock hideout of the last of the major Western gangs was occupied now only by the ghosts of Black Jack Ketchum, Flat-Nose George, Deaf Charley, Sundance Kid, Butch Cassidy, and Peep O'Day. They had "gone west," and we felt lonely without a litany of underworld nicknames to rattle off. But within a few years we were in business again, this time watching with fascination and even sometimes with applause the antics of such fellows as Mossy Enright, Sunny Jim Cosmano, Greasy Thumb Guzik, Short Pants Campagna, Machine Gun Jack McGurn, Snorky Capone, Dutch Schultz, Porky Dillon, Legs Diamond, Paul the Waiter Ricca, Golf Bag Sam Hunt (he carried his shotgun in a golf bag), Camel Humphreys, Bugs Moran, Basil the Owl Banghart, Terrible Touhy, and Pretty Boy Floyd.† With nicknames like that, why shouldn't America think of them as just "the boys"? America's own mischievous brood.

---

* Richard O'Connor *Wild Bill Hickok* (Doubleday, 1959).
† Most of the nicknames originated in the inflamed imagination of newspaper feature writers—and were not the natural product of the underworld—but the public loved them none the less for that.

Indeed, so fond was the public becoming of its wayward gunsels—a fondness nurtured perhaps by the fact that, at the bottom of the Great Depression, there was a better than usual reason for admiring anyone who could, even with a gun, get money from a bank—that the godfather of law and order, J. Edgar Hoover, laid aside his previous shyness and began to publicize himself and his FBI as the avenging hosts of righteousness. Crime was getting too much applause; it was, Hoover felt, time for the symbol of Anti-Crime (as he saw himself) to take the stage. The great public-relations battle began, FBI scholars say, as a direct result of Hoover's unhappiness with the public's response to two bloody skirmishes.

On June 17, 1933, FBI agents and local gendarmes were escorting Frank Nash, a mail robber, back to prison. They hustled him across the street from the Kansas City railroad terminal and crammed him into the front seat of a car, G-men sitting on both sides and behind him. Another car full of cops, riding shotgun so to speak, was parked to the rear. Before this two-car caravan could get away from the curb, three of the era's top gangsters—Vern Miller, Charles (Pretty Boy) Floyd, and Adam Richetti—converged on them and went to work with two tommy guns. "Methodically," writes Fred Cook in *The FBI Nobody Knows*, "the machine gunners walked around the car, pumping out such a steady stream of lead that the car top was nearly severed from the car body. In that scythe-like hail, men were literally cut to pieces." Indeed, "shredded" is not an extravagant description of the results of the tommy gun when put to its ultimate use. A demonstration for newsmen in 1922 left this impression with a New York *Herald* reporter: "The three guns, pounding out steel jacketed .45-caliber bullets at the rate of 1,000 a minute, sliced the tires off the machine, cut through the spokes and chewed their way through the body, radiator, lamps, steering gear, tanks and woodwork," and, switching to incendiary bullets, "converted a solid looking seven passenger touring car into a flaming mass of junk in less than a minute. Nothing in the machine larger than a mouse could have survived the fusillade." But delicate operations were not for the tommy. One did not use it to rip apart an auto with a surgeon's selectivity, as the rescuers of Kansas City discovered: Nash, whom they had hoped to free, died in the fusillade along with four lawmen.

A little more than a year later, at 10:30 P.M. on July 22, 1934, John Dillinger walked out of the Biograph Theater in East Chicago where he had just been entertained by *Manhattan Melodrama*, a gangster movie starring William Powell and Clark Gable. Walking beside Dillinger were two girlfriends, one of whom had helped G-men set up the trap. As fifteen agents closed in on him, Dillinger, realizing that the air was wrong, went for his Colt automatic. But it was hardly out of his pocket before he was brought down by one bullet through his left side and another that entered his lower back and exited through his right eye. Dillinger left his mortal body on the sidewalk between a tea store and a chop-suey restaurant.

The public's reaction to these two episodes was not entirely what Hoover desired. Just as some had felt that the Jesse James holdup of the Kansas City fair showed marvelous courage, some felt that the gangster triumvirate's boldness in trying a daytime rescue of Nash was something to be admired. And just as one Missouri newspaper had called for the assassination of the public officials who had persuaded Robert Ford to kill Jesse James, a Virginia newspaper editor denounced FBI agents as "cowards" because so many had set upon Dillinger and because they had shot him down in an alley rather than making their arrest—like "gentlemen law officers"—in the movie theater. But the public's disenchantment with the FBI had other causes. There were suspicions after the Dillinger scene—suspicions reinforced by subsequent FBI gunplay—that the federal gumshoes were something less than efficient. In taking Dillinger, they had fired wildly, even hysterically, and had wounded two women on the street. The wildness of the marksmanship could be accounted for by confessions like that made by Melvin Purvis, who led the FBI ambush:

My throat was parched from the cigar, from fright, and

from nervousness. My knees wouldn't stay still. . . . I stood with my cigar shaking in my mouth. . . .

I had one gun stuck between my trousers and shirt on the left side and another gun in the same fashion on the right. Later, after leaving this scene, I tried to button up my coat and found both buttons gone. Apparently I had grabbed for my gun without thinking, and I am frank to say that I do not know how it came into my hand.*

And did not know where the bullets went.

The G-gunmen were still up to their wild gunplay two years later, as evidenced in a raid on the hideout of the bank robber Harry Brunette. *Newsweek* reported:

A sharp clatter of gunfire echoed through the placid neighborhood. Federal men in the hall outside were firing through the door [of the apartment where Brunette and his wife were hiding]; somebody was shooting back. As the battle raged, an army of police arrived. Later, a tear-gas bomb set fire to the apartment and brought fire engines screaming to the scene.

Amid the hubbub, a flustered G-man poked a submachine gun at a husky fireman. "Dammit, can't you read?" growled the fireman, pointing at his helmet. "If you don't take that gun out of my stomach, I'll bash your head in."

For 35 minutes, the shooting continued. Then a lull. "Give up, or we'll shoot," shouted a G-man—as if they had been throwing spitballs up to then.†

The public was hardly inclined to give its heart to these police clowns. And anyway, hard times had turned the social gyroscope on its side. Law-abiding though most Americans were by habit and instinct and desire, the 1930s gave them momentarily a perverse perspective: caught in the drab, broke depths of the Depression, they found it hard to sympathize with the bankers who were foreclosing on mortgages right and left, found it equally hard to

---

* Quoted in Max Lowenthal, *The Federal Bureau of Investigation* (Harcourt, Brace, 1950), p. 410.
† Quoted in Lowenthal, *op. cit.*, p. 412.

sympathize with the upper crust who had so much money that they could pay big ransoms. Bank robbers and kidnapers were bad men, to be sure, but at least their naughtiness supplied the cheap thrills by proxy with which the dreary breadline years were somewhat "brightened."

It was an era when the hoky biographies of badmen filled the ten-cent movie houses—badmen who seemed to be in much more danger from stoolies and rats and finks (the vocabulary of the underworld that was becoming popular in those days) in their own ranks or in rival gangs than they were from the bungling police. The 1930s were the movie years of the glorious gat and the pathetic prison inmate. Everyone who went to the movies—and everyone did—was instructed that gangsters lived by a code, lowly though it might be; they saw that prison inmates were much more civilized and worthy than the screws, who were invariably bestial; they saw that most hoodlums were the product of Hell's Kitchen, victims of their environment, and that if they had had any luck they might just as easily have turned out to be priests (Pat O'Brien).

From such hokum were spun the careers of men who were much more admired by the public than were the politicians of the day. Would you rather be Vice President John Garner or James Cagney (*Doorway to Hell, Public Enemy, Mayor of Hell, Angels with Dirty Faces*)? Would you rather be Senator John Bankhead or Humphrey Bogart (*The Petrified Forest, Bullets or Ballots, San Quentin, Crime School, King of the Underworld*)? Would you rather be Congressman Sam Rayburn or Edward G. Robinson (*Little Caesar, The Last Gangster, A Slight Case of Murder*)? To most Americans, it wouldn't have been a hard choice to make.*

Edward G. Robinson (Nick Donati), with his enemy Hum-

---

* There was poetic justice in George Raft's being launched toward stardom by that famous coin-flipping scene in one of the most famous of the gangster films, *Scarface*. After all, Raft had once actually been an ambitious smalltime racketeer, working for the bigtime liquor racketeer Owney Maddon, an experience Raft recalls with nostalgia: "I had a gun in my pocket and I was cocky because I was working for the gang boss of New York." Could it be that the actors wrote their own worst lines?

phrey Bogart (Turkey Morgan) pointing a snubnosed .38 special at his belly: "You're so used to a machine gun, Turkey, you're liable to miss with that peashooter."

Now there was a line to make you forget the milk bill!

In their cruel world of make-believe, as in the real world of Pretty Boy Floyd's submachine gun and Dillinger's automatic, there was a philosophical conclusion to be drawn that meant much in the stagnant Thirties: with such tools a man could, despite all the imposed discouragements of the Establishment, carve out his own future, even if it included prison and death. With a gun a man was still not totally subject to Wall Street and the bureaucracy and the politicians.

People didn't *say* such things, but the feeling was so palpable that it made an ominous crackling sound that rolled up to the highest offices of the FBI where The Great Man heard it and frowned.

"The vast weight of public opinion was on the side of Hoover and the FBI," writes Don Whitehead in *The FBI Story,* the authorized history of the Bureau, but "the sympathy poured out for the dead gangsters and the criticism of the FBI outraged J. Edgar Hoover's Presbyterian concept of right and wrong."

Whitehead fails to mention that it also outraged Hoover's concept of how to expand the powers of the then relatively insignificant FBI into a superpolice force, a *Geheime Staatspolizei* modeled after some of the national police forces of Europe. He wanted the jurisdiction (at that time the FBI had to operate timidly in most interstate law enforcement) and the budget to go with it. So he decided to go public—to sell himself and his agency, to outfox the underworld at public relations.

Among other things, this entailed concocting the most godawful crime wave and the most inhuman criminals possible. Hoover and his slavish sideman, Attorney General Homer S. Cummings, had to manufacture some desperadoes to prove that only a bigtime federal law enforcement agency girded with all sorts of federal laws and with a bigtime budget could do the job. (As it turned out, bureaucratic hyperbole worked very well for inflating the FBI's powers and budget. Between the mid-1930s and the mid-1940s the FBI assembled an infinite series of new laws allowing it to butt into the lives of Americans and also saw its budget soar sevenfold.)

Among the most useful of the manufactured bogeymen were George (Machine Gun) Kelly, who was described by Cummings' Justice Department as a "desperate character" but whose record consisted mainly of such frightening offenses as bootlegging and vagrancy. Finally convicted of kidnaping, he disappeared over the waves to Alcatraz without having fired a machine gun to knock off anything except, as J. Edgar Hoover conceded, "a row of walnuts from the top of a fence and at a good distance."

Undismayed by such facts, Hoover was capable of writing of his G-men that they were true "soldiers," although, to be sure, "There was no martial roll of drums to buoy up their spirits as they went to face their death, no crash of cymbals, no blare of bugle or trumpets—only the vicious rattle of a machine gun." It wasn't all hokum: dozens of desperadoes were indeed armed with submachine guns and some did indeed fire at the G-men. But these widespread skirmishes and isolated guerrilla encounters hardly added up to a war, except perhaps to the readers of *Liberty* and *Collier's* and *Saturday Evening Post* whose editors were all too receptive to the Hoover-Cummings cataclysmic view of crime. So, realizing apparently that they would have to get away from the specific criminals—get away from the faces on the post office bulletin board—and start talking in broad statistics if they were to impress anyone with the need for more jurisdiction and a bigger budget, Hoover and Cummings rose to the occasion. Hoover warned of "a horde of vandals larger than any of the barbarian hosts that overran Europe and Asia in ancient times . . . roving bands of plunderers moving swiftly from city to city and state to state, their machine guns clattering death. . . ."

One day Hoover would see "armed forces of crime which number more than 3 million active participants." Shortly thereafter his count had dropped to "a whole half-million of armed thugs, murderers, thieves, firebugs, assassins, robbers, and hold-up men." A year later his count had soared to 4.3 million felons, among whom were "150,000 murderers roaming at large."

The irrationally fluctuating count was no wilder than Attorney General Cummings' statements on the same point. To the House Ways and Means Committee in 1934 he pronounced his criminal census thus:

> I stated in a moment of zeal on this question that there were more people in the underworld armed than there were in the Army and Navy of the United States. On the basis of the records of crimes of violence which have been perpetrated, taken with our statistics of the number of persons in prisons for crimes of violence, and such other collateral data as it is possible to secure, I am prepared to say that the statement was exceedingly conservative. It would be much fairer to say that there are twice as many people in the underworld today armed with deadly weapons, in fact, than there are in the Army and the Navy of the United States combined.*

If Cummings' estimate was correct, it meant that one out of every two-hundred-forty-four persons was an armed ruffian prowling the streets. Although this wasn't by any means as high a percentage of undesirables as Congress contained, it was a deadlier one.

But a census of evildoers, even though highly exaggerated, left incomplete the crime picture that Hoover wanted to present. As any good propagandist knows, the public will respond with more excitement to a villain with an evil instrument than to one who is evil only in himself. That's why right-wing propagandists used to talk about Godless Communism's sinister plan to destroy us through fluoridation. Something concrete to go with the shadowy ideology.

Hoover, one of the greatest propagandists ever to grace the

---

* Ways and Means Committee, House of Representatives. 73rd Congress, 2nd Session. Hearings on H.R. 9066 (National Firearms Act), April–May, 1934 (U.S. Government Printing Office), p. 4.

federal bureaucracy, took the same tack. The most oppressive crimes of the 1930s, as today, were white-collar and corporate—not bank robberies but bank embezzlements; not "contract" murderers but contracts to swindle consumers; not muggers but juggled corporate books; not kidnapings but antitrust violations. It was the bank robber, the murderer, the mugger, and the kidnaper who made the best and biggest headlines, however, and headlines were what Hoover sought. To make his actors seem suitably fierce, he talked about them as though they possessed an armory of the deadliest weapons of the day. That's why he always described the underworld army as having "blazing machine guns." The machine gun, or rather the submachine gun (which is what he meant), was not nearly so useful to the underworld in getting money out of its victims as the instrument was to Hoover in getting money out of Congress. As one of the most effective propaganda weapons of the 1930s, the submachine gun deserves special respect and attention.

TOMMY'S GUN

John T. Thompson, a military man of unusual creativity and foresight, having seen the wretched weaponry with which our men went into the Spanish-American War and anticipating the need in World War I for a firearm as light as a rifle but with the devastating power of a machine gun, envisioned a "one-man, hand-held machine gun," and set out to perfect what came to be known as the tommy gun. Thompson certainly had the expertise to develop it. He had held the highest ordnance position in the Army during the Spanish-American War (and was to do so again during World War I); between the two conflicts he had helped develop the Springfield Model 1903, based on the Mauser bolt-action. Many gun buffs believe the Springfield '03 to be the best bolt-action military rifle ever produced. Equipped with a Redfield telescopic sight, it was used by our snipers even into World War II; and for a brief time after the outbreak of the war production of this rifle was revived.

Thompson's financial backer was Thomas Fortune Ryan, who, after helping to exploit Belgian Congo mining properties and to develop the American Tobacco Company into a monopoly and after a series of other buccaneering achievements, had retired in 1910 worth one-quarter billion dollars. The few hundred thousand dollars he put into the submachine gun's development was not sorely missed. The company they formed in 1916 was the Auto-Ordnance Corporation. While none of the submachine guns was finished early enough to help American soldiers in World War I, several hundred later found their way into the hands of soldiers to whom Ryan felt closer, the Irish Republican Army.

The first model, the 1921 model, was changed very little over the years. The gun, which had a detachable butt stock, could be fired either semiautomatically or automatically, using magazines holding 20 or 50 or 100 cartridges. With the standard .45-caliber ammunition used in the U.S. Automatic Service Pistol, the bullet could be expected, at 100 yards, to penetrate six ¾-inch yellow-pine boards spaced one inch apart; 4 at 500 yards. The effective range of the submachine gun was 600 yards. Considering its firepower, it was a very light weapon, variously advertised at from 8½ to 10 pounds. It was also a trim weapon: without stock the gun was 23.2 inches long, with the stock 31.8 inches.

The first public showing of the Thompson was at the National Rifle Association/Army's Camp Perry National Matches in August 1920. With an Auto-Ordnance official doing the firing, the gun, on semiautomatic, ran up a perfect score for 20 shots in 10 seconds at a distance of 200 yards; switched to automatic, it poured out 600 rounds in 70 seconds and of these 100 hit the target. The distance for the last was 500 yards. The experts were impressed.

And so was the Colt Company, which tried to buy the rights to the gun. Thompson wouldn't sell, but he did convince Colt to produce the gun for him. Colt charged him $45 per gun, and the list price for the first model off the line in 1921 was $225.

But the military showed so little interest in the Thompson that within two years the company dropped the price to $175, still with few takers; among the quibbles was that it fired "too fast," so the designers cut the prototype's 1,000–1,500 rounds a minute down to 800 rounds per minute for the production model and to 600 to suit the Navy.

An ad in the January 31, 1922, New York *Herald* offered the gun as "A Sure Defense Against Organized Bandits and Criminals." The argument: "The old time safeguards are inadequate to foil the carefully planned raids of heavily armed bandits, whose 'getaway' is assured by high powered automobiles. Improved and more powerful methods of defense have become necessary."

Thus, the appearance of the Thompson Anti-Bandit Gun. "The gun is a powerful deterrent. It strikes terror into the heart of the most hardened and daring criminal. The moral effect of its known possession is an insurance of its own."

Despite such nifty advertising, however, the gun just wasn't moving with either the military or the police, though among the three thousand Thompsons sold by 1925 were a handful to the cops in New York, Boston, and San Francisco as well as the state police in half a dozen Eastern and Midwestern states, plus the Texas Rangers. But the most satisfied customers were the sheriffs' departments in mining and manufacturing towns where the city fathers feared strikes. It was promoted in advertisements as the "ideal riot gun," and for that purpose Auto-Ordnance sold a cartridge containing .20 pellets of No. 8 birdshot which, so the advertisements read, will "allow serious occasions or disorders to be handled by officers of the law in the most humane manner possible." Mine and mill operators interpreted that as referring to those lousy malcontents on their payroll who were pressing for better pay and working conditions, and so they happily supplied the local sheriff's department, which the companies virtually owned, with these fine new weapons.

It should have been quite clear that the Thompson was an ideal military and police gun. It should have been equally obvious that in the wrong hands it could also be an excellent antimilitary and antipolice gun—a little drawback that the authorities ignored, with their usual foresight, apparently thinking that because they didn't want the gun, neither would the gangsters. When Auto-Ordnance advertised in *Army and Navy Journal* that the tommy "can be carried under the coat for instant use," it did not impress the authorities; but the concealability of the tommy certainly impressed the bank robbers.

Although Auto-Ordnance tried to keep sales honest, it couldn't. Phony "dealers" bought some and passed them along to crooks; bad cops bought some for their friends in the underworld. Many were stolen from National Guard armories and police stations and even from some consulates.

By the time the problem of the tommy gun came before a Congressional committee in 1934, Colt officials were thoroughly embarrassed by their connection with it. When W. B. Ryan, president of Auto-Ordnance, and Frank Nichols of Colt appeared before the House Ways and Means Committee that year, there was a curious conflict in their testimony as to whether Colt was still turning out submachine guns. The merchants of death, to use that quaintly accurate label of the Thirties, were always pretty slippery in their public dialogue, and in this case one had trouble following their verb tenses.

Ryan testified, "As far as I know, there *is* only one company which actually manufactures the small type machine gun, the Colt Firearms Co., who manufacture for us, and they also manufacture a small gun called the 'Monitor,' a gun of their own." Present tense. Did he mean the gangster-type submachine gun? Yes, said Ryan, he meant just that. Once again he was asked if Colt was manufacturing the gun and once again he said, "That is right, sir."

Yet when Nichols came on to testify, he stated flatly, "We do not make submachine guns." No more. Once, yes, but no more. "We manufactured fifteen thousand of those in 1921 for the Auto-Ordnance Co. . . . How many they have left, and what their method of merchandising was, I do not know. . . . I think we can state correctly, they were a bit careless in their method of merchandising." Having washed his hands of the deal (and, in a way, accurately, for Colt made only that one batch of fifteen thousand tommies; but one can comfortably assume that if the gun had sold better, Colt would have been happy to go on making them), he then wiped his hands on Ryan's shirt. Although the Army dumped thousands of his company's .32 revolvers on the civilian market for as little as $4 after World War I, Nichols brushed that aside as of little consequence; what *really* mattered, he implied, was that Auto-Ordnance was so dollar-hungry that it sold tommy guns to "anybody that wanted them." *Colt* would never do a thing like that.

The first mobster use of the tommy gun in Chicago was in the beer wars of 1925, and its performance was so unqualifiedly successful that almost immediately no Chicago gang felt fully equipped without it. Its appearance in the New York underworld was a bit later, 1928, and William Helmer, whose book *The Gun That Made the Twenties Roar* is the most thorough and entertaining biography of this weapon, thinks that one reason for the lag was that

> while the Chicagoans were still fighting beer wars, New York gangsters were busy developing the higher forms of "racketeering" that would become the mainstay of organized crime following Repeal. Men like Lucky Luciano, Joe Adonis, Lepke Buchalter, Bugsy Siegel, Meyer Lansky, Albert Anastasia, Longy Zwillman, and Frank Costello were a new breed of gangster-businessmen and operated out of paneled, carpeted offices instead of flower shops and garages. Their criminal activities not only were organized, but "syndicated." . . . The Syndicate came to power in the early 1930s, and it was during this period of transition—from Prohibition-era gangsterism to nationally organized racketeering—that murder by tommygun made New York the country's new "crime capital." *

* (Macmillan, 1969), p. 127.

But culture of every sort will eventually trickle down to the boondocks. In the criminal roadshow of the 1930s even the small towns in the Midwest and South and Southwest could sometimes share the entertainment. And for a while, out of this flamboyance and new gadgetry, the status of lead reached a new high.

To get mowed down in an alley, as Dillinger was, or to be among the several who died in the St. Valentine's Day Massacre via tommy guns, was the modern equivalent to putting up a good fight but losing to Nero's lions. Machine Gun Kelly was far better known and revered than Felix Frankfurter. The place of firearms on the people's scale of entertainment preferences was evident from the fact that women like Winnie Ruth Judd, who did their work with poison and axe and butcherknife, were looked upon as balmy, while the true mad dogs like Bonnie Parker, who did their work with guns, were considered to be merely exciting—or, for an even better example, Ma Barker, who lived incestuously with her gangster sons and died (after a six-hour gunfight with G-men) beside her son Fred—he, riddled with eleven bullets but still clutching his tommy gun like a good soldier; she, $10,200 in her purse, a bullet in her heart, and her trusty Thompson still cradled in her arms. Ma went out the way any red-blooded American mother would surely want to go, lullabied forever with the sweet singing of lead.

The eulogy of the masses was accurately captured by Herbert Corey's description of the scene in *Farewell, Mr. Gangster!* published in 1936: "They had died in the old Oklahoma tradition, empty guns in their hands. With one final filial gesture Fred Barker had given his old mother the gun which carried a magazine holding one hundred rounds. The good son kept the 50-shot machine gun for himself."

To counteract the silly romanticizing of the weapons of outlawry as well as of the outlaws themselves, Hoover and Attorney General Cummings put together the first concerted effort to pass federal gun-control laws. But, as they immediately discovered, it is one thing—and relatively easy—to persuade Congress to pass new laws to control criminals, and quite another matter to get Congress to control guns. Not even the industrious imagination of the top G-man could counteract the tide of overblown pageantry and pseudopatriotism that had been enjoyed for so many years by so many Americans.

Hoover was becoming a beloved grandmother to most Americans, but they loved even more the myths of the Minuteman and Civil War Sharpshooters and Wild West buckos. There had been too many generations of literary hucksters parlaying their melodramatic hot stuff, like the historian of the Pinkerton National Detective Agency who had conceded "it is difficult to find any nobility or splendor" in the lives of outlaws, but still "we do come to admire, however grudgingly, the vitality, self-confidence, recklessness, and gusto of these men." And saying amen to that was an industry that creamed many millions of dollars from the gun-loving boobocracy of America.

It was too strong a tide to buck, and those first gun-control efforts were, to put it gently, very paltry indeed. But for those who enjoy cyclical history, the events leading up to the failure of the 1930s will be read as an interesting pattern for the 1960s: a great furor over rampant criminality, slayings in the headlines, a crisis atmosphere—all of this seeming to push toward an inevitable stiff gun-control law; but resisting from the other side a well-organized, crafty, fanatical group; and muddling along in the middle, an ill-informed and mismanaged bureaucracy.

THE DISARMAMENT DODGE.

Consider first, for amusement, the National Firearms Act of 1934. As originally written by the Justice Department and presented to Congress, the National Firearms Act required that sawed-off shotguns, sawed-off rifles, all pistols and automatics, all submachine guns, all gimmicky weapons like "pencil guns"—in other words, all concealable firearms—plus such unclean auxiliaries as silencers, be taxed on sale or transfer and that records of sale and transfer be kept for inspection by agents of the IRS's Alcohol and Tobacco Tax Division (ATTD).* The purpose obviously was to

---

* Now known as the Bureau of Alcohol, Tobacco and Firearms.

keep track of where the gangster-type guns came from and went to. But bear in mind, the law's emphasis was supposed to be on pistols and revolvers. The framers of the original legislation had proposed that if a gangster was caught with a pistol or revolver for which a permit had not been obtained, he could be sent to prison for five years. The reason for this provision was simple enough, as explained by Assistant Attorney General Joseph B. Keenan: "When we catch a criminal, we usually find the machine gun, but we always find a half dozen or eight or ten Colt automatics or some easily concealable firearm. It is a matter of convenience. In addition to the machine gun, the modern gangster is not technically well equipped if he does not have several concealable small arms for use instantly."

It was a good piece of legislation, and Keenan's explanation of the pistols and revolvers portion made good sense. Tommy guns made headlines, but handguns were by far the most used and the most useful weapons in crime.

Unfortunately, there was the National Rifle Association, that ubiquitous organization that pops up inevitably to oppose gun controls and whose response to logic is much like stomach acidity's response to sauerkraut. The NRA did not want its heavily armed members to run the risk of a five-year jail rap, so at its insistence "pistols and revolvers" was knocked out of the language of the bill.

The National Firearms Act as originally written would have included under its taxing and registration requirements "any firearm which shoots automatically or semiautomatically more than 12 shots without reloading." The NRA browbeat Congress into rewriting the bill so that it would include only weapons that fire multiple shots "by a single function of the trigger"—one continuous pull. This eliminated semiautomatic rifles and pistols, which require an individual pull for each bullet.

As if the NRA's opposition weren't enough of a burden, the government screwed up from the beginning. It introduced the bill on the Senate side, forgetting that tax revenue legislation always *must* originate on the House side. Discovering his blunder,

Cummings backed up and tried again, this time dropping his bill where it belonged, in the Ways and Means Committee; but that was not exactly the most hospitable depository for a gun-control bill, considering that twelve of the fifteen Democrats and five of the ten Republicans were either from the South or from the Midwest, both regions whose politicians have traditionally believed that God gave man a trigger finger for a sacred reason that no one should attempt to inhibit.

Cummings, attempting to keep his gun drive quiet so that those pesky fellows at the National Rifle Association would not be aroused, persuaded Ways and Means Chairman Robert L. Doughton of North Carolina to hold secret hearings on the bill for a couple of weeks. But it was in vain. Naturally the NRA's friends in Congress passed along detailed information as to what was happening, and sure enough here came the deluge of angry letters from NRA members followed closely by NRA officials themselves, testifying against the legislation in no uncertain terms. Cummings suggested making dealers pay $200 for a license to handle submachine guns. NRA President Karl T. Frederick called $200 "burdensome" and suggested that "twenty-five cents is ample, or fifteen cents, or ten cents."

Cummings tried to bluff, but he wasn't very adept at it. He threatened that if the NRA and its allies were not willing to accept legislation such as he had proposed, Congress would take over the manufacturing and disposition of all firearms in the country, which would put the government in a position to sell to nobody but the military and the police if it so desired. There was not, of course—and he must have known it—no, not the slimmest chance that a United States Congress would ever take such an anti-private-industry position.

Flooding Congress with a tidal wave of opposition letters and telegrams, the riflemen won handily. Pistols and automatic hand-guns were removed from coverage. Semiautomatic rifles were removed from coverage. Only sawed-off shotguns and tommy guns were kept in the bill. And indeed there might not have been a new

law to cover even those handy weapons had not John Dillinger and
his boys showed such poor timing as to help the Hoover-Cummings
reform by using a tommy gun to blast their way out of the FBI trap
at Little Bohemia (several people were killed but they had been
killed by an FBI error, not by gangster's intent) and President
Roosevelt decided to help the FBI save face and to throw his
personal weight behind the gun bill. That passed it.

But so what? Did the new law requiring a transfer fee for
possessing an automatic rifle or a sawed-off shotgun take these
weapons away from the criminals? Not at all. It takes no special
talent or intelligence to cut off a gun barrel. When cops cornered
an escaped mental patient from St. Elizabeth's Hospital in Washington, D.C., he had just knocked over a bank and was carrying a
.32 pistol, a 12-gauge sawed-off shotgun concealed under his
overcoat, and twenty-five shells. It was hardly surprising equipment. Sawed-off shotguns are today one of the most popular
holdup weapons: any veteran Safeway supermarket cashier in
Washington knows exactly what they look like.

There are statistics to indicate that the tommy gun is still
around. The usually inaccurate Treasury Department claims that
there are two hundred thousand items registered under the updated
National Firearms Act; tommy guns are in that number, but it also
includes sawed-off shotguns, sawed-off rifles, silencers, and such
"destructive devices" as cannons and bazookas as well as submachine guns. During a one-month amnesty in 1968, sixty-five
thousand more "gangster-type" weapons were brought in and
registered. How many remain unregistered? Plenty, if the Ohio
experience is any example. Ohio police officials complained in 1973
that there were probably 9,000 submachine guns in that state alone
but that only 3,000 of them were registered under the National
Firearms Act and, as of midyear, only 177 were registered under
state law. No doubt the underground market in other states is just
as brisk. But they are getting more expensive. Writing in 1969,
Helmer reported,

A couple of years ago anybody who knew somebody could
pick up a good Thompson for under $300, and Sten guns and

M-3's [two other types of automatic weapons] were selling briskly for as little as $75. Since then prices have doubled or tripled, and the $5 hand grenade now belongs in a class with nickel beer. Now and then you find somebody running a special on full-automatic carbines for $150, but in 1966 you could still get M-2 conversion kits for an even $25.

Whatever the price, they keep popping up everywhere. Blacks have allegedly attacked New York cops with submachine guns and other automatic weapons several times in recent years. The Indian militants at Wounded Knee thought it was hot stuff to show off a Russian-designed submachine gun on television; federal agents claim the Indians often fired automatic weapons at them. Like an endless Easter-egg hunt, the feds here and there uncover a cache of a hundred or so illegal submachine guns. The New York Drug Task Force occasionally finds organized narcotics syndicates that protect their merchandise with submachine guns. In mid-1966 the fellow suspected of trying to ambush Mafia underboss Salvatore Bonanno was wounded by submachine-gun fire. In November 1967 three soldiers in the army of Mafia boss Paul Sciacca were killed by submachine-gun fire. The two youths who held twenty hostages briefly in Dallas in early 1973 were armed with a submachine gun and a sawed-off shotgun. Albert Lee Nussbaum, after being sentenced to five years for transporting a machine gun across a state line, emerged from prison to pick up where he left off: he used his tommy gun to murder one bank guard and almost got a police officer (the bullet lodged in his shield pin) while leading eight bank robberies totaling $248,541. Back in prison, he recently had the good humor to send out word that he opposed any gun-control laws.

Whether or not the National Firearms Act helped shrivel the submachine gun market, the use of that weapon did decline. There were at least a couple of other reasons for this. Few crimes require a gun capable of chewing up a car or unhinging the side of a saloon. Why lay oneself open to a prison sentence for an auxiliary crime—carrying an unregistered tommy gun—when a semiautomatic rifle or a semiautomatic shotgun, ownership of neither requiring a federal license or a local license, would do the average crime job just as well. If you aren't too particular about where the bullets go, you can get off a couple of shots a second with either. Apparently little experimentation has been done by the gun industry to find out just what the speed capabilities of the semiautomatic rifle can be when coupled to a fast finger. I wrote to a number of manufacturers to see if they had done any research along this line but could find none that had. The nearest thing to an estimate came from little Commando Arms, Inc., of Knoxville, Tennessee, which specializes in equipping .45-caliber carbines (fifteen- or thirty-shot magazines) with stocks to resemble commando weapons. They are also reminiscent of the tommy gun. A spokesman for Commando Arms said the weapons had never been timed but that a thirty-shot clip could be emptied "pretty durn fast." In contrast to Commando Arms's normal acceptance of the fact that firearms are for shooting, one of Connecticut's important manufacturers, Sturm, Ruger & Co., was strangely outraged even to be reminded that semiautomatic rifles can be used for fast firing. E. P. Nolan, Vice-President for Marketing at Sturm, Ruger, replied to my query about the speed of Ruger semiautomatic rifles that it was not a sporting question; he said he hoped I would never buy a Ruger rifle and he made it quite clear that he wanted never to hear from me again. Considering the kind of publicity some firearms are getting these days, the sensitivity of the Connecticut gun industry is understandable.

A few days after Nolan denounced me for asking questions about his merchandise, Mark Essex, a twenty-three-year-old black whose shafting by the U.S. Navy had made him hate all whites, went to the roof of the Howard Johnson Motel in downtown New Orleans and started shooting. Maybe he had help from others and maybe he didn't; the police, as usual, weren't sure. But of one thing they were sure, ballistically: his .44-caliber Ruger semiautomatic carbine had killed at least two of the seven victims that day, and his Ruger weapon was also ballistically linked to the shooting of two

New Orleans policemen on New Year's Eve. He must have been firing his Ruger pretty fast from the motel roof because at one point in the gunfight New Orleans cops said they thought there were *five* men shooting at them.

The crazy ex-Pinkerton guard who went into the New Jersey employment agency in 1972 equipped with two semiautomatic rifles and a pocketful of extra ammunition demonstrated clearly enough that the tommy gun isn't needed: in what witnesses said took only "six or seven minutes" he got off between fifty to seventy shots, killing six and wounding six. In the opinion of some experts of the tommy-gun era (Johnson and Haven, *Automatic Arms*, for example), "the semiautomatic rifle is capable of laying down a barrage in much the same manner as a light machine gun." And the semiautomatic rifle was then, and still is, considered a "nice" weapon, even a sporting weapon. Well, maybe not by everyone, but it takes more than harsh words to put obliging gun merchants out of business. In 1965 California Attorney General Thomas Lynch appeared before the Juvenile Delinquency Subcommittee to denounce a weapon called "The Enforcer"—"one of the most fantastic weapons I have ever seen in my life, and I have been in this business a long time. This weapon is an M-1 carbine in reality, cut down [the stock is cut off and a pistol grip attached; the barrel is cut off too]. It is well made, as you can see. It has no legitimate purpose except that it can be carried under your coat in an appropriate sling which need be no more than a sling or piece of rope. It can be completely concealed. I know of only two uses for it. One is robbery, and the other is murder." Harsh words, but flip open a gun magazine today and you'll find the same .30-caliber semiautomatic "having the mobility of a handgun and firepower of a rifle" still being sold by Universal Firearms Corp. of Hialeah, Florida, the company whose product had infuriated Lynch. Indeed, the heirs of the tommy are to be seen in all the popular gun literature, sometimes described in such a way as to suggest that somebody is trying to skim close to the limits set by the tommy-gun law: a barrel length of not less than 18 inches and a minimum

overall length of 27 inches. A recent issue of *Guns* magazine touts a
Remington Model 870P police riot gun weighing only 7 pounds,
ten ounces, with a metal stock that folds up to make the gun only
28½ inches long. You can get it with a pistol grip, just like tommy
had. It's all legal.

But the main reason for the decline in the use of the tommy
gun was undoubtedly that the men who plied their trade behind
guns had discovered that good public relations is worth almost its
weight in booty. For a while, particularly during the Chicago beer
wars, the flame and sweep of the tommy gun signaled another
"American first"—something to be proud of, or at least to tolerate
in the name of progress. But after the newness wore off, the public
began to view the tommy gunman as irresponsible. It was quite all
right for the hoodlum to wipe out six or seven of his mischievous
colleagues within the confines of a garage or saloon, but when he
began to use it as a sidewalk broom—with baby carriages and
children falling by the wayside—the Mothers of America finally
began to squawk. And when that happens, the police must—over-
coming their usual reluctance to hunt criminals—go forth and do
their duty. Why risk it? Why stir up the moms and cops? It was
senseless, when the .38 or .45 roscoe would do the job just as well, if
not better, and in a much more socially decorous fashion. Why
overkill? Why lug along a gun that you can hide only under an
overcoat? Speaking for the advantages of all semiautomatic pistols
was the Charter Arms advertisement of the gun selected by Arthur
Bremer: "Shoots five shots as fast as you can pull the trigger. So
small, it can hide in your drawer, pocket or purse." Most mod
criminals prefer to travel light. As for the trigger speed, Charter
Arms did not exaggerate. Bremer needed only 2.7 seconds to put
four bullets into Wallace's arm, chest, and stomach.

Next: the Federal Firearms Act of 1938. It was supposed to
prohibit the interstate shipment of handguns to felons and to
fugitives from justice. Like the 1934 Act, it was originally written to
require both the licensing of owners and the registering of guns;

both provisions were knocked out by the NRA. The 1938 Act required that dealers have a license. The cost of this license—which made the holder virtually immune from state and local gun laws—was set at a dollar. For that buck he got the privilege of getting guns through the mail, something the unlicensed citizen could not do. To obtain the license, one filled out the simplest of forms, available at any post office. There was no minimum or maximum age restriction. There was no penalty for lying on the application. One didn't have to be a legitimate dealer to get a license, and in fact the alleged administrators of the law, the ATTD, subsequently admitted that probably two-thirds of the federal dealers' licenses were held fraudulently. The IRS didn't seem to mind.

As for the portion of the law forbidding interstate shipment to criminals and possible criminals, it was ruined before Congress even saw it. The Federal Firearms Act of 1938 was written by a committee of three: a representative of the Senate Special Committee on Crime, a representative of the Department of Justice, and a representative of the National Rifle Association. The NRA member, President Frederick, was far and away the most influential member of the troika. He pressured the others into inserting into the bill a phrase to make it unlawful for a dealer to ship to a criminal only if he did it "*knowing or having reasonable cause to believe*" that the recipient was a criminal. Proving that a dealer shipped a gun to a hoodlum is sometimes not so difficult; proving that he *knew* his customer was a hoodlum is always difficult and often impossible. That phrase destroyed the law. Or at least the Justice Department claimed the law was destroyed, and consequently not a single dealer was prosecuted under the clause in the next thirty years. To be more exact, the Justice Department covered up its failure for thirty years and said nothing about the quality of the law or its own alleged helplessness until its officials, testifying before a Senate subcommittee, were forced to admit that they had done nothing during the entire life of that law; after this was publicized, the embarrassed bureaucrats went scurrying about until they finally made one pinch and conviction in 1968. Their first.

The pattern successfully established by the NRA in this instance—first total opposition, later modified only if the government submitted to NRA-mangled legislation—was to be the pattern by which gun legislation was written in Congress from that day until the present.

For his heroism in penetrating the Congressional lines and shafting the Federal Firearms Act with the magic phrase, Frederick was later awarded the NRA's highest accolade, Honorary Life Membership, a laurel that as of 1971 had been conferred on only six persons. Another to receive it, for playing a "leading role in removing restrictive features of federal firearms bills of the 1930's," as the citation reads, was Lt. Gen. Milton A. Reckord (Ret.), a hardfaced fellow who had come out of the Meuse-Argonne slaughter of World War I a much-bemedaled hero. Reckord, as Executive Vice President of the NRA, worked with Frederick to almost wipe out the earlier gun-control law, the National Firearms Act of 1934. Their efforts may have spared sportsmen from being badgered by federal laws, as they claimed was the only intent of their lobbying; but the effective result of their work on Congress was also to leave America's criminals quite as free to buy and own and use guns as ever before. The gun controls passed in the 1930s were a washout.

CONNECTICUT'S GIFT TO DOMESTIC TRANQUILLITY

And so we say farewell to the failures of the more distant past and come to the gun-control failures of the 1960s, which were led throughout by our little Senator with the big head of brilliant white hair and a taste for Scotch, none other than Tom

Dodd himself. For ten years he carried the flag, posing as the great reformer. He was the author, at least the author of record, of the major gun-reform legislation, such as it was. He was chairman of the Senate Juvenile Delinquency Subcommittee, whose staff—despite their devious boss—conducted a number of first-rate investigations into the heart of the problem. On the surface, he looked very, very good.

Though he had little seniority, having won his seat in the Senate only in 1958, the reputation he brought with him from his pre-Senate days made up for that. Among other things, he had been a gamecock special assistant to a U.S. Attorney, prosecuting wayward Deep South public officials for civil rights violations twenty years before the beginning of the civil rights movement, and prosecuting them with such tenacity that on at least one occasion he had to be escorted to the state line to assure his personal safety.

In the early 1930s, he spent about a year in the FBI, which was enough to give him a permanent patina of law and order. He reportedly was at the battle of Little Bohemia, where the federal agents goofed and allowed Dillinger to escape. Far from pretending heroism, Dodd was honest enough to admit it was during this fight that he first decided the FBI wasn't the place to spend his life "because I was scared silly."

During World War II he had won fame prosecuting officials of the German-American Bund and executives of the Anaconda Wire and Cable Company for cheating the government's war effort by supplying defective telephone wire to the Army. After the war he became executive trial counsel at the Nuremberg trials of Nazi war criminals; he was the assistant to Robert Jackson, chief prosecutor and later Supreme Court Justice, but some felt that Dodd was the man who held the prosecution together.

Elected to Congress in 1952—the only Congressional Democrat from Connecticut to survive the Eisenhower landslide—he began putting together the record of a typical "national Democrat" with just a touch of anti-Communist kookiness, enough to keep him politically safe during the McCarthy years. But apparently it was not an artificial attitude: he really thought that way, and by the time he was elected to the U.S. Senate in 1958, on his second try, Dodd was a full-fledged anti-Commie zealot—as well as being what Representative Thomas O'Neill, Jr., of Massachusetts once called "the second nastiest drunk in town"—and there were times in the years ahead when he almost seemed to have lost his marbles on the subject, as when he accused *The New York Times*, the New York *Post*, the St. Louis *Post-Dispatch*, the Providence *Journal*, and the Washington *Post* of being the "Red network," a Communist-front machinery of newspapers in cahoots to smear and defeat him. Though he often voted the "liberal" way on civil rights and civil liberties and economic issues, he suspected liberals and thought of himself as a true conservative. He had paranoid intimations that Robert Kennedy, when Attorney General, was bugging his telephone. He was convinced that Kennedy and "other fellow travelers" would someday try to frame him by "dumping a naked blonde in my hotel room and then taking pictures." He was convinced that a professor at Georgetown University who gave one of Dodd's sons a D in a course must be a subversive, and he ordered a security check run on the man.

In other words, Dodd was often pickled and always slightly unbalanced on some topics. Furthermore, despite his many successes, he was extremely unsure of himself, and overly defensive. Carl Perian, the staff director of Dodd's Juvenile Delinquency Subcommittee and the man who kept the Senator's integrity publicly patched up and wired together on the gun-controls issue, describes his former boss: "Dodd was always very, well, he was very short and felt inferior about it. He didn't like academicians. He didn't like bright people. He didn't like good debaters. He thought Hruska [Senator Roman Hruska of Nebraska, leader of the pro-gun forces on the subcommittee and Dodd's constant tormentor] was bright, and he was just psychologically terrified at the thought of matching wits with Hruska. He'd make up all kinds of excuses not to do it. We went out to California in the middle of the Watts riots, set up an entire hearing on guns, and then when Dodd heard Hruska was there, he canceled the hearings. He wouldn't sit on the podium and match Hruska, tit for tat. The old man would squirm and say, 'Roman's going to be up there, and we've got to sharpen our pencils.' "

Making Dodd's life even more unhappy was the common misfortune that he combined the desires of the playboy and wastrel without the funds to be either legally. By the time he had been in the Senate three years, he was in debt the equivalent of five full years' salary. The next step was automatic: he went on the take. His Juvenile Delinquency Subcommittee staff was investigating the impact of TV violence on youth, and they had worked up a pretty good case against Metromedia. Then Dodd got some money and gifts from Metromedia executives and he dropped the investigation. His investigation of the movie industry fizzled after he received a five-hundred-dollar contribution from a Motion Picture Association lobbyist. (You could say one thing for Dodd: he sold cheap.) Two committees of which Dodd was a member were investigating drug industry abuses; but Dodd himself never worked up much enthusiasm for the investigations, perhaps because he was using a private plane supplied by the McKesson & Robbins drug company and received a thousand-dollar contribution from a McKesson & Robbins vice president. Dodd was also chairman of an antitrust subcommittee investigating the insurance industry, which is extremely potent in Connecticut. The investigation never got off the ground. At the same time as he was supposed to be doing something about it he was taking heavy payoffs for services rendered to a wide variety of insurance companies; his law firm represented Maryland Casualty, Standard Accident Insurance, Phoenix of Hartford Insurance, American Insurance Group, American Fidelity, Reliance Insurance, Fire Association of Philadelphia, Northwestern National Casualty, Central Mutual Insurance, and Norfolk and Dedham Insurance. Also, Dodd had large insurance policies on which he paid no premiums.

This was the sterling chap who led the gun-control fight in the Senate, and with an awareness of that background one can more easily understand why, though no legislation has been pushed so emotionally for so long, there were so few results.

There had been gun-control bills eddying around the back-washes of Congress for years. The big emotional tidal wave that set them going was President Kennedy's death; the momentum was perpetuated by the assassinations of Robert Kennedy and Martin Luther King, Jr., and by the massacre of fourteen people by Charles Whitman, shooting from the top of the University of Texas tower. Also, from Watts to Newark, rioters did a good job during the 1960s of suggesting that maybe everybody should disarm before a few nuts triggered a race war.

Along with the lobby of emotional events there was an official list of advocates that was so impressive one might suppose it would have been easy to pass a law to assure control over the 200 million or so guns in 50 million homes.*

Most major newspapers, most judges, most penal officials, J. Edgar Hoover, some big-city police chiefs and most big-city mayors urged Congress to require that all guns be registered and owners licensed; some wanted to outlaw *all* handguns and even prohibit their manufacture except for use by the military and police. Backing them in a general way throughout the 1960s and right up to the present were public-opinion polls that regularly showed a majority of the people wanting the gun market to be freed of its anarchy. In urban America the gun was now widely seen as nothing but a plague.

And yet, mysteriously enough, little came of the mood. Only once in the 1960s were gun-control advocates successful in Congress, and then only in a most limited fashion. Why? The usual explanation has been that further reform was blocked by the

---

* Among the advocates: the National Crime Commission, the National Riot Commission, the American Bar Association, the National Council on Crime and Delinquency, the General Association of Women's Clubs, the National Association of Sheriffs, the American Civil Liberties Union, the AFL-CIO, the United Auto Workers, the Americans for Democratic Action, the Leadership Conference on Civil Rights (forty affiliated organizations), and the Women's Clubs of America.

National Rifle Association, possibly the most powerful grass-roots lobby in America. Reformers have made the NRA the standard villain, and the NRA—because it profits from the appearance of power—has done all it could to promote this reputation, but the National Rifle Association is not the omnipotent fraternity it would like you to think it is.

The real reason that America observed the tenth anniversary of John Kennedy's death without being able to point to any significant gun reform is that too much hypocrisy and fraud was mixed into the Congressional effort. And perhaps the main source of that mixture, or at least the most flamboyant individual source, was Senator Dodd, who behind his reformist front continued to put one stone upon another in building a memorial to corruption. "Congressmen on the make," Drew Pearson once wrote, "have discovered a number of shortcuts to the easy dollar, and Senator Thomas Dodd has tried most of them." To Dodd, gun controls were just another shortcut.

Connecticut, Dodd's base of operation, has more than a casual relationship to the gunmakers. It is, in fact, along with Massachusetts, the bellwether of the New England gun industry, and the New England gun industry has almost a corner on the market. Connecticut is headquarters for Remington, Colt Industries, Sturm, Ruger & Co., O. F. Mossberg & Sons, Winchester-Western, Charter Arms, Marlin Firearms Co., and High Standard, as well as such major manufacturers of ammunition as Winchester-Western, Peters Cartridge, and Connecticut Cartridge. And the firearms side of Colt Industries—one of the two hundred largest businesses in America—brings in only about 15 percent of that conglomerate's income. According to their annual report, Colt Industries' other divisions that have headquarters in Connecticut include Pratt & Whitney and Chandler-Evans Control Systems. Winchester is owned by Olin Corp.—another of the top two hundred—which also owns a bevy of companies manufacturing everything from skis to power tools to pharmaceuticals. The voices of Colt and

Winchester indirectly carry the weight of other giant industries to which they are tied.

And when they spoke, Dodd—like all federal politicians from Connecticut—listened, and parroted their wishes to Washington. But he did so only for a price.

Former aides of Senator Dodd tell how an official of the Colt Firearms Company became alarmed when he was approached by an emissary from Dodd in what appeared to be a shakedown. After an especially bountiful contribution from the gun industry, Dodd would make cracks to his staff that the "gun issue is good to keep alive." Carl Perian says the agent for one of the larger gun manufacturers once told him—rubbing his fingers in the classic sign for money—"We've got Dodd in our pocket."

But they didn't have him there as thoroughly as they thought. He was shifty. Because it was profitable for him to keep the gun-control debate going as long as possible, Dodd dillydallied.

James Boyd, the Dodd staffer whose exposé of the Senator brought about his downfall, says, "Dodd never really devoted any personal efforts to the gun problem. He didn't give it day-to-day leadership. Once or twice a year he would run the problem through his subcommittee for an executive session in which the legislation would be lethargically mashed this way and that, with no results. Nor would he hold a public hearing unless he wanted some publicity. Once or twice a year he would make a statement on the floor of the Senate, but very pro forma."

And when Dodd did speak out publicly on his gun legislation, he was often in error about what it contained. Once he gave an interview with CBS that his staff diplomatically had to have canceled, it was so faulty. Anything of substance that went into the gun-control fight was done by his staff, under the leadership of Perian, a tough, articulate strategist whose dress and temper are those of a riverboat dandy with a derringer in his boot. But often the staff's best efforts were canceled by Dodd's behind-the-scenes deals with the opposition.

Perian recalls that on the very day Martin Luther King was

assassinated—but before it happened—Dodd "went into the committeeroom without asking me to accompany him. That was very unusual. The way I interpret it was he didn't want me in there because he was going to sell us out. One of Senator [Joseph] Tydings' staffers who was in there later told me, 'If you ever wanted a blueprint of how to defeat a piece of legislation, you would have had to see your chairman in action at this meeting.' In other words, Dodd apparently did everything he could to aggravate and irritate the other members of the subcommittee so that they would kill the bill. Then he could have denied he had anything to do with the results."

Later in the day came King's death and Dodd saw that he would have to push some kind of gun-control bill, so he ordered Perian and his other staffers to fix up a bill—"but leave out rifles and shotguns." A rifle was used to assassinate King. Dodd also ordered his staff to catch up with Senators George Smathers of Florida, Edward Long of Missouri, and Hugh Scott of Pennsylvania and get their votes—although Dodd knew that they could be expected to vote *against* letting a gun-control bill get out of committee. (Scott fooled him and voted for it.) Meanwhile, leaving his staff to handle the details, Dodd announced, "I have to go home to attend a party." It was a typical gesture.

VIRTUE BY OVERKILL

Dodd was not always devious just because he wanted to keep the golden debate going. He was under tremendous pressures from more than one side, and some deviousness was perhaps necessary to bring about a compromise. To be bought off by the gun industry was not enough, for the gun industry is just one of the powerful conflicting forces in the gun debate. If he was to get any kind of legislation through his subcommittee and through the parent Judiciary Committee and then through the Senate, he knew

that he had to satisfy some of the most sensitive of opponents. Or
at least they were opponents on *some* of the major points. It was
very, very complicated—and still is—and so perhaps it would be
best at this early point in the narrative to make clear that the
conflict in the gun-control debate has not been simply between
those who want controls and those who do not. It has also been
between those of conflicting commercial interests; in fact, the cash
register has been the key battlefield. But spectators to the battle
have heard very little about that. Instead, they have been subjected
to the most pious sermonizing from every direction. The lack of
candor has, in fact, been the most pitiful result of it all, because
deception has not been necessary. Every side has a sizable amount
of good sense and logic to depend on; but instead of simply saying
they want to have a good time with their guns—something not
frowned on even in Puritan America—the hunters have concocted
all sorts of weird Constitutional and conservation arguments to
defend their position. Instead of saying simply that they want to
make as much money as they possibly can—which has never been
considered a sin in America—the gun merchants also throw up
great cloudbanks of patriotic fluff. And the antigun people, who
could effectively restrict their argument to showing that guns are
not an absolute necessity for the American way of life, have instead
clobbered the senses with distorted statistics hysterically interpreted.

To oversimplify, the major divisions in the debate have been
the Antiguns, the Sports, and the Hucksters—in foreign affairs
their counterparts are the Antiwar forces, the Militarists, and the
Defense Industry. The most visible and noisiest division, of course,
finds the Sports and the Hucksters teaming up against the
Antiguns. But as will be shown, the Sports and the Hucksters
sometimes have their sharp differences too, as do elements within
the Hucksters.

The Antiguns are a varied lot. Some would simply like to make
it more difficult to own guns by requiring the licensing of owners
and the registration of firearms. Others would like to limit the use

of guns to police and military, or perhaps also—in their more generous moments—to target-shooters, if their guns were kept locked up at the firing range. The Antiguns are adept with statistics and love to point out that more Americans have been the victims of domestic gun murders, accidents, and suicides since the turn of the century than have been lost in all our wars. Here is one of them, talking in 1972: "Every four minutes someone in the United States is killed or wounded by gunfire. Every three minutes someone is robbed at gunpoint. A new handgun is sold on the average of every thirteen seconds. Used handguns are traded at the rate of one every thirty seconds." They are quick to point out that two of every three homicides, over a third of all robberies, and one out of five aggravated assaults are committed with a gun, usually a handgun. And, of course, the Antiguns are never without a dramatic gun tragedy to relate—some teen-age gunsel knocking off a cop with twelve children, or a six-year-old boy finding his father's shotgun and wiping out the family while they sleep, etc. Here is another, again in 1972, giving the latest bloody report from Los Angeles: "A carpenter working on the roof of a house was allegedly shot by juvenile snipers practicing their marksmanship, a swimming pool guard was shot to death for reprimanding an unruly swimmer, and a fourteen-year-old boy was killed over a fifty-cent robbery." The Antiguns can make the mere possession of firearms sound like a very gory proposition.

SPORTING PROPOSITION

The Sports—who include hunters and target-shooters and collectors—are an equally flamboyant lot. They begin by plucking their rhetoric right out of the Constitution—the Second Amendment (Article II of the Bill of Rights): "A well-regulated militia, being necessary to the security of a free State, the right of the people to keep and bear arms, shall not be infringed"—and with this they damn the Antiguns as un-American. To be sure, the United States Supreme Court has repeatedly said that this Amendment has nothing to do with the right to personal ownership of guns but only with the right of a state to establish a militia; but in saying so, the Supreme Court has not in the slightest degree discouraged the Sports from using this line of argument, which in fact they have done during every appearance before Congressional committees for at least the past thirty-five years. Indeed, even when the Congressional objective was simply to make it more difficult to buy submachine guns (hardly a sporting weapon) and sawed-off shotguns, many Sports went to Congress and said that it was every American's right to own a submachine gun if he wanted to. Even as recently as the March 1973 issue of *The American Rifleman*, the NRA argues that the sawed-off shotgun is a legitimate weapon that should be made available to "all able-bodied young and middle-aged males and perhaps many more." When efforts were made to restrict the sale of bazookas and mortars and antitank guns in the 1960s, once again many Sports went to Washington and said that it was the right of every American to own a weapon with which he could blow up a house or a truck if he wanted to. Some Sports are unbudgeable on this point.

TIN CAN ALLEY

Target-shooters are the gun world's masters of hallucination. They can stand all day plinking at a tomato can and dreaming that they are Buffalo Bill who could *break onetwothree-fourfive pigeons justlikethat*. Occasionally, grown men will actually tell you that when they shoot at a target, they really are seeing an outlaw. That kind of juvenilia is a deep and endless vein of gold for the industry. Any serious target-shooter will own at least $500 worth of guns—that's the barest of minimums—and will spend $100 or so on ammunition each year. What this means to the industry can be sampled at Winchester-Western, a corporation that had $250.7 million in arms and ammunition sales in 1972 and could thank stationary-target-shooters for 25 percent of that; ten years ago they were contributing only 10 percent to the corporation's income. Winchester has all sorts of come-ons, including father-son and father-daughter seminars that cost from $150 for an over-the-weekend outing that includes church services to $1,780 for a goose-hunting trip to Iceland. The target-shooter, however, is a simple person who does not require such embellishments. He will go out weekend after weekend to engage in a pastime that is about as gripping as a fast game of mumblety-peg. The target-shooters' less lethargic cousins, the trap- and skeet-shooters, are big spenders too. In 1972 they blasted away at half a billion clay "birds" costing $125 million. Avid is the only word to describe these Sports. Some of the seventeen thousand participants in the Grand American Trap-Shooting Tournament in 1972 couldn't climb out of their wheelchairs, but shoot they did.*

Naturally, these people have their heroes. One of them is the late Adolph P. Toepperwein, who holds the record for wasting ammunition with accuracy: in a ten-day period in 1906 at a fair in San Antonio he is reported to have hit 72,491 wooden blocks out of 72,500 tossed into the air. Toepperwein used .22 rifles supplied by Winchester-Western, for whom he was an exhibition shooter. Think of it: ten days shooting at wooden blocks. The target-shooter is little different today from what he was at the beginning of the sport, which dates back to the martial feasts of early-fifteenth-century Germany at which young men met to drink ale all day and belch and shoot their arquebuses; the fellow who hit the target most often won a fair damsel, the loser got a pig. Today they don't even get a choice. The NRA promotes target-shooting with great enthusiasm because that's where the industry's big money comes from.

---

* Lots of goodies about this and other features of the industry are packed into Marilyn Bender's "The Gun Business on the Defensive," *The New York Times*, March 4, 1973.

A YEN FOR GOTHIC-FLUTED BARRELS

To those of us who would just as soon collect old hubcaps or broken bottles, the collecting of guns as it is done by the average collector is difficult to get very excited about; but at the top of the fraternity a more rarefied and costly air is breathed, evidenced by the fact that in 1972 thirty-eight lots of firearms brought $543,525 in an auction at Sotheby's, the highest bid being a record $150,000 for the early-eighteenth-century silver-mounted flintlock repeaters made by Michele Lorenzoni of Florence; the pistols are covered with finely engraved battle scenes and classical figures. Even an "ordinary" fine pair of dueling pistols made by the celebrated Paris firm Gastinne-Renette sells for $1,500 to $2,000 these days, and one of their handsomest dueling sets—made in 1844, richly ornamented with gold and with the ebony halfstocks inlaid with silver wire and Gothic-fluted barrels—went for $20,000 at Sotheby's a couple of years ago. But that is collecting art, not guns. "Nobody in his right mind would shoot them," said Leo Martin, gun buyer for Abercrombie & Fitch, with his eye on one of the store's prize offerings, a $20,000 sixteenth-century wheel-lock army pistol. Some engraved stocks are as beautiful as anything produced by Dürer. That's a different matter, as are guns in which are buried something of history or mores. One can become mildly enamored of the fact, for instance, that gunsmiths who specialized in dueling pistols avoided using metals that might catch a ray of the rising sun (sunrise, or just before, being the common time for duels) and momentarily dazzle the shooter, thereby causing him to delay his shot just long enough to be brought down himself. I might even like to have around the house, for no good reason except that he sounded less interested in guns than in some other things, one of the rifles turned out by the eighteenth-century Pennsylvania gunsmith who advertised: "J. T. Sackett, manufacturer of and dealer in rifles, shot guns &c. Also Horse shoer and Blacksmith. He also manufactures a very superior Violin, which has attained much celebrity for its excellense. These have been used by some of the best violinists in Boston, that center of American Musical culture." Some unusual Lugers sell for $10,000 and up, but your average collector is always panting over an ordinary hundred-dollar Luger or worrying if he bought a fake 1851 Colt, or burying himself in esoterica about the minimatics of Francis Pfannal, which are concerns that only another collector can appreciate. Even more mysterious is the collector's willingness to spend large sums of money even on ersatz guns, copies of the real thing, Disneyland museumlike. In 1972 alone gunmakers produced and sold 825,000 commemorative guns. Every time somebody or someplace has an anniversary, Colt quickly cranks out a batch of anniversary guns, and it never gets stuck with them, even when it reaches for the absurd: it made 104 derringers to celebrate the hundred and twenty-fifth anniversary of Genesco, Illinois, in 1961. All were sold at $27.50 each, and reportedly could be resold today for twelve times the original price. The American Bicentennial is an obvious excuse for milking this market: one manufacturer is already peddling a copy of the Brown Bess, the famous long gun used by the British. At $585 they are reportedly selling fast. Eternal childhood.

In any event, collectors have little to do with the gun problem except that they are often ill-informed about the debate and boisterous in their ignorance, and their super-American red-bloodedness contributes its share to the heavy atmosphere within which we operate. When asked why men collect guns, Dr. W. R. Funderburg, past president of the American Society of Arms Collectors, replied, "To one who has studied guns, loved guns, and avidly collected guns for twenty-five years, the question seems absurd. It is like asking why men like apple pie, risqué stories, Scotch whisky, or curvaceous gals in bikinis. How is it possible *not* to like and collect guns?"

A PENNY FOR YOUR WOLF

Far more influential than that kind of Al Capp simple-mindedness is the hunter's generic conviction that he should be free to use any kind of firearm to blast away at just about anything that flies, runs, swims, or slithers. National Rifle Association records show that in a typical year a couple of thousand hunters will mistake a person for a deer or rabbit. But this is privileged shooting: a survey by the Associated Press of thirty-three states shows that rarely is there either prosecution or conviction. The stiffest penalty in recent years, says the AP, was six months on probation plus a charge of $229.67 for jurors' wages, levied against a hunter in Colorado who had shot and killed two children riding by on their bikes.

Generally speaking, hunters are a swinish lot, always have been, and are the same throughout the world. Let us leave America for a moment to look elsewhere—to the pleasant meadows and groves of the Encomienda estate at Santa Cruz de Mudela, where in early January 1973 Generalissimo Francisco Franco of Spain and President Americo Thomaz of Portugal led a hunting party that bagged 1,791 partridges in a two-day shooting orgy. Or let us turn our eyes upon romantic Italy, where we see nearly 2 million slightly insane Italian hunters bobbing across the countryside dressed in feathered hats and flashy hunting suits and boots. Before their slaughter is finished this year—any year—they will have killed an estimated 200 million birds and 50 million animals. They have killed so many insect-eaters that the Italian government and farmers have to bury the fields under increasingly heavy dosages of pesticides. They have specifically killed so many falcons and other heavy birds of prey that snakes and mice are taking over in some rural areas. And what is the Italian hunters' response? "Italian hunters," writes Yorick Blumenfeld in *Editorial Research Reports*, "constitute a powerful, well-heeled force. Lobbyists for extension of the game season include stores that sell hunting gear, rifle and ammunition producers, and the Italian Hunting Federation. The federation places advertisements in the press showing virile male models brandishing powerful firearms and inviting the reader to 'join the ranks of men.' "

If one substitutes "American" for "Italian" and "National Rifle Association" for "Italian Hunting Federation," Blumenfeld's remarks would be just as accurate.* Despite their sentimental protestations to the contrary, hunters have almost no regard for the preservation of wildlife or wildfowl, except to the extent that by preserving a certain number of them, they preserve the "sport" of shooting wild things. And there have been plenty of times when they didn't even show enough sense to protect their own selfish interests, which is why we have seen the last of the passenger pigeon, the Carolina parakeet, the Labrador duck, the Great Plains wolf, the heath hen, the sea mink, and the great auk. For "sport" or for a few bucks (or a few cents: the first bounty in America, a penny per wolf, launched an extermination of the wolves from the East Coast) our great hunters have also driven the Everglades kite, the whooping crane, the golden-checked warbler, the California condor, the mountain lion and timber wolf, the grizzly bear, the polar bear, the osprey, the pelican, and two hundred or so other species into the "endangered" category or even to the brink of extinction. Not all of the damage was done with the gun, but most was.

One of the unique depredations committed by hunters is due partly to the fact that most waterfowl hunters are such lousy shots. Experts say that the average hunter fires five shots before bringing down a duck or goose. But that doesn't mean the "missed" shot is safe; it falls in the marshland—about 6,000 tons of spent lead are

---

* The likenesses between Italian and U.S. hunters include the slaphappy destruction of the balance of nature. For example, men who hunt foxes from light airplanes in South Dakota (they fly the plane with their knees and shoot out the window with a 12-guage shotgun) have knocked the wildlife environment off kilter. "The foxes are shot so bad on my property," a farmer told *The New York Times*, April 3, 1972, voicing a common complaint, "that there is nothing left to control the jack rabbits, which are eating all the bark off the trees. Have you ever watched a plane run down a fox? The animal doesn't have a chance."

deposited in the marshes and ponds of the United States each year, and in the public hunting area near duck blinds it has been found at an estimated density as high as 120,000 pellets per acre—where the waterfowl eat it, grind it in their gizzards, and get lead poisoning. Even the most optimistic researchers believe that 4 percent of the mallard population annually dies from lead poisoning and another 1 percent is sickened. Some biologists estimate the nation is losing up to a million waterfowl to lead poisoning each year; others believe it may be as high as 2 million. It's been going on for a long time, and now they're worried. So are some hunters, about their own welfare, for between 5 and 10 percent of hunter-killed waterfowl are found with ingested shot in the gizzard, which means that to some extent the flesh of the bird is contaminated and can contaminate the eater.

Many hunters make up for their stupidities and clumsiness as marksmen by taking unsporting advantage of the birds. The Chesapeake Bay is winter home to about a million migratory waterfowl. Among these is the canvasback duck, very popular with hunters. It is quite common for hunters to bait the waters with corn, which makes the ducks easy prey. U.S. Attorney Michael E. Marr of Baltimore, who has handled numerous cases against the cheating sportsmen, points out that "a canvasback on corn is like a human being on heroin. It takes away all of their wariness. It really is a tremendous assistance to the hunter." This kind of cheating is, naturally, most common among the affluent and powerful, who don't mind paying fines and are willing to spend considerable money in order to make the ducks helpless in this way. Only 5 of the 670 baiting convictions in Maryland last year drew jail terms. Among those arrested were such fine fellows as Senator Edmund Muskie, former Senator Eugene McCarthy, and Emile DuPont of the industrial clan. Typical of these sportsmen was the wealthy Washington patent attorney who was convicted of shooting 13 canvasbacks in one day (the limit was one bird) and shortly thereafter (though on probation from that conviction and not supposed to be hunting at all) was arrested for baiting the 7 miles of shoreline he owns by dumping 300 pounds of corn into the water every other day and thereby holding virtually as prisoners about 9,000 of the 40,000 canvasbacks wintering in the Chesapeake; the corn temptation was placed about 1,200 feet from a hunting blind.* Because of such tricks the canvasback duck is now an endangered species: there are only about 240,000 still in existence nationally.

American hunters have never shown more than the dimmest sort of wit about managing wildlife. Within eighteen years after the colonists landed at Plymouth they were running out of deer. In 1646 Rhode Island had to order a closed season on deer and by the start of the Revolution only Georgia still allowed deer killing year round. But our forefathers, whose genes are so evident all around us today, paid little attention to closed-season laws. Between 1755 and 1773 Americans shipped to England 600,000 deerskins through the port of Savannah alone.

Best known is the handiwork of riflemen who wiped out the herds of bison. Once the plains bison numbered an estimated 60 million; by 1890 fewer than a thousand remained. You can credit the advent and popularity of the breech-loading rifle, which made reloading on horseback much easier, as the mechanical reason for the bison's demise. Perhaps. But it was just plain greed ($2.50 a hide) and pigheadedness that did it, not the gun. There was no real sport to buffalo hunting. They could be picked off from a safe distance with no trouble at all. Indeed, shooting buffalo was even less of a sport than trap-shooting, as it was done in the early days, around 1830, when passenger pigeons or English sparrows were used as targets and when it was common for some of our great sports of the period to hood the birds to make them fly more slowly.

There are amazing byways and corridors in the psyche of the hunter that most normal people would never be able to follow. It would probably be difficult for them to comprehend, for example,

---

* Philip A. McCombs, "Wardens Hunt the Hunters," Washington *Post* January 18, 1973.

the attractions of the shooting ranch in west Texas that caters to wealthy hunters who want to shoot exotic quarry but don't want any risk or inconvenience. Say the shoe manufacturer from Massachusetts wants to bag an ibex goat but he doesn't want to travel to Asia to do it; he can visit this ranch, which has transplanted a number of zoo castoffs to its 3,000-acre range. There the shoe manufacturer can borrow a gun if he has none and climb aboard a jeep to be driven to within 100 yards of a grazing ibex. Bang. His guide dresses the animal, and within a couple of hours the shoe manufacturer is on his way home with a trophy. For that he pays $1,000. If he doesn't bag an ibex, there's no charge. Because the ranch is fenced and crossfenced, the cover sparse, and the jeep driver relentless, sooner or later just about everyone but the most advanced alcoholics will come away with something to put over the mantle. Of course, one does risk sunburn.

But the very best example of the mind of the hunter that I have heard is told with great relish by Elmer Keith, a well-known writer on guns, in *Shotguns by Keith*:

> Walking back toward the spring wagon for the cold drive home in the gathering winter dusk, Dick suddenly stopped, spread his long legs on either side of a big sage brush and slowly pushed the muzzle of his long full-choked pump gun down into the bush. Then he shot, and out kicked a big white bunny, sans head and ears. Dick said he intended to make sure of that one, so shoved the gun down within two inches of the Jack's neck and let her go. Just why that fool rabbit thought he was still hidden will ever remain one of the dim mysteries.*

That is the true hunter's sense of humor. It is equaled only by the hunter's sense of pride, which was effectively appealed to recently by Canadian bureaucrats, who offered to reward wolf hunters by encasing their victim's jaws in a plastic block.

This is the fraternity that is loved and admired so much by the "conservation" crowd who survive by getting a legal rakeoff from

* (Stackpole Books, 1967), p. 89.

what the hunters of America pay for licenses and ammunition. Each state has a fish and wildlife department, and more than 99 percent of the money they get for wildlife law enforcement, research, management, land acquisition and development comes from the hunting licenses and permits. Less than 1 percent comes from general revenues. Additionally, the hunter indirectly pays the manufacturers' excise tax of 11 percent on sporting arms and ammunition. Under the Pittman-Robertson Federal Aid to Wildlife Restoration Act of 1937, this goes into a special fund in the U.S. Treasury and is thereafter divvied up among the states on a matching-grants basis for wildlife restoration projects. As of 1970 a 10-percent excise tax on handguns goes to the same cause (about $7 million a year). Since recordkeeping began in 1923, hunters have put more than $1.6 billion into "wildlife restoration work" via state hunting licenses, $472.5 million via Robertson-Pittman since 1937, and $124 million via the federal duck-stamp sales started in 1934.

It's better than nothing. But it makes for a wild and unbreakable daisy chain. The hunters feed the conservationists (who constitute a bureaucracy of eighteen thousand at the state level, four thousand at the federal level) a pittance, but that pittance is all the conservationists get, so they fight like demons to let the hunters have perfect freedom with their guns.

The supreme demonic defense from this group always comes in the person and voice of Thomas L. Kimball, Executive Director of the National Wildlife Federation, who becomes quite incensed when any laws are proposed that, by discouraging the ownership of guns, might discourage hunting. And he's right to worry: any gun-control law has a dampening effect on gun-ownership. When Maryland passed a law requiring a permit to carry a handgun, handgun sales dropped 10 percent. Well, Mr. Kimball is going to do everything in his power to see to it that rifles and shotguns don't suffer likewise anywhere in the country. Immediately after John Kennedy's assassination, Dr. E. U. Condon, then a professor of physics at the University of Colorado, proposed that *all* firearms be licensed and *all* private firearms be left in the custody of police except when taken out for a specific purpose and for a specific period, and that anyone taking his private firearms from police custody should be compelled to wear distinctive garb—like the colors required on trucks carrying explosives. That would certainly discourage hunting; so here came Kimball with his tarbrush. Condon had had a very distinguished career in earlier years as director of the National Bureau of Standards and president of several important professional societies. But that was during the Trumanesque "domestic security" and the McCarthy if-you-smile-you're-a-Commie periods when eggheads, especially eggheads of science, could get in trouble with such organizations as the House Un-American Activities Committee. Condon did. HUAC, in 1948, described him as "one of the weakest links in our atomic security." Fifteen years later, proposing something that might inconvenience hunters, Condon still looked suspicious to Kimball, who was only too happy to try to discredit his proposal by going before a Senate committee and reading the old HUAC allegations into the record.

THE MAUSER MENACE

The overlapping, or transitional, interest that links the Sports with the Hucksters is that relating to profits and pocketbook, and here lies the real crux of the gun-control debate. The Sports naturally want as broad a selection of guns as possible at the cheapest prices, and it was this desire that fired them into such an understandable rage over the effort to cut off mail-order gun sales, an effort that was finally successful in 1968 but that, considering the opposition, may be overturned by some Congress of the future. Going back to the bitter wrangling of the pre-1968 period, one could hear the litany of concern for the Sport's pocketbook expressed like this, swaddled in the sonorous voice of Senator Hruska:

There is a big mail-order business in guns in this country, is there not? We have not been able to determine how big, but I imagine it runs into the tens of millions a year. I would think so. Now, if that avenue is foreclosed and the purchaser of a gun must buy that gun from a local dealer, what will happen to the prices of the guns for the man who wants to use them? They would go up. A small dealer cannot stock guns and sell them the same as a mail-order house, can he? He has his money tied up in it and turnover is not very great, and he has to charge more, and he will.

Thirty percent of the people still live in rural areas. As a matter of fact, do you not find that there are many large areas in the United States where there is less population now than fifty years ago? Businesses are rapidly disappearing from the countryside. It would involve many miles of travel to get to the place of business of a licensed dealer. Once there, the purchaser would very likely find a monopoly of one or two dealers. A monopoly—for all practical purposes, a monopoly, and he must buy at their prices.

Now, he might ask the dealer to special order such and such a gun by mail, and he will get it. But will he pay the mail-order price or will he pay the dealer's price? He will probably pay the dealer's price. It is very likely; it is very likely.

My mail indicates that the people are afraid of the impact on the mail business all over the United States. They say, "Why should we legislate a monopoly, a restraint to trade in a well-known business method; namely, mail-order sales, for legitimate, lawful, wholesome purposes?" *

Wholesome purposes. To hear Hruska is to forget for a moment the urban hoodlum and to think only of the Nebraska sodhouse frontiersman taking aim at a ground squirrel.

But what he said about the cheapness of the mail-order houses, compared to their retail competitors—and especially the retail competitors who depend on supplies from the old-line New England gun manufacturers—is quite accurate. Flipping back through gun magazines of the mid-1960s, you will find the largest mail-order outlet, Hunters Lodge of Alexandria, Virginia, which

---

* Juvenile Delinquency Subcommittee, Judiciary Committee, Senate, Hearings on Amendments to Federal Firearms Act (U.S. Government Printing Office, 1967), pp. 250–251.

was a conduit for Interarmco, the largest importer, selling German Mauser rifles for as little as $22.95, Belgian Army M-50 "NATO" Mausers for $39.95, U.S. M-1 carbines for $59.95, Swiss M-11 rifles for $19, most of the rifles using ammunition capable of bringing down deer at a reasonable distance. The end of each World War had dumped millions of guns on the international market that no country but America was rich enough or dumb enough to buy up; and then this glut was added to when NATO forces switched to a uniform cartridge and discarded their old reliables. Handguns too, of course. Interarmco was importing Colt and Smith & Wesson military revolvers that were identical in construction and quality to, and selling for half the price of, the Colt and Smith & Wesson commercial revolvers peddled in the classiest retail stores.

It's estimated that between 1959—about the time the New England manufacturers really began to get their anti-import propaganda going—and 1963, 7 million foreign weapons, mostly military surplus, were imported into the United States. Because of the potential markup (the kind of Italian rifle used on John Kennedy was imported for $1.03 and sold, without scope, for $12.78), they were enormously popular with the dealers who sold them: the large outlets like Sears and Montgomery Ward, as well as thousands of smaller dealers. Because of their cheap price, the surplus guns served as good come-ons, and once hooked, the typical customer spent an estimated $10 and $20 on accessories— cartridges, slings, sights, reloading tools—on the spot, and over the life of the gun would buy gadgets and ammo worth several times the gun's original purchase price.

Around the cheapness of these firearms was to whirl all sorts of erroneous claims in the years ahead. The big American gun manufacturers argued that the castoff military weapons were unsafe, unreliable, not worth even their cheap price, and gave the industry a bad name. Some of the imports deserved the insults: most of the cheap new pot-metal handguns pouring in from Spain and Brazil and Italy were hardly quality stuff. In fact, if you held them over a Bunsen burner, they would melt in half a minute. And a few of the military surplus items—the Kennedy assassination gun, for instance—were of terrible quality. But for the most part, the military surplus guns were not "junk" at all, except in the bookkeeping sense that some of the importers cheated and labeled them as junk so that they could avoid the higher tariff that applies to guns.

Just because some were old did not mean they were junky. The Springfield 1903 surplus rifle, which sold commercially for $40 and which members of the National Rifle Association could buy in a special deal with the government for $15, was a perfectly serviceable gun. The Mauser military rifle, manufactured abroad twenty or thirty or forty years earlier and sold through the catalog for $35, usually turned out to be just as fine a gun as the new American-made commercial rifle selling for more than $100.

Most of the military rifles were manufactured to specifications that were higher and more rigid than those that apply to most sporting firearms. In 1966 the H. P. White Laboratory, America's leading independent firearms-testing agency, tested sixteen types of military rifles and six types of U.S. commercial rifles. All passed. In its report the laboratory praised surplus foreign military rifles: they were

> generally of good design and construction, and usually have safety features not found in many rifles made specifically for sporting uses. There is good reason for that. A rifle must be subjected to GIs of all sizes and shapes for long periods of very rough use, and they do not have some of the refinements that sporting rifles have, and hence they can be much more regulated.*

But the quality of the competing firearms was hardly an issue that would be sufficient to inflame Congress. If the New England gun manufacturers wanted to block the imports of both the pot-metal trash handguns and the military surplus weapons, they

---

* Testimony of William D. Dickinson before Senate Judiciary Subcommittee on Juvenile Delinquency, Aug. 1, 1967, *op. cit.*, p. 255.

would have to fall back on something simpler and more easily understood by the layman. Not surprisingly, they used the "national security" gimmick. Our national security was being imperiled, they argued, because the flood of cheap imports cut so drastically into the sale of new American-made weapons that the manufacturers had to economize by firing skilled labor who were needed to maintain production schedules on combat weapons for the United States armed forces.

Typical of the sad plaints heard from this group was the 1962 letter from C. R. Hellstrom, President of Smith & Wesson, to Los Angeles Police Chief W. H. Parker. Parker had wondered where all the cheap military surplus guns (including Smith & Wessons) were coming from. Hellstrom replied:

> During the First World War our plant was commandeered by the Federal Government, and in the Second World War we were, by Presidential order, directed to the manufacture of service arms exclusively, and there are probably some 2 million surplus arms floating around in the commercial markets.
>
> We made over three-quarters of a million lend-lease guns for Great Britain alone, not to mention contracts with Canada, South Africa, Australia, and other Commonwealth countries. After the war these guns were sold by their respective governments as surplus, and through devious channels they have found their way into the United States where they are being rebored and converted to popular calibers and sold at cut-rate prices.

But the main thrust of Hellstrom's complaint was in the last sentence of his letter:

> We are heartily in sympathy with any action to curtail such imports . . . as they are a threat to the legitimate arms industry so necessary as a standby for national defense.*

---

* Juvenile Delinquency Subcommittee, Judiciary Committee, Senate, Hearings on Interstate Traffic in Mail-Order Firearms (U.S. Government Printing Office, 1963), pp. 3227–3228.

On other occasions Hellstrom became so incensed by the import gun dealers that he called them "troublemakers and pulp magazine gun runners" and "shabby hangers-on and junk peddlers," who should be shaken "from the coattails of an old and honorable industry and sport."

Even before Dodd got to the Senate, the "old and honorable industry" had been working desperately to cleanse its coattails. In 1958 the New England firearms industry had tried to persuade the U.S. Commerce Department to throw its weight against the imports on the grounds that if the New Englanders went broke (not suggested as a likelihood), the nation would be short of gun manufacturers. The same plea had been taken to the House Foreign Affairs Committee by E. C. Hadley, President of the Sporting Arms and Ammunition Manufacturers Institute, a trade organization made up primarily of outfits like Winchester and Remington.

Also in 1958 Senator John F. Kennedy came to their assistance, but he did so candidly, admitting that the bill he introduced to ban the importation of military arms was meant to keep the cash registers jingling in his home state, Massachusetts (headquarters for Savage Arms, Harrington & Richardson, Iver Johnson, Smith & Wesson). The imports, he said, "have helped spoil the domestic market," and his bill was "of particular importance to five arms manufacturers in Massachusetts," which was as close as any politician will come to telling the truth: the legislation was written by the interested parties.

In 1958 and 1959 the gunmakers—aided by Senators Leverett Saltonstall of Massachusetts and Prescott Bush of Connecticut—tried to get the Defense Department, the State Department, and the Office of Civil Defense Mobilization arbitrarily to cut off the imports. Each time they were rebuffed; they also were rebuffed when they tried to get Congress to attach an embargo to the Mutual Security Act. Twice in 1960 Dodd succeeded in attaching as a rider to other legislation a "sense of the Senate" amendment urging the State Department to "prevent the importation of all military firearms," and twice the Senate-House conferees killed the amendment.

By that time it had become clear even to the uniquely obtuse gun industrialists that they were taking the wrong tack, that nobody in his right mind was about to believe that whether they stayed in business was of much significance to the national defense, and that furthermore the imports were not the kind of competition that seriously imperiled them anyway.

So they needed a new attack. And that's when Dodd came up with crime in the streets. Yes, true, to be sure—crime in the streets already existed; but it is significant that the gunmakers of New England didn't discover crime until they needed it. One can search the records of Congress and also the records of the bureaucracy from the mid-1950s until 1963 and find hardly a suggestion that easy gun access might be contributing to urban turmoil and crime. Everything was couched in terms that *Barron's* would understand: profit and loss and competition. Moreover, the usefulness of crime as a new propaganda pitch in their trade-protection effort was brought to the gunmakers' attention—or rather, to Dodd's attention—quite by accident.

It happened one day that Dodd got a letter from the Los Angeles Police Department complaining about several mail-order importers of the cheap guns, the real sleazy stuff, that they in turn were peddling to sleazy L.A. hoodlums. And it so happened at the time that Dodd had just hired the son of an old friend but didn't know what to do with him. Although he was something of a misfit in the office, he was also a gun genius—knew everything about every kind of weapon—and this looked like a good query to send the fellow out to check on. At least it would get him out of Dodd's hair.

Instead of its turning out to be just another Congressional makework junket, however, something came of it. The aide did a marvelous job. He came back loaded with data, so much that in fact, with a carefully detailed explanation from Perian turning the switch, the lightbulb went on over Dodd's head and, lo, before him, illuminated in mystic fashion, was the new ploy: Imported Cheap Guns Equal Street Crime!

On this theme was to be launched the 1963 gun-control hearings. How very clever of Dodd to pinpoint the evils of guns and the tie between guns and crime just about as far from the gun-manufacturing factories of the East Coast as he could get: in Los Angeles. Of course when the hearings opened, he gave profuse public assurances that in preparing for them his investigators had considered the social impact of firearms from every production source, including those "produced in the state I represent, the State of Connecticut." Only obliquely were these ever his target, and then only accidentally, either in 1963 or in the clamorous, quarrelsome hearings of the years beyond. The restrictions that Dodd sought to impose on firearms would have little effect on the manufacturers of America's old-line guns but would, he hoped, cripple the importers of foreign-made weapons. As for the evils of gun-ownership—the risk, the social devastation, the bloody grotesqueries resulting from gun-ownership—these he never even indirectly attempted to pin on Colt and Smith & Wesson and Sturm, Ruger, and Remington and Winchester and other "elite" guns. The arguments he made for restricting sales were aimed at shabbiness and secondhandness. Dodd never opposed guns generically—he never opposed the sale of a firearm across the polished counter of Abercrombie & Fitch—it was only the cheap mail-order gun that really got him worked up, or the surplus war weapons from overseas.

This was his attitude until he left the Senate in 1970. He never changed. He wanted to "tidy up" the gun traffic; he wanted a "responsible" gun traffic. He didn't want to keep guns from Americans—"I want to emphasize that we do not intend to tamper with the Constitutionally guaranteed right of a free people to keep and bear arms," he said in his opening statement of 1963, showing both his ignorance of the Constitution and his bias in favor of the gun traffickers. He wanted only to put a higher pricetag on guns, and to make them most easily available to people who had a good income and who could sign their names legibly: "nice" people.

There was little logic to this, in terms of reducing crime. Experience had shown again and again that so long as guns were available to nice people, not-so-nice people would get their share of them. They steal them. It's that simple. Most of the submachine guns that made the 1920s and 1930s so merry were stolen by enterprising bandits from the arsenals of the National Guard and the police. Most of the guns making the black-market rounds of the underworld today were stolen: many as part of the take in burglaries; literally tons from wholesale warehouses and from the piers; more tons from gunshops and pawnshops. The "shoppers" are always on the prowl, as Queens District Attorney Thomas J. Mackell discovered when he returned home one evening to find burglars had passed his way and had taken the .38-caliber from his dresser. To freshen their arsenal: that's why the four bandits went to John & Al Sports, Inc., and triggered the famous shootout. Also freshening up a bit were two other bandits who dropped in on the Valley Gun Shop in Towson, Maryland, and left with two Thompson submachine guns, AR-15 and AR-180 rifles, two .38-caliber revolvers, and a large supply of ammunition. Those grim underworld reapers know where the best harvests are to be found. So many guns are available to the underworld right now that if not another weapon were added to the market and if every gunshop in the nation closed its doors tomorrow, plenty of cheap guns would be available on the street corner—which is where two out of every three gun purchases are made, according to New York cops—for another generation. In some New York pool halls guns sell for a dollar a caliber: a .38-caliber, $38. In the poorer neighborhoods of every city a gun is communal property, passed from hand to hand for income.* And where crooks don't have

---

* Albert Seedman, former Chief of NYPD detectives, says, "Sometimes you arrest somebody for a job that was pulled last week, say. And you ask, 'Well, where's the weapon?' 'Ah,' he says, 'I gave it to Joe.' And Joe says, 'I gave it

either a friend to lend them a gun or enough money to buy one, they can rent. An inmate of Joliet Penitentiary told a CBS reporter that guns can be had for a percentage of the take: "In other words, if you rob a bank or something for about ten or twenty thousand dollars, it might cost you a good five hundred dollars for a gun. In other words, the more money you make, the more the gun would cost you. You can rent any kind of gun. A machine gun, a sawed-off shotgun, any make of pistols, .45s, .38s, any kind of gun you want."

Dodd was operating under no illusion that he could price the underworld out of the market. He simply wanted to cleanse the market of as many competitive guns as possible, and clear the way for those nice firearms made by those nice manufacturers back home who got a nice price for what they turned out.

---

to John.' And he says, 'I gave it to Jimmy'—and it's passed through four or five hands while we're actively engaged in looking for it."

THE SATURDAY NIGHT SPECIAL

In the City of New York a handgun of any price and any description is simply a "piece." Whether it shows a democratic spirit or lack of imagination, to a New Yorker all guns are called by the same nickname, used by cops and hoodlums alike.

But in some other parts of the country where the little issues of life and death inspire more jocularity, a cheerful special name has been reserved for the low-class gun that draws heavily on the emotions but lightly on the purse. The discrimination is quite deserved; guns are as identifiable by caste and class and even ethnic features as people are. The design of the Luger, for example,

could have come only from the national mentality that gave birth
to Nazism. The design of the Berreta looks like something out of
Leonardo's notebooks. Where else but in America could the Colt
Peacemaker have been conceived, where else but in Britain the
Webley? You look at such guns, and you know.

The low-caste gun is the "Saturday Night Special." It is the
nigger, the white trash, the untouchable of gundom; and like its
human counterpart, nothing can stamp it out. It is especially
impervious to salvation.

Though it has something of a Gay Nineties ring to it, the term
Saturday Night Special has actually been around for only a few
years. Fittingly, its place of birth was Detroit. Something is always
happening there in the way of firearms. When Sidney Hillman, the
labor leader, visited Detroit in the mid-1930s to help settle a strike,
a group of union men met with him in his hotel room. He noted the
bulges under their coats. "Guns! Always guns!" he cried despair-
ingly. "Why is it there are always guns in Detroit?"

Not that Detroit is the easiest place to buy a gun; it's just that
a determined Detroiter won't be stopped when he wants one. So it
was that in the late 1950s and early 1960s, when mischievous
residents of Detroit could not get their hands on guns in their
hometown, they would simply hop in their cars and tool down to
Toledo, Ohio, less than an hour away, where guns were sold in
candy stores, flower shops, filling stations, shoeshine stands,
anywhere at all. Since a great many of these purchases were made
to satisfy the passions of Saturday Night, Detroit lawmen began to
refer to the weapons as Saturday Night Specials. And thus the
language of Americana was enriched.

Like many folk terms, it does not have a fixed meaning. Like
most targets of snobbery, its definition depends largely on who is
talking. To the major American gun manufacturers, who naturally
don't like competition, any cheap import is a Saturday Night
Special, as is any cheap American-manufactured gun not a product
of their assembly line. To the cops and to some members of
Congress, just about any gun that causes trouble is a Saturday

Night Special. They were even using that designation on the gun Arthur Bremer bought at the Casanova Gun Shop in Milwaukee for his assassination attempt on George Wallace. It was an $85 Charter Arms "Undercover-2," a steel pistol with a barrel only 1⅞ inches long; the gun weighs 16 ounces and measures 6½ inches overall—one of the smallest, lightest .38 special steel-frame revolvers made. If that's a Saturday Night Special, then the police of America are loaded down with them, for Bremer's gun was very similar to the style and quality gun preferred by many cops.

The caliber doesn't disqualify it: .38s can be Saturday Night Specials if they're junky enough. But most Saturday Night Specials are .22s and .25s, or at most .32s. Nowadays the cruddy assembly line just seems to gravitate in that direction.

For about the last fifty years the small, inexpensive, easily concealed handgun has been getting an increasingly bad reputation, subjected to such denigrating nicknames as "murder special," "suicide special," "7-11," etc. The genre wasn't always judged that way. The Saturday Night Special's proud predecessors, considered highly practical articles of personal equipment, almost as necessary as garters and belts at every level of society, included the little pearl-handled whatsis that ladies of the evening carried in their handbags to ward off non-paying drunks; the derringer that the professional gambler whipped from his sleeve to defend, or protest, a deal; the tiny gun concealed in the sheriff/outlaw's boot which he drew after he had been otherwise disarmed; the vest-pocket pistol the judge carried to reduce the possibility of unorthodox appeals. They are as commonplace on the late, late movie today as they were once in reality. And they were not scorned.

Congressmen and men of business were as grateful to Henry Deringer, Jr., for producing his handy little pocket pistols as were the thieves and gamblers and whores of the pre-Civil War period. So popular was the Deringer, some of which were only 3¾ inches long, that very soon dozens of manufacturers were copying it (Deringer had forgotten to take out a patent). Some were two-shot guns, the barrels over and under; but the one-shot pistol was the most popular. Eventually all small single-shots came to be referred to as "derringers," to disguise slightly the theft of the design. One bullet from it was big enough to stop an opponent permanently— .33 to .51 caliber, but usually around .41. Because of their short barrels, derringers were not accurate, but the kind of quarrel that they figured in was usually the short-range kind, over a card table or a saloon table or a bed, and at that distance aiming by gesture was quite adequate.

Equally popular in its day was the pepperbox pistol, such as the four-barrel sweetie, smaller than a woman's hand, that Christian Sharps began manufacturing in 1859. Though Sharps has a far more impressive place in gun history for the big-bore buffalo rifle he produced, his pepperbox pistol, which came in .22, .30, and .32 calibers, was the most popular handgun of its type: Americans bought 150,000 of them over a twenty-year period. In the 1870s the price for the .32-caliber was $5.75—very much in the Saturday Night Special price range. (Until they were embargoed by the 1968 Gun Control Act, a Japanese copy of the Sharps four-barrel using .22 long ammunition could be imported for $27.50, which put it at the upper range of SNS prices.)

Perhaps the most remarkable feature of the Saturday Night Special's bad reputation is that the major U.S. gun manufacturers have managed to channel most of the odium onto their less ritzy competitors while engaging in exactly the same commerce, appealing to the same market.

If you thump the piety of such outfits as Colt and Smith & Wesson, you'll find it is pretty hollow. All their talk about wanting to get rid of the Saturday Night Special because cheap guns entice the uninitiated and the violence-prone sounds good until you look back at some of the cheap little guns they were only too proud to push before the Pentagon came along with its unending contracts and made gentlemen out of these companies.

Many of the old-line respectable companies got into the equivalent of the Saturday Night Special market as early as possible. (I don't know why I use "respectable"; they didn't really become respectable until they became rich, and the big manufacturers are neither more nor less "respectable" than the "cottage industry" gunmakers who employ Social Security retirees on their assembly line.) Indeed, if it wishes the credit, Smith & Wesson could claim to have invented the first real Saturday Night Special, for when Horace Smith and Daniel B. Wesson took out a patent for their metallic cartridge in 1854 and began to produce pistols with a patented bored-through cylinder to go with their ammunition in 1857, they specialized in .22-caliber revolvers—producing 126,000 during the next dozen years in which their patent held. Although many other companies cribbed from their cylinder design, it was during this period that the small S & W seven-shot pistol became enormously popular, preferred over the derringer by many ladies and gents of beleaguered occupations. In the 1870s and 1880s small cheap revolvers were turned out by at least fifty companies—many of them peddling their wares by mail order; many of them producing such shoddy pistols, albeit at bargain prices (some went for as little as sixty cents, new), that they were ashamed to put their own company's name on the gun but instead would stamp some catchy, frivolous name on the barrel, like Protector, Little All Right, Little Giant, Tramps Terror, and Banker's Pal.

Marlin is best known these days for its quality rifles and shotguns, but one of the company's earliest production firearms a hundred years ago was a .22 single-shot pistol about as long as a king-size cigaret—a perfect Saturday Night Special. Its first model was called Little Joker. Remington came out in the late 1870s with a runt .22 revolver easily hidden in the palm of the hand.

To understand the sermons against the Saturday Night Special being delivered today from the executive boardrooms in the major gun companies, one must ask for definitions. Would Colt have put into that category the seven-dollar derringer it was turning out in the 1870s and 1880s—the derringer that was constructed in such a way that it could also be used as a knuckleduster? Today one gathers from the remarks made by the officials of such outfits as Colt and S & W that while they consider cheapness and shoddiness great evils, they do not see anything wrong about some other characteristics of the Saturday Night Special, such as ease of concealment; perhaps that is because they have been making easily concealed guns for so many years.

Here's an ad in the Colt catalog of 1909, for example, pushing a six-shot .25-caliber hammerless automatic pistol with a two-inch barrel: "Being flat and compact (only 13 ounces in weight and four and one-half inches long) this arm can be conveniently carried in a vest pocket (or other easily accessible place), ready for instant use, with perfect safety, and has no equal in its size for Power, Accuracy, and Effectiveness." Here's an ad that Colt carried in its catalog from 1933 to 1940, for the Bankers' Special: "This powerful, compact pocket revolver has a dozen important uses—ranging all the way from personal protection to service as a snug little all around arm for camping and outdoors. It handles . . . the .22 High Speed Hollow Point for those who want knock down and stopping power . . . can be easily tucked away in the pocket—ready for service at an instant's notice. $28.50 walnut stock."

Just so there won't be any illusions about the manufacturer's suggestion, remember that the hollow-point bullet mentioned above is the dumdum, which spreads on impact and carries a fist of flesh with it; it's the kind of bullet that blew open the back of Robert Kennedy's head.

Colt also had the Pocket Positive Revolver, six shots, with a 2½ inch barrel, "small enough to be almost concealed in the palm of the hand. . . . It is an ideal lady's revolver . . . for the Home, Office, Store or Pocket—wherever concentrated energy is desirable. . . . A favorite with travelers as it may be packed in small space and is safe under the pillow or in the pocket as in the dresser drawer"; and a .25-caliber automatic pistol, overall length only 4½ inches, six-shot, "conveniently carried in vest pocket or a lady's hand bag . . . fits the feminine hand. . . . May be safely carried in any convenient pocket or easily concealed in the hand." *

---

* In Charles Haven and Frank Belden, *A History of the Colt Revolver and*

Today Colt is said to be among the world's leading suppliers of .25-caliber pocket automatics, one of the most popular being its six-shot automatic that weighs only 12½ ounces and measures 4⁷⁄₁₆ inches overall. You could keep that one hidden in the palm of your hand until you got right up next to the banker, and even then he probably wouldn't see it until you nudged him in the ribs. Colt looks down its nose at the small-caliber cheap foreign import, but until the 1968 Gun Control Act interrupted the flow, it was only too happy to make use of the cheap labor of Spain to have the weapons manufactured there and then shipped to America. Since then, Colt has been making them in this country.

When gun buffs talk to each other and don't feel the outside, critical world is listening, they sometimes are quite candid. Thus, in the September 1972 *Gunsport & Gun Collector* magazine, Harvey Hurwitz wrote of the Saturday Night Special market competition:

> The year 1968 will always be remembered by those who follow and engage in shooting sports but anyone with a little foresight could read the handwriting on the wall in 1967. Apparently the design and marketing group at Smith and Wesson foresaw the changing times and forecast the rules that would be promulgated by the Internal Revenue Service, whereby tons of small foreign automatic pistols that were literally inundating these shores would be turned back. Based on these facts, and the greater truth that a huge market existed for handguns of this nature, a concentrated effort was made [by S&W] to create a new gun that would plug the coming gap.

Among the items offered by Smith & Wesson to supply the enormous market for small handguns is a $46.50 five-shot .22-caliber automatic called the Escort, 5¼ inches long and weighing 14 ounces. S & W advertises it in the usual derring-do tones as "small enough to fit in a uniform pocket, yet packs enough fire power (.22 Long Rifle) to pull you through when the going gets rough." That

---

Other Arms by Colt's Patent Fire Arms Manufacturing Co. from 1936 to 1940 (William Morrow, 1940). Reprinted by Bonanza Books, *passim*.

is, if it goes off. A *Gunsport & Gun Collector* expert tested the gun and found "it jammed up solidly on the first shot."

Which is rather funny, for the old-line gunmakers in this country have a long solemn catechism they run through at the slightest opportunity to persuade you what a perfectly efficient product they turn out. I asked an official at Smith & Wesson what differentiated his company's products from the typical Saturday Night Special. Drawing in an executive breath, he replied without pause:

> Item one. We drop-forge all the major parts of the revolver. In this way we control the granular structure of the steel and compress this granular structure for very fine grain and great strength.
>
> Item two. Where the cheap guns, especially the cheap imports, are made of whatever metal is handy, the guns of our manufacture are made of aircraft-quality steel. We use the very finest ordnance steel available to us for the purpose. We spare no horses there.
>
> Number three. We heat-treat all of the major parts to give them great strength and keep a very close check on this, because hardness is a very important factor.
>
> Number four. I'll give you a specific. One form of heat-treating is case-hardening. We case-harden all hammers and triggers in our revolvers. In fact, this is so important to us that it is a copyrighted procedure. It is sometimes called pack-hardening. It is a surface-hardening process that gives a mottled blue-gray finish to the exterior. Its value to us is that we can get a glass-hard exterior, so hard that it will cut a piece of glass, yet beneath this—about a ten-thousandth of an inch beneath this—is a steel that is more resilient. In hammers and triggers, where there is a considerable amount of vibration and impact from firing and continuous snapping, this is exclusive with us. The resilience absorbs the jarring.
>
> Number five. In the manufacture of the ordinary standard revolver of our production, there are approximately eleven hundred inspection operations on each gun. There are ninety inspection operations on the hammer alone. These are not productive operations. They don't make any money for you. They just make sure your production is up to standard.

Number six. Every gun that we manufacture is tested in three different ways. It is function-tested with standard commercial ammunition to make sure it is a working machine. It is tested by an inspector who is also a shooter. Next, we spot-check with definitive proof loads to make sure the gun will handle everything it is supposed to handle in the line of ammunition, everything in its caliber. The proof loads will be 50 to 55 percent over normal working pressures. Not *every* gun. Where we have been making a gun for forty years without trouble, we do this test on a spot-check basis. If it is a newer gun, we'll check each individual gun until we are satisfied that everything is running fine. We also target every gun. And the guns are fired by qualified men with normal eyesight, who use a forearm rest to prevent fatigue, and they fire every gun on a target at a prescribed distance. Every gun that leaves our plant has been targeted and it shoots where it is supposed to shoot.

From the world of the acknowledged Saturday Night Special, one hears much more modest claims. In this realm one finds executives praising their product because it does *not* shoot where it is supposed to shoot. Harry Friedman, President of Arms Corporation of America in Nashville, a modest little company that puts together about thirty-five thousand .22-caliber MARK-059 revolvers every year, speaks of his $16.95 product as though it were no more deadly than a scarecrow:

No, we don't test-fire our guns. Our pistols aren't for heavy-duty use. But the American people are entitled to this market. If you are a dollar-sixty-an-hour workingman and your wife is scared and you can't afford a $95 Colt, you may want ours for $16.95. Your wife will never use it. How many women get raped, percentagewise? How many houses get broken into?

I find that most people buy guns for their wives, for the table beside their beds. Not to shoot. Just to make their wives feel good, to feel like they've got protection. I had a gentleman call me yesterday who said, "I want one of those inexpensive guns to give to my wife *to make some noise,* to make her feel like she's got protection." She doesn't know how to shoot it.

She takes it out once and shoots it to see if she can do it, and that's the last time the gun is fired.

Anybody who wants to take up crime seriously would be stupid to buy a Saturday Night Special, said Friedman. "These guns are not accurate. A holdup man would have to be right next to a man to hit him. Criminals aren't going to buy our guns, but if they did we'd be lots safer than if they carried .38 Colts. If you want a gun to give to your wife to make a noise, or a gun to stick in your tackle box for killing snakes on fishing trips, okay, this one is okay."

Though he didn't go into other "safety" features of the Saturday Night Special, Friedman could also have pointed out that the little gun is notoriously erratic. This can be both bad and good. Sometimes, though rarely, the cylinders have been placed so close together than when one bullet is fired, it accidentally sets off the adjacent bullet as well, a potentially dangerous situation; sometimes, though again rarely, the bullet will stick, exploding the cylinder, a piece of which will go whizzing off like shrapnel. On those occasions, admittedly, the marksman is in more danger than the target. But the erratic nature of the Saturday Night Special also has an accidentally benign side: more common, much more common, than two bullets firing or one bullet firing and getting stuck is *no* bullet firing; the hammer and firing pin are often so far out of alignment because of faulty craftsmanship that they don't discharge the bullet—and of course when that happens, the Saturday Night Special is the safest gun on the market.

"LEAD BELLY" AND OTHER WOUNDS

But the Saturday Night Special is not quite so innocuous as Friedman makes it sound. After all, the basic potential deadliness of a gun is not in its machinery but in the bullet. The neighborhood zip-gun manufacturer has proved that often enough. Commercial "specialty" gun manufacturers also have proved it in all sorts of weird ways for hundreds of years: spears that also shot bullets, sword guns, dagger guns, cane guns. In the 1920s S. P. Cottrell & Son of Buffalo, New York, was selling a seven-shot .22-caliber revolver built into and disguised as a workable flashlight: "Aiming is unnecessary as the bullet must travel to center of the light. The most practical defense arm ever invented. Absolutely dependable. Price $12.00." There were belt-buckle pistols used by the Nazis, umbrella pistols (not, however, used by Neville Chamberlain), pipe pistols, pen pistols, whip pistols. The jackknife pistol was always a favorite commodity of the gimmick-gun dealers in this country. A typical advertisement, placed by the American Novelty Company of Chicago in the March 1922 issue of *Popular Science Monthly* offered either the "Huntsman" jackknife, four inches long and selling for $4.45, or the "Defender" pocketknife, three inches, $3.25. The ad illustration showed a man—but left it to the reader's imagination as to whether he qualified primarily as a Huntsman or Defender—using his jackknife pistol to shoot an angry dog. The jackknife gun used .22 cartridges; trigger, coiled mainspring, and firing pin were built into the knife parallel with the blades. It was a ludicrous little tomboy gadget, but it could kill as well as any high-priced launcher of bullets.

People who know guns have known this all along, though once in a while they have hoodwinked Washington officials into thinking otherwise, because it was to the gun industry's advantage to pretend that the small-caliber guns were just "peashooters" and "popguns." In the 1934 gun-control hearings, Assistant Attorney General Joseph B. Keenan, who had swallowed the industry's yarn on this point, said that the Justice Department was willing to exclude the .22-caliber rimfire pistol from the proposed gun-control bill because it was looked upon as "not being a deadly weapon as compared with the other-calibered pistols and weapons included."

There are some deadly serious gun users who would disagree. Thus one reads in the extremist paramilitary Minuteman publica-

tion *On Target*: "Suppose the reader has no gun at all and is
planning to buy one gun only. . . . What shall it be? Though it will
surprise many people, my recommendation is a .22 caliber semiautomatic pistol. . . . It's true that the .22 lacks the shock effect of
a more powerful cartridge, but this is largely compensated by the
ease of putting a well-placed shot into heart or brain." Not all
National Rifle Association experts agree on the best home-defense
weapon: in back-to-back articles, at the height of the rioting in
1967, one NRA expert advised keeping a shotgun loaded with No.
4 buck, twenty-seven pellets per round, or "at the very close ranges
usually encountered inside a home, a skeet load of No. 9 shot
would be almost as effective"; the other NRA expert, while
admitting that "a light shotgun is probably the most efficient
firearm for home defense, because it demands less precision in
aiming and is safer to handle than a pistol," nevertheless concluded
that "Most women will be happier with a medium-weight, .22
rimfire, either revolver or auto. Why the .22? True, a .38 or .45
makes a much more effective single hole in an assailant, but a
half-dozen .22 hollow points in the chest will stop a would-be rapist
or murderer better than a .45 slug that goes whistling over his head
because the shooter closed her eyes."

From police departments come endless stories and scientific
and quasi-scientific anecdotes to bolster the status of the small-caliber bullet.*

Lt. Paul E. Murphy of the New York Police Department, who
has had a lifelong love affair with guns, knows them well, and
whose own marksmanship was sufficiently developed to enable him
to put a bullet through the rear vent window of a getaway car and
into the head of a fleeing holdup man to win the NYPD's second
highest medal, the Combat Award, says of the little guns, "The .25

---

* The .25-caliber even got a quiet kind of endorsement from the White House
in 1973 when it was disclosed that this was the caliber Colt that E. Howard
Hunt, one of those implicated in the Watergate burglary, kept in his office at
the White House. A former CIA operative, Hunt must have been familiar with
its capabilities. However, so far as is known, it was never tested on a
Democratic hide.

and the .22 are very underestimated weapons. It's a small bullet but it has a tremendous velocity. If you shot one of those weapons at 125th Street, you could kill somebody in Jersey. Most people say, 'What can happen with a .22?' A .22 bullet hit one of our policemen in the eye; it went inside and around his skull three times—just cored his brain like you core an apple."

Any bullet that travels faster than three hundred feet a second is capable of penetrating flesh and bone. The run-of-the-mill .22-caliber bullet—depending on whether it is a short, long, or long-rifle variety—will travel between nine hundred and fourteen hundred feet a second in ideal conditions. Some of the hotshot .22 ammunition is still doing better than two thousand feet per second at a hundred yards. Even though many of the Saturday Night Specials are so poorly constructed that much of the gas generated by the burning powder leaks past the bullet, thus reducing the velocity, there is still more than sufficient energy left in the bullet to kill. Moreover, the lightweight high-velocity bullet has a special deadliness. Charles V. Rorke, who runs the ballistics office at the New York Police Academy, explains: "When the larger-caliber bullet hits the body, it tends to go right on through. If a person is shot in the shoulder with a .38 bullet, that ordinarily wouldn't be a lethal wound. It might tear half his shoulder off, but the wound would probably be restricted to the shoulder. But the .22-caliber, because it is small in size but traveling at great velocity, is easily deflected. You have a big bullet's velocity with a pellet that is very unstable. So the .22 might hit the shoulder and then rip off in another direction, maybe dropping into the chest area and doing some fatal damage there."

That is exactly the kind of thing that happened to the most damaging of the two .22 bullets fired into Senator John Stennis. One struck him in the left thigh and fragmented when it hit the femur, but it seriously damaged neither the bone nor any major blood vessel or nerve. The other .22 bullet was a much more serious matter: it hit him in the lower rib cage, then apparently bounced off a rib and plowed downward through his body toward the right side—passing through the stomach, the pancreas, the portal vein (an important vessel that carries blood away from the intestinal tract), the colon, and finally lodging within the fleshy portion of the right flank.

Richard Lis of the Chicago Police Department Intelligence Division says, "If I have to get shot in the line of duty, I hope that the guy has a .38 or .45. I have been on the street with kids that have been shot with a .22 or .25; your chances of living are little as compared to a .38 or .45. I do not know if you have seen pictures of people shot with these small-caliber guns, but it does a hell of a job inside of your guts, and it tears your intestines and ricochets over the bones. Your chances of living are not there as compared with a higher-velocity handgun, a .38 or .45.

"I have a partner who was shot by a .45, and he lived. The slug went right through him, and it did not hit any vital parts. But I have seen policemen hit with .22s and .25s—and kids on the street—that could not make it; the bullet would ricochet inside of your abdomen too much, hitting vital organs, mainly intestines, the colon and the kidneys. This is what I have seen."

William L. Cahalan, prosecuting attorney in Detroit, says the waywardness of bullets is another danger inherent in Saturday Night Specials, which "are more deadly than the well-manufactured gun because they do not expel the bullet through the barrel in a true line. Rather, after four or five shots the rifling is worn out and this causes the bullet to come tumbling out of the barrel. It creates what doctors call a 'keyhole' wound—several perforations, and much more difficult to treat."

THEY WORK FOR THE ESKIMOS

It should also be pointed out before we go further that cops talk like experts but actually are not expert on the killing power of bullets. There are no experts on the subject, nor has there ever been anything remotely resembling an authoritative study on whether it is more dangerous to be shot by one bullet than another. There are standard methods to determine velocity and energy—what happens to the bullet in flight. In his *Textbook of Pistols and Revolvers*, Maj. Julian Hatcher works it out:

> A moving object tends to keep on moving, and the heavier it is, or the faster it moves, the harder it will be to stop. For example, a bullet that weighs 200 grains will be twice as hard to stop as one that weighs 100 grains, and is moving at the same speed. Thus the energy of bullets varies directly as the weights of the bullets.
>
> Velocity, however, works differently; if two bullets have the same weight, and one is moving twice as fast as the other, it will not be twice as hard to stop, as might be expected, but four times as hard. And if a bullet is moving three times as fast as another of the same weight, it will be nine times as hard to stop. Thus the energy varies with the square of the velocity.*

But trying to figure out scientifically what weight will best take life is another matter. On the night of December 21, 1972, Patrolman James Pafford of the Monticello (Arkansas) Police Department was attacked by what he assumed to be a mad dog. Pafford whipped a .38-caliber pistol from his pocket and shot the dog twice, and then pulled his .45-caliber police pistol (Arkansas cops apparently travel well armed) and shot the dog "at least" twice more, but the animal just galloped off, still full of life.

Hunters who are competent enough to be candid will acknowledge that killing power cannot be defined. Hunting literature is replete with articles about the successful pursuit of elephants or lions with ammunition that some hunters would consider too lightweight for elk. Hundreds of Eskimos have kept their larders filled with caribou using nothing but .22 Hornets. Jack O'Connor, quite a name in the hunting fraternity, says he is frequently asked whether a .270 is a better killer than a .30-'06, or a .264 a better

---

* (Small-Arms Technical Publishing Co., 1935), p. 182.

killer than a 7-mm. Magnum; his answer is that any of them is a killer if the bullet is placed correctly and not if placed incorrectly. He suspects that "caliber, velocity, foot-pounds of energy, and all the other hocus-pocus that we rifle nuts set so much store by is far less important than many of us think."

The greatest wisdom to achieve in the study of guns is that the experts simply don't agree on killing power because it isn't an absolute. Testifying before a Senate committee, arms merchant Sam Cummings stated, "The World War II carbine was a useless weapon. It was light. Everybody loved it because it was light, but it was a dog." Asked why it was a dog, he continued, "Ballistically, you can have a hatful of cartridges in your stomach and still live long enough to blast the man who fired at you. It is as simple as that." At this juncture the male stenographer who was recording the committee dialogue jumped up and said, "He's right! He's right! I was in the Battle of the Bulge and I shot a German six times with a carbine and he was still able to shoot me." Yet many military experts claim it was a good weapon. Apparently it comes back to where the bullets land.

The .32-caliber is supposed to be a lousy man-killer, but .32-caliber bullets in the head were sufficient to wipe out the banker, his wife, and his daughter in the woods near Grandin, Missouri, early in 1973. And a .32-caliber bullet in the head was sufficient to end the career of narcotics wholesaler Servio Winston Agero as he slept in Oakland.

Police, who get to do a lot of firearms experimenting on people, can't make up their minds about what kind of bullet is the best killer. They used to feel that nothing proved the potency of a bullet more than the fact that it went through the body. Now they are hung up on the idea that the bullet that stays inside and diddles around is the deadliest. They used to swear by the .38 special bullet: for many years it was far and away the most popular with the cops. But now they complain about its penetrating power. Lately they have become faddish about the dumdum, which spreads on impact and usually chugs around inside the body without passing through. Maybe the dumdum has more stopping power, and maybe it hasn't. In the man-stopping business a case can be made for just about any kind of bullet you favor. It's such an arbitrary matter that many misconceptions and distortions have been accepted and spread, even by professionals. Recently a writer for *Playboy* interviewed a guy named "Joey," identified as one of the underworld's most active gunmen, a man who claimed to have thirty-eight kills to his credit. Three of his murders, he said, were of men who had killed his wife, and he was more interested in torturing them to death than in dispatching them speedily, so "I carried .22 long-range flat-nosed bullets, because I wanted them to suffer. At short range they won't kill you, but they will smash your bones and make you bleed." The gunman obviously couldn't read; even a lip-moving reader of the tabloids can cite dozens of cases to prove that flatnosed .22 bullets can kill you very nicely and quickly at short or long range, and they know also that the .38-caliber bullet—which this allegedly renowned gunsel swore by and ordinarily would use none other than—often does a less than efficient job. Police annals are full of stories about suspects who walked away laden with .38 bullets somewhere under the fat. Of course, they are also full of stories about suspects who were laden and didn't walk away. There's just no dependable rule of thumb for hunters of men. *Playboy*'s taped gunman assured his audience that a .38 bullet in the head can be guaranteed to "end the argument quickly." Maybe. Five .38-caliber bullets in the head, as Mafia chieftain Thomas (Tommy Ryan) Eboli would tell you if he could still talk, will almost assuredly do the trick. *Almost* assuredly. One of the victims in the mass murders in a Washington, D.C., Black Muslim headquarters late in January 1973 was shot with a .38 pistol seven times in the head, but she lived. The student who shot Columbia College Dean Henry Coleman with a .38 should have checked with the cops first. They would have told him not to be surprised at what happened: though hit six times, once in the lung, Coleman was back at work in three weeks. Although .45 slugs are supposed to be much better as man-stoppers than .38s, not even .45s can always live up to their reputation when the target is a tough, determined fellow.

Baby Face Nelson was hit by seventeen pieces of lead—buckshot and .45 slugs—but stayed alive long enough to kill the two FBI agents and steal their car. Pretty Boy Floyd reportedly lived for fifteen minutes after being hit by fifteen .45-caliber bullets—lingering long enough to set the atmosphere for his exit in true gangland style, swearing at the FBI agents who had shot him and vowing, "I won't tell you nothing."

Attempting to fix a scale of killing power is especially difficult at present, for there is a great deal of experimentation going on among cartridge manufacturers. If a .22 can bring down a moose, what lesser cartridge may not be about to challenge the .22's ability to bring down, say, a man? A new caseless, primerless cartridge has such a playful appearance that its manufacturers (Daisy/Heddon) don't even like to call it a cartridge. Call it what you wish, it travels at 1,150 feet per second muzzle velocity—about the same as the high-velocity .22 short, though because of its lighter weight it hasn't the long-range accuracy or the penetrating power of the latter. Most of the first-class air arms or pellet guns send their missiles along at 500 feet per second or better; the more powerful air arms can put out a .177 pellet at a velocity of more than 700 feet per second. On the killing powers of these weapons the experts are again in disagreement. Manufacturers of some of the better pellet guns advertise their ability to kill squirrels and rabbits and "varmints"; I've talked to a number of pellet-gun owners who say this is no exaggeration and that they have dropped small game at 15 or 20 yards. The owner of a pump rifle tells me that with eight pumps he can deliver a pellet at short range with the same impact as a .22 short—or, to give it the kind of informal measurement we can all understand, he added, "let's say it will go through both sides of a coffee can at 15 yards."

What would these pellets do to a man at five yards? William

Blizzard writes* that "such a silent, accurate weapon could be dangerous to humans and of value to an assassin, except that its short effective range rather cancels out its potential." This ignores the fact that some assassins, Bremer for example, have nothing against operating at short range.

On the other hand, Russ Moure, director of technical services at International Armament Corp., scoffs at the idea of depending on the best pellet gun on the market to kill even the smallest game, much less man. But if pellet guns are not dependably dangerous, why was G. Gordon Liddy, the ex-FBI agent who masterminded part of the Watergate burglary, packing a pellet pistol in an attaché case the night of the break-in? An expert pistol marksman who often carried and brandished guns in a bullying and reckless fashion, Liddy was not reputed to be the sort who would employ a weapon that couldn't do considerable damage. Indeed, the "harmless" firearms missile is getting so difficult to find that it becomes quite easy—shifting one's thinking back to the cartridge—to believe all the horrible possibilities of the .22 and .25 Saturday Night Special. At the same time, one can play that game so enthusiastically as to come out the other end thinking that .38s and .45s are *less* harmful, which is probably what the police would like you to think.

If ever tempted to draw that conclusion, recollect the little drama down in Bee County, Texas, about twenty years ago. One of two handcuffed robbers drew a hidden .22 pistol from his boot and emptied its five bullets into the Bee County sheriff, a gentleman who, though by far the toughest fellow in that corner of Texas, assumed that he would not survive those five bullets. He did not want to die unavenged, so he emptied his two .44 pistols into the robbers, reloaded, and emptied them again. The sheriff survived after all, but the robbers didn't. The Saturday Night Special is not always the deadliest gun in the room.

* "Tycoon in the Pellet Gun Department," *Gazette-Mail State Magazine*, December 27, 1970.

OLD HANDGUNS NEVER DIE

In short, it is quite easy to make an elaborate and accurate case against the Saturday Night Special, proving that it is very often both a menace and a gyp. But inasmuch as abominable gyps abound in almost every type of commodity for sale in America—autos, toasters, deodorants, furniture, packaged foods: where is the product that does not disappoint?—the only characteristic that could justifiably subject the Saturday Night Special to banishment would be its menacing qualities. But as a matter of fact, there is no proof that the Special is more of a threat to society than a gun of superior quality; and there is indeed some testimony and evidence to indicate that it is less a menace than the better-quality guns in which Americans take such pride.

Patrick V. Murphy, New York City's Police Commissioner, appeared before the Senate Juvenile Delinquency Subcommittee in September 1971 to testify about the dangers of the Saturday Night Special. He said:

What kinds of guns are used by our criminals? . . . Of the 8,792 illegal weapons seized by the New York City Police Department in 1970, 24 percent of them were classified by our ballistics section as of this type [the Special]. In one recent sixteen-month sampling we were able to establish that such weapons, retailing for as little as five or ten dollars, were used in at least 36 murders, 68 robberies, and 117 felonious assaults.

There is absolutely no legitimate reason to permit the importation, manufacture, or sale of these weapons, or their parts. They are sought only by people who have illicit motives, but who may have some difficulty securing a better gun. No policeman, no Army officer, no security guard, no businessman or merchant, and no sportsman would purchase one of these weapons for any lawful purpose [this isn't true, but let Murphy exaggerate to make his point]. . . .

But Saturday Night Specials are only one part of the handgun problem, and by no means the most significant part. Most of the *guns we seized are quality weapons manufactured by reputable foreign and domestic companies . . .* [emphasis added].*

Police officials in other cities have had very much the same experience. They have had troubles from the Specials, but they have had a great deal more trouble from the "quality weapons manufactured by reputable foreign and domestic companies."

So why pick on the Special? Apparently those who do the most aggressive picking—apart from the true gun-control advocates who want the Special outlawed simply because it is a handgun—are motivated by the fact that the cheapest Saturday Night Special increasingly became, after World War II, an irritating competition to the major gun manufacturers. Before the passage of the 1968 Gun Control Act, many thousands of military surplus weapons were imported into this country. They were dismissed by some critics as "junk guns," but actually most of them were well made and highly serviceable and durable. The handguns among them were so cheap and easy to get that they easily qualified as Specials, even though few of them were less than .38 caliber. They're still around, they never die, these military surplus weapons that reached our shores fifteen or twenty years ago and have since passed through a dozen pawnshops and two dozen poolhalls before being sold on the street corner by junkies who need a five-dollar fix. In any event, the 1968 Act cut off that supply from overseas, just as it cut off the supply of the very cheap, poorly made .22-, .25-, and .32-caliber foreign handguns—mostly produced by the second-rate factories of Brazil and Italy and Spain and Germany—that retailed for as little as $3.50. But until their import was halted in 1968, millions of surplus and trash guns flooded this country each year. And though young thugs bought some of them, just plain people—housewives, fishermen, storekeepers—bought many of them too. They were taking trade away from the elite gun manufacturers, who, naturally, went to Congress to have the hole in their pocket sewed up.

---

* Juvenile Delinquency Subcommittee, Judiciary Committee, Senate, Hearings on S.2507 (1968 Gun Control Act to Prohibit the Sale of Saturday Night Special Handguns) (U.S. Government Printing Office, 1971), p. 177.

CAPITOL FOLLIES

And so it came to pass that the modern fiasco of gun control as played upon the soiled stage of Congress and as it was observed by a largely misled public began at exactly 8:19 A.M. on January 29, 1963, in a conference room of the New Senate Office Building when Senator Thomas Dodd, who only five years later was to be censured by his colleagues for illegally pocketing campaign money, opened his hearings into the morality of the gun traffic and the evils of misspent youth. It was called Hearings on Interstate Traffic in Mail-Order Firearms—which, by no accident, were often the kind of firearms that cut into the profits of the gun manufacturers back home in Dodd's Connecticut.

As the chairman of the Senate Subcommittee to Investigate Juvenile Delinquency, Dodd could be expected to wrap his activities in a warm concern for youth. And so he did, his first words sounding much too solemn for that sleepy hour: "The hearings beginning today are on the readily available supply of firearms to juveniles and young adults. . . . We are concerned here with the threat to law and order presented by the 'irresponsibles,' the youths and young adults who feel more secure in approaching life's problems when they have a gun or other lethal weapon concealed on their persons. As we proceed, I am confident you will all be startled by their numbers and appalled by the destruction they wreak on their communities." *

Why should they be surprised? Youth, after all, is youth; and as he droned on, one realized that his feigning of shock was only part of an act. Dodd was canny enough to have realized, or his advisers were wise enough to have persuaded him, that nothing

---

* Our federal legislators are always leading us to a neat deductive conclusion, and then drawing back in fright. In this instance Dodd showed us, without putting it in so many words, that the final solution of the youth/gun problem would seem logically to be a super-Herod experiment: the extermination of all young males living in cities of 250,000 and over. Get rid of urban young people and you get rid of virtually all violent urban crime.

In fairness, society could supply each person of sound mind over the age of thirty with a handgun and a kind of gift certificate awarding him one free *prima-facie* legal assumption that the shooting of anyone between the ages of fifteen and twenty-four was done in self-defense.

That solution is probably too extreme to find widespread acceptance when we are still feeling our way, so more deft arrangements must be made. An alternative would be to supply *free* narcotics to all males in the above category. It has been well established that the inroads of narcotics addiction broke up the zip-gun gangs of the 1950s, and there is now increasing evidence to show that narcotics are once again assisting society in killing off its troublesome youths. In a recent story about youth gangs *The New York Times* came back with this hopeful report from the front: "More brothers gettin' killed,' said a former 'gang-banger,' as warring gang members are known on Chicago's black West Side, 'because there are more guns. But gang-bangin' itself is dyin' off. Now, too many brothers are too busy noddin' on the junk.' "

Aw, I'm only kidding—I think.

offered more certainty of incandescent headlines than the specter of dangerous young crazies. The youth/gun combination has always—or at least throughout this century—been enough to paralyze the cerebrum of anyone of middle age.

Forty-eight years ago, William McAdoo, Chief Magistrate of New York City and former Assistant Secretary of the Navy, complained: "The gunmen in this city are nearly all young. The whole dangerous army of criminals are rarely over thirty years of age, and most of them in the early twenties, and all determined never to do any honest work. In the late outbreak all over the country of holdups and shootings, many of these fellows were beginners, cowardly, cruel, reckless, emotionless, pitiless, selfish, lazy, lustful, incorrigible, hopeless, irreverent, and much more dangerous to encounter than an experienced professional. The latter would hesitate to take life, whereas these fellows, nervous, heartless, cowardly, and frightened, possibly drug addicts, are apt to shoot on the slightest provocation." *

This was not the first time a Congressional committee had entertained the plea that interstate traffic in guns be stopped. If you go back to what is charitably considered the Congress of 1930, you discover the legislators laboring in their usual style with the same problem. There you will find, for example, the testimony of Miss Katherine B. Blake, of the Women's International League for Peace and Freedom, producing for the education of a House Commerce subcommittee a dogeared booklet and proclaiming angrily, "I hold in my hand here a catalogue. It says that it is a catalogue of 'Surprising novelties, puzzles, tricks, jokes, games, useful articles,' and so forth, and among them there are listed a number of pistols. I have turned down the pages at one in particular which is a combination of a knife and a pistol which shoots a .22-caliber bullet and is only three and three-quarter inches long, and is an excellent pocketknife at the same time. Our boys ought not to be tempted with such things," and she begged for

* *When the Court Takes a Recess* (E. P. Dutton, 1924), p. 119.

a law to prohibit the interstate shipments of all concealable firearms.*

But then those male rascals on the committee teased her into arguing her position as "the first step really toward world peace," which of course caused much tittering. They thought her a nut, though in fact she was quite levelheaded and by far more rational than, say, the Honorable Hamilton Fish, Congressman from New York, who had introduced his own bill to curb interstate gun shipments, turning away the suggestion that his bill might be unconstitutional with the typically Fishy argument, "You have a right to stretch the Constitutional provisions to a considerable degree," which "I for one am strongly in favor of, even if it were aimed solely against the Communists." He meant domestic Communists. In the early years of this debate, the advocates of gun control were too often burdened with his type. As was true of the reformers who came after the riots of the 1960s, insurrection—not general brutality and crime—was his hangup.

Dodd's hearings were conducted with much more decorum, and into them were poured data a great deal more impressive than those at the hearings of the 1930s. He put on a very fine show indeed, replete with hideous gun stories and a troop of witnesses that included spectacularly lawless gun dealers, lawless bureaucrats, and dumb cops.

But gun-lawless youth had both a very powerful appeal and a weakness—or at least a weakness at that stage of the gun debate. Its power came from the fact that, without exaggeration, non-young people are scared witless by the unrestrained frolicsomeness of young people—and for good reason, considering that more than half of those arrested for the seven FBI Crime Index crimes (murder, forcible rape, robbery, aggravated assault, burglary, larceny over $50, and auto theft) are citizens who have not yet

---

* Interstate and Foreign Commerce Subcommittee, House of Representatives, 71st Congress, 2nd Session, Hearings on several bills pending before the committee to regulate the interstate shipment of firearms, April 1930 (U.S. Government Printing Office, 1930), p. 30.

reached the august age of nineteen and *one-fifth* of those arrested
for the most serious crimes are fourteen years old or younger. In a
typical recent year, 72 percent of those arrested for serious crimes
were between the ages of thirteen and twenty-nine. If the age is
lowered to include those under thirteen, the percentage soars to 82.
Not counting traffic offenses that the community has come to
expect from its brood, like drag-racing at seventy miles an hour
through a hospital zone, some crime will be committed by each
member—on the average—of the twelve-to-seventeen age group
during the next six years.

The relationship between the crime rise and the birth rise is
too apparent to miss. The FBI reports that between 1955 and 1971
the number of committed crimes listed in its Uniform Crime
Report *doubled,* from 3 million to 6 million (that's just all it knows
about), and it admits that while murders and auto thefts are pretty
well reported to the police, no more than two-thirds of all robberies
are reported, and only half to three-quarters of rapes, assaults,
burglaries, and larcenies are reported.

At the same time as this lawlessness rate was soaring, so was
the number of products of all that bedroom activity in the 1940s
and 1950s: the number of citizens within the fifteen-to-twenty-four
age group—the one that is most dangerous to the community—rose
47 percent in the 1960s and continued its ominous climb into the
1970s; this, according to the experts, explains at least one-fourth
the crime spurt.

James Q. Wilson writes in *Law and Order in a Democratic
Society*:

> Why then are there more serious and violent crimes every
> year? *Simply because there are more young people every year,
> and because young people have always had a higher crime rate
> than adults.* Because the size of the younger age group is
> increasing twice as fast as that of the older age group, over the
> next ten years California [for example] can expect an increase
> in the number of serious crimes of 55 percent. The "crime
> susceptible" age group will at the same time increase in size by

110 percent. What appears to be a crime explosion may in fact be a population explosion [emphasis added].*

Moreover, confirming the fears of all of us honkies who are convinced that the darkies will eventually do us in,† 62.2 percent of the murder arrests, 66.4 percent of the robbery arrests, 50.3 percent of the rape arrests, and 46.9 of the aggravated assault arrests in 1971 were black. These percentages are rather impressive when one considers that blacks make up only about 12 percent of the total population. And if black youngsters can be counted on to continue their mischief, it is not at all comforting to note that the black birthrate far exceeds the white. According to the National Advisory Commission on Civil Disorders (NACCD), the nation's white population is expected to have increased by 9.5 percent between 1966 and 1975, while the black population increase will have been 17.7 percent. More than that, the number of fifteen-to-twenty-four-year-old blacks will grow much faster than the black population as a whole and much, much faster than the white population of that age group: up 40.1 percent for the former, 23.5 percent for the latter. The NACCD observes with restraint: "This rapid increase in the young Negro population has important implications for the country. This group has the highest unemployment rate in the nation, commits a relatively high proportion of all crimes, and plays the most significant role in civil disorders." To say the least.

Washington, D.C.'s general population declined a bit between 1960 and 1970, but its crime-prone population, aged fifteen to twenty-four, increased 33 percent—and serious crime in the capital shot up 350 percent during the same period. A few years ago the

---

* Marvin R. Summers and Thomas E. Barth, eds. (Charles E. Merrill, 1970), pp. 10–11.
† Like: Two black youngsters walked into an East St. Louis tavern called The Spot one night in early 1973 and, one saying, "Here's to you goddam whites," and the other announcing, "I'm going to kill every white sonofabitch in here," they began unloading two guns into the patrons. Why, lawdy! it's enough to make you believe that line from Grier and Cobbs's book *Black Rage:* "Because of his experience in this country, every black man harbors a potential bad nigger inside him."

conclusions to be drawn from such statistics in every major city might have sounded a bit racist, but fright has been so thoroughly integrated that now we hear from the likes of New York NAACP President Carl Lawrence urging the "good people" of every harassed community to arm themselves and "take the streets away from the hoodlums."

Bad as the youngsters' behavior has apparently always been, authorities insist it is getting worse. Police across the country say it's much commoner these days for a holdup to end in death, because it involves youths who just don't seem to care, even a little. In Chicago the number of persons fatally shot during armed robberies rose from 12 to 117 between 1965 and 1970; most of the killers were ghetto blacks between the ages of fifteen and twenty-four.* The number of persons under the age of twenty-one who used a gun to commit murder in Chicago rose from 38 to 171 during the same five-year period—a 613-percent increase. Although the young free-lance is more likely to be the chap who shoves it into your ribs, the urban street gang is also on the upswing. Some areas are beset by packs of youths who roam like wild dogs, as in south central Los Angeles and Watts. Philadelphia street gangs reportedly contributed significantly to that city's 34-percent increase in major crimes in 1971.

In looking to youth for the kind of scare appeal that would bring Congress around to outlawing mail-order guns, Dodd was relying on something that, in its fright, America had grown used to. This was the weakness of his appeal. The preceding statistics of

* Different figures are given by George Newton of the Chicago Bar Association and Professor Franklin E. Zimring of the University of Chicago Law School. But their investigation includes deaths from all types of weapons, not just guns. On that basis, they report that the number of robbery killings in Chicago increased from thirty-three in 1965 to a hundred and forty-seven in 1970—a 345-percent increase—and that eleven of the thirty-three killers were in the fifteen-to-twenty-four age group in 1965 and ninety of the hundred and forty-seven in 1970; most were blacks. They also noted that in 1970 the homicide rate among blacks of this age group was nearly thirty times that of whites of the same age group. (By the way, when Mr. Newton visited Washington to explain his findings, he was waylaid by an armed robber on the way to his hotel.)

youth/gun crimes may not have been known precisely by the typical non-young citizen, but he had always felt the statistics in his bones. Should he interpret them to mean that guns must be taken from the young, or that the old must arm in self-defense? It wasn't clear. The situation was too familiar to be clear. What Dodd needed to shatter the public's equilibrium of terror was an exceptionally dramatic massacre by some young guy; but there hadn't been a really hopping massacre of that type for five years, and there wouldn't be another one, as it turned out, for three years more.

DON'T TRUST ANYONE UNDER THIRTY

What he might have found useful, in short, was the kind of morality lesson that was ultimately to be acted out by Charles Joseph Whitman during that hour and a half of an August day in 1966.

No wonder his psychiatrist, looking back, said Whitman had seemed "an all-American boy." He loved his mother and hated his father; had become an Eagle Scout three months after his twelfth birthday and years later served as a Scoutmaster; was a gung-ho Marine; was handsome and lively company; had a B average as an architectural student at the University of Texas, and was a devout Catholic. To be sure, he sometimes beat his wife (the ex-Queen of the Fair of Needville, Texas), just as his father before him had done, but was that un-American? Or were the facts that he wrote bad checks to cover gambling debts or peddled pornographic pictures on the side when he was in the Marine Corps?

So one night he climbed into his brand-new Chevrolet Impala (another good American touch) and went to visit his mother for the last time, leaving her dead from a butcherknife wound in the chest and a bullethole in the back of her head; he then returned home, visited with friends, fed the dog, went to pick up his wife from her job at the telephone company, brought her home and tucked her in bed, and there he polished her off with three deep knife wounds in the chest.

So far, four stab wounds and only one bullet wound. This wasn't like Charlie, because he loved guns and preferred using them. ("I'm a fanatic about guns," his father later told reporters. "My boys knew all about them.") * Charlie proved this the next day when he hauled a footlocker full of guns onto the observation ramp at the top of the University tower, 307 feet above the campus, which was crawling with students at the lunch hour. On his way to the top he had shot and killed the receptionist, and immediately after arriving at the observation platform, he killed two tourists who happened to step out behind him. Now he was ready to display the sharpshooting his father and the Marine Corps had prepared him for.

He wanted to do the job right and was obviously in no hurry, having brought along Spam, Planter's peanuts, fruit cocktail, sandwiches and boxes of raisins, several water containers, a transistor radio, a roll of toilet paper, and a plastic bottle of Mennen spray deodorant. He would, after all, likely get to sweating, and a young man does not want to have underarm odor in his moment of glory.

Although he had left three rifles and two derringers at home, Charlie, always the good Boy Scout, was fully prepared. Aside from the machete and Bowie knife and hatchet, he removed from his footlocker a .357 Smith & Wesson Magnum revolver, a Galesi-Bresca pistol, a 9-mm. Luger pistol, a 35-mm. Remington rifle, a 6-mm. Remington bolt-action rifle with a 4-power Leupold telescopic sight—all of which he was familiar with from long practice —and a brand-new 12-gauge shotgun that he had bought that

---

* Charlie's younger brother, John M. Whitman, may have thought he already had learned all about guns at his father's knee, but he had one final lesson on July 3, 1973, when he was shot and killed by someone using a .22-caliber weapon outside a Lake Worth, Fla., bar. John was twenty-four and had had several brushes with the law.

morning from Sears (on credit) and a .30-caliber carbine he had bought from Davis' hardware store, also that morning. He had about seven hundred rounds of ammunition.

He relied primarily on the scope-fitted 6-mm. Remington, with which a marksman of Charlie's talents was capable of hitting a six-inch target consistently at three hundred yards. This is why most of his early victims—during the first fifteen minutes when nobody was shooting back at him and he could take leisurely aim—were hit in the head and chest. Thanks to the scope, it was no accident when he shot the pregnant student right through her pregnancy—in fact, shattering the unborn baby's head with the 6-mm. Remington's high-velocity soft-nosed bullet. The 35-mm. Remington pump, which hunters call a "brush-buster," spewed out bullets that just plow through anything. All in all, he scored with one out of every three shots, which, under the pressure he was facing, was extraordinary indeed.

Charlie knew he would finally be attacked at his own level, and for that eventuality he had the shotgun (which he had sawed off, gangster-style) and the light fast-firing carbine. There's absolutely no close-quarter weapon like a shotgun, which virtually aims itself and, with heavy shot, can take down three people at once. But when he was killed, he was holding the carbine.

Politicians and wise men were quick to seize upon the Whitman episode for moralizing. Senator Ralph Yarborough of Texas said it was all the sinful result of TV violence. Texas Governor John Connally demanded that the legislature pass stiffer punishment for insane criminals (intimating that Whitman's coffin should be put behind bars). And then, of course, there were those who read into Whitman's actions the sickness of a nation, or even the sickness of the human race. And some, adapting the Whitman episode to their premise that stiffer gun-control laws were needed, pointed out that 57 percent of the 9,850 homicides in the United States the previous year were committed with guns.

But nobody dwelt upon the most obvious cause of the crime—Charlie's age—apparently because most adults are parents, and parents don't like to mention such things. Because they have spent so much money and worry and sweat on their male monsters, parents much prefer to speak of the teens in terms like those Oscar Wilde used—"the morning dawn of boyhood with its delicate bloom, its clear pure light, its joy of innocence and expectations"— and are not much less rhapsodic about their male issue when they pass into their twenties; there's supposed to be something romantic about the age of "one and twenty," as A. E. Houseman pretended, that just doesn't apply to one and forty. But the age of the supposedly delicate bloom is most assuredly also the age of the nastiest barb, and what it really comes down to is a simple equation: youth equals its bloodier kind of insanity. Not the other sort. Charlie may not have been as mentally sound as one would have liked—he had actually gone to the university's staff psychiatrist four months before and acknowledged a hankering to "be up on the tower with a deer rifle and start shooting people," but that sort of aggressive blathering was heard every day from the youths who passed through the psychiatrist's office. Charlie wasn't insane by any commonly accepted definition; he was just a mean sonofabitch who flailed madly about in a futile effort to keep from drowning in the fiery juices that rose in his twenty-five-year-old gullet.

His madness was in being under thirty. Bible-quoting Howard Unruh, who shot and killed thirteen people in twenty minutes in Camden, New Jersey, in 1949; Charles Starkweather, who toured through Nebraska and Wyoming in 1958, knocking off ten people; Richard Speck, who, a month before Whitman went to work with his arsenal, killed eight student nurses in Chicago; Lee Harvey Oswald, John Kennedy's assassin; Sirhan Sirhan, Robert Kennedy's assassin; Arthur Bremer, George Wallace's would-be assassin—all under thirty years of age. Harvey McLeod, who bought a .22-caliber semiautomatic carbine and killed three and wounded eight in Raleigh, North Carolina, before killing himself—twenty-three years old. Charlie Simpson, who killed three and wounded three in Harrisonville, Missouri, before sticking his M-1 rifle in his mouth and finishing himself—twenty-one years old. Edmund Kemper III, who shot his grandparents ("I just wondered how it would feel to shoot Grandma") in 1964 and, having been released by the state psychiatrists as cured, proceeded to kill six young girls, his mother, and one of his mother's friends—fifteen years old when he committed the first and twenty-two when he accomplished his last murders. Edmund is a Santa Cruz, California, crazy. Another Santa Cruzer is Herbert Mullin, recently convicted of killing 10 persons; Mullin is certainly in the right age bracket—twenty-six years old. The Memphis man who strolled down the sidewalk with his .30-.30 carbine spraying bullets in May 1973, leaving five dead—thirty years old. (Okay, but he was *just* thirty.) The Los Angeles chap who, the previous month, had walked from his home with a .20-gauge shotgun to kill six and wound nine—twenty-five years old. The AWOL sailor who killed four and wounded a deputy sheriff in Maryland in early 1973—twenty-two years old. On and on and on. Most of the slaughter in this country is committed by people under thirty. It's true of those who commit the massacres and it's true of those who, more modestly, commit simple murder.

THE POST OFFICE ACCOMPLICE

Dodd's first objective was to uncover some seedy mail-order dealers and focus on them to such an extent that the public would assume they represented the entire class. To that end he could not have gone to a better harvesting ground than Los Angeles. One of the first rocks lifted revealed, for example, George William Rose, President of Seaport Traders, Inc., Madison Import Co., George Rose & Co., and Merchanteers, Inc. These were, in practice, one and the same company, but when disgruntled customers or federal officials came calling, it was always convenient to have a different hat to wear.

Rose would in 1963 achieve a footnote in history through Seaport Traders, which supplied Lee Harvey Oswald with the .38 Special Smith & Wesson revolver he used (or so the Warren Commission said) on Patrolman J. D. Tippit. Another Los Angeles dealer in cheap guns had public-relations problems in the post-assassination period. This was Martin Retting, whose company imported and sold the telescopic sight attached to Oswald's rifle. Later a fifteen-year-old Baltimore boy would use a .38 revolver he bought by mail from Retting to polish off his father, mother, and sister; when the cops came to pick him up, Railway Express was delivering another Retting gun.

At the time Senator Dodd first met Rose, the Los Angeles gun merchant had little to set him apart from a number of other shady dealers. In addition to trading in cheap guns, he had had experience in other commerce of questionable social value. In 1951 he was found guilty of selling "indecent writings," fined $50, and sentenced to ten days in jail. Actually, the commodity was not "writings" but pictures, tame by today's standards, of nude women; he also sold ashtrays depicting couples in the act of fornication. Rose's father and another employee were arrested, too, for selling obscene pictures, but the charges against them were dismissed.

Those were the early days, when Rose was trying to establish himself in the novelty business. Shortly thereafter he decided that guns would be more profitable than girlie photos, and less risky, so he obtained a permit from the Los Angeles Police Department to sell concealable firearms. He prospered. By the mid-1950s he was reputedly taking in an estimated $300,000 a year. By 1962 he was the nation's biggest importer of foreign-made Saturday Night Specials.

Rose was not exactly the type to be elected president of the Los Angeles Chamber of Commerce, but he was no worse than most of his colleagues in the mail-order gun business of that era, and if one likes to engage in fine measuring, he might even be considered better than some.

Charles F. Stocker, a former vice squad sergeant who turned rogue, was fired from the Los Angeles Police Department on July 6, 1949, and was immediately charged with burglary but freed by a hung jury. Subsequently he became a successful, and extremely controversial, gun peddler under a number of different names: Sutter Import Co., Kent Imports, Kent Sporting Goods, the Pacific Weapons Co., the Sierra Arms Corp., and Sierra Import Corp.

But Stocker had other interests. He headed companies that sold breast developers, lotions to remove facial lines, and a hair grower. He was occasionally in tax trouble with the federal government, and on March 22, 1962, a grand jury indicted him on fifteen counts of mail fraud. By that time hundreds of complaints had been filed against him by dissatisfied customers for failure to deliver paid-for weapons that he had advertised in pulp magazines. It seemed a perfect chance for federal officials to push ahead with an airtight case and rid the market of a very unsavory character; instead, when Stocker promised to reimburse his clients $10,000, the government dropped its charges.

One of the most infamous of the gun peddlers was Hayward Hunter, better known by his trademark name, Hy Hunter, who first entered the mail-order business in 1946 in Los Angeles to sell photographs of nude women. The next year he pleaded guilty to contributing to the delinquency of a minor after the cops caught him allowing a thirteen-year-old girl to help in the shipping of the photos. He got a one-year suspended sentence and, like Rose in similar circumstances, thereupon turned to guns for a living. He also shuffled his business affairs under a number of corporate names: H. H. Hunter & Co., Hy Hunter, Inc., General Arms Corp., American Weapons Corp., Crown International Firearms, Inc., and Krone Internationale Waffenshandelsgesellschaft mbH, the last based in Hamburg and all the others in California.

Hunter's entry into the bigtime came when he purchased for $50,000 the American Weapons Corp., which he claimed—a claim never denied by the government—was originally set up by the CIA and headed by Leo Lippe, who also established an outfit called

Western Arms Corporation; it was with Western Arms that Sam Cummings got his start in arms. Cummings established International Armament Corp. (Interarmco), the nation's biggest importer of surplus weapons.

Hunter was recognized as an especially flamboyant dealer, even in a business known for its advertising flamboyance. It was difficult to separate the real Hunter from the hoopla Hunter; he encouraged all sorts of wild stories, as he later admitted, "to make a bigshot of myself." Whether he actually outfitted border raiders in eastern Burma, and Iraqi rebels, and Central and South American revolutionaries is hard to say; after talking with him, writers would put such things into the articles they wrote for "men's magazines," but he later denied that the stories were accurate. Hunter was reputed to deal not only in sidearms but in bazookas and tanks; but when government investigators confronted him with these tales, he said he was "shocked" to learn that anyone could think such a thing of him. The truth might have eventually come out if Hunter, when Dodd's staff began closing in on him, had not shipped most of his records to Germany—in violation of the 1938 Federal Firearms Act, which requires that dealers have their records available for inspection at all times.

It was certainly known, however, that Hunter did deal in submachine guns. On one occasion he imported twenty-four Beretta submachine guns from Singapore; the box was marked "scrap" and its declared value was $481, but in fact the guns and parts were in perfect shape and were worth $6,501. Customs officials grumbled, but they did no more than grumble. The government's tolerance of Hunter was instructive. He was apparently one of the shadiest dealers in the business, but federal agencies not only let him get by with it for years, they even broke the law on occasion to help him get off the hook. He was caught importing guns without a license, and the guns were seized by the government; at that point, under the Federal Firearms Act, the feds could legally do one of three things: destroy the guns, sell them to a state or local government, or turn them over for the use of a federal agency. Instead, the illegally imported guns were brought into the country and turned over to Hunter's debtors.

Most of the submachine guns he peddled were what dealers called—with straight-faced humor—"DEWATS," deactivated war trophies. As everyone in the business is aware, a deactivated submachine gun can be activated by anyone with even a moron's grasp of mechanics. Ashley Halsey, Jr., then a writer for the *Saturday Evening Post* and now editor of *The American Rifleman*, realized the excellent story potential of this situation. He ordered a DEWAT .45-caliber Thompson submachine gun from a mail-order dealer in the name of his two-year-old daughter and put it in good working condition. The normal method for "deactivating" a submachine gun is to weld the opening of the barrel and weld the barrel to the frame. Some people have put their submachine guns into operating order simply be dislodging the welding material from the barrel—which can be done in a couple of minutes. Halsey used the other approach: he ordered a spare barrel from the same mail-order house, and then, using dimestore-variety tools—a hacksaw blade, a couple of files, a bench vise, and a large wrench—he removed the plugged barrel and installed the good barrel in a little more than an hour. Thousands of these DEWAT submachine guns—Thompsons, the Schmeisser "burp" guns loved by the Nazis, Berettas and Brens and Stens—were sold to the public and many have undoubtedly been reactivated. One was spotted in the hands of a member of the Diplomats, a New York juvenile street gang, on the prowl for members of an outfit called the Colts.

Hunter's trafficking in submachine guns brings us back to Mr. Rose and Seaport Traders, for he bought more than a hundred DEWATS from Hunter and resold them, using an ad that was to become something of a landmark in soft-sell. The opening kicker was "Submachine Gun for Father's Day?" The gun cost $49.95, complete with magazine and sling.

Rose, who claimed he did not know the guns could be put in killing order, sold one to a student at the University of Mississippi in April 1962. Fortunately, the student was too dumb to figure out how to get the gun to shoot and he felt that he had been swindled. Dodd subpoenaed records of all submachine gun sales and induced Treasury agents to get off their asses and go find the guns; they found the unhappy Mississippian's still in its wrapper.

When Senator Dodd subpoenaed Rose to testify about his business, he asked him, "Do you remember what was going on in that area in April of 1962?"

"No, sir," said Rose.

"You don't have any recollection at all?"

"No, sir."

That exchange was less than seven months after the Ole Miss riots. But a hazy memory was a hallmark of the mail-order dealers. Rose also couldn't remember the Chief of Police of Fallsburgh, New York, who, like the Ole Miss student, was dissatisfied with a plugged submachine gun and asked for his money back. Rose tried to mollify him by offering to send him a 12-gauge shotgun instead of a money refund, and when the Chief wouldn't take that, Rose—never one to give up easily—offered to send some equipment the Chief could use for repairing watches.

One of the wonders of Rose's operations was that he seemed to have such a friendly relationship with the United States Post Office Department. According to the testimony of a Los Angeles Board of Police Commissioners investigator, Rose had managed to become the target of more than four hundred complaints from unhappy mail-order customers in the United States and Canada between 1956 and 1963, most of them complaining formally that Rose had sent them weapons other than those he had advertised and they had ordered. The inspector added, "It should be noted that a representative of the Los Angeles office of the Better Business Bureau estimates that only about 1.5 to 2 percent of the persons bilked by mail-order operations of this type will protest in writing. This indicates approximately twenty thousand individuals have been so victimized, victimized by this particular dealer." One might suppose that this would have been a sufficient hint of fraud to prompt the postal inspectors to cut off Rose's mail-order business, but they didn't seem to notice.

If Rose sometimes seemed especially slick, it may also have been because the laws written to confine his ambitions were written so loosely and enforced so lightly that he could make sport of them. For instance, the Customs laws under which he originally operated required that he pay $1.35 per imported gun plus 30 percent of the gun's value; but a *blank* or "starter" pistol with a solid barrel could be imported for a Customs fee of 11.5 percent of its value. So Rose simply had the foreign manufacturers put a solid barrel on the guns before they were shipped; he also had them send along a *regular* barrel for each gun in a separate shipment. When everything arrived in this country, the solid barrels were taken off and the regular barrels were substituted.

Rose made no attempt to hide what he was doing. "The entire operation," he said, "was purely to save on duty." And then he added a comment of the sort that is basic to understanding what has been going on in the gun world for the past decade: *"Customs knew exactly what was being done because invoices were submitted to them."* Very little of the questionable gun marketing has been done without the knowledge and often the approval of some agency of the federal government.

The Customs laws were eventually changed so that Rose and his colleagues could not take advantage of the tariff differential between blank and regular guns. But a tariff advantage remained for the importation of gun *parts,* as compared to the duty on assembled guns. So Rose (and other companies) adjusted quickly: the new technique was to buy guns in Germany, dismantle them there, then ship the parts to this country by various means. The barrels and the frames were serially numbered to match, and when they arrived at his plant in Los Angeles, his staff simply reassembled them. In this fashion he saved many thousands of dollars, but, as he put it, "I did not beat the tariff law. I took advantage of the tariff laws as they are now on the books."

The mail-order gun peddlers were unloading their wares in the most irresponsible manner, sending them into cities and states which had laws prohibiting the purchase of guns without a permit or at least without a waiting period. Most of the mail-order dealers made little or no check on their clients. Most would ask their customers to fill out a form "certifying" that they had not been convicted of a felony, were not under indictment for a crime of violence, were not a fugitive from justice, were not an alien, and were at least twenty-one years old. But no proof of any of these was required, by the dealer or by law. Consequently, as one Los Angeles cop put it, "The 'certification' is a mere formality, having no regulatory effect over the flow of gun traffic. In fact, any nine-year-old can fill out the form and secure a gun as long as he has a piggy bank for the payment, can draw the numerals 21, and scrawl his name."

Recognizing the mail-order-purchase certification process as a time-consuming farce and wanting to sidestep local gun-ownership restrictions, some dealers (Rose among them) advised their customers to take the easy route and buy a federal dealer's license. It cost only a dollar and with it a person could (1) buy and sell almost any type of weapon, ammunition, and explosive; (2) ship via parcel post at about half the cost of Railway Express (which the ordinary customer had to patronize); (3) circumvent waiting periods and also circumvent local police and city permit requirements.

No fingerprints were required for a federal dealer's license; nor did the Treasury Department, which issued the licenses, check to see if applicants had criminal records. So long as an applicant signed the piece of paper affirming that he was not a fugitive and had no felony record, the government was only too happy to take his word for it.

An estimated half to two-thirds of the holders of federal dealers' licenses were *not* in fact bona fide dealers.

This semifraudulent law was part of the Federal Firearms Act of 1938. Like all portions of the Act, it was ostensibly aimed at making it more difficult for the wrong people to lay their hands on guns and ammunition. The practical effect of the law, however, was to make it much easier for anyone—especially anyone willing to lie a bit—to buy any arms he wanted, more swiftly and at a cheaper price. A license could get guns at discount prices.

The result of this kind of indiscriminate peddling of arms by mail could easily have been foretold: many of the weapons fell into the wrong hands. There were cases of ex-mental patients found wandering around town, carrying several automatics they had ordered through the mail; ex-convicts caught "practicing" with mail-order guns just for old times' sake; bank robbers so heavily laden with their mail-order arsenal that they couldn't run fast enough to escape; youngsters who knocked off their dads with mail-order roscoes because they wouldn't let them have a Coke. Those little pulp-magazine ads seemed especially attractive to boys. The cop who said a nine-year-old could order by mail if he could scribble his name wasn't exaggerating by much. Dodd found an eleven-year-old boy who had ordered a .22-caliber Saturday Night Special pistol; it blew apart in his hands, as they occasionally do, and "it was just a miracle it didn't severely injure him," said Dodd, scolding Rose.

"Well, you know children can do all kinds of things," said Rose philosophically. "They will crawl into refrigerators and kill themselves. It doesn't necessarily mean. . . ."

Dodd interrupted. "You don't sell refrigerators, do you?"

"No, I don't."

Checking Rose's records of 104 purchasers in the Philadelphia area, Senate investigators found—with the assistance of local police—that 15 of the gun buyers had criminal records. In Chicago, police checked on the 1,857 residents who had purchased guns from Rose—guns which Rose maintained were largely used for "the pleasure of target-shooting and plinking"—and found that "90 percent of the addresses are located in the 2d, 3d and 7th, 10th, 11th or 12th districts, the highest crime-rate districts in the city of Chicago," and that 428 of the purchasers, or 23 percent, had criminal records—"at least one involved in a murder, several others involved in robberies, and any number of these persons having spent time in a penitentiary for an assortment of felonies."

Confronted with these statistics, Rose responded with the one argument that federal, state, and local officials could not answer without an admission of laxness at least the equal of Rose's own.

"Mr. Rose," asked Senator Dodd, "is this the first time you ever heard that you had sold guns to juveniles and to criminals in Chicago? Is this the first you ever heard of that?"

"Let me put it this way: I have not been notified by the Chicago Police Department," he answered. "I think it would be their duty to notify me if they have had so much trouble with my guns that I should cease from shipping my guns into their city. Why did they wait until this investigation to let you know that all these guns are coming into the city of Chicago?"

"Well, I do not know why," said Dodd. "But I asked you if this is the first time you have ever heard of the fact."

"Yes, sir."

"You never knew before that you sold guns to criminals in Chicago?"

"I must again say that if I was not informed that there are any criminals that my guns were sent to—I certainly have taken all the precautions that are necessary under the Federal Firearms Act."

This was almost accurate; except for keeping sloppy records, contrary to the requirements of the Act, he did most of the things that were absolutely "necessary" to comply with its provisions. The failure lay in the provisions of the Act and in its enforcement as much as it lay with Rose and other dealers of his sort. When Dodd's staff director, Carl Perian, gigged Rose for encouraging his purchasers to become federally licensed "dealers" for a dollar, he and Rose engaged in an exchange that cut to the heart of the problem.

Perian pointed out that the phony dealerships were being handed out even to people with criminal backgrounds.

Replied Rose, "It is certainly up to the federal government to check them out, or they shouldn't issue them a license."

"You are a highly technical man with the federal law," said Perian, getting sarcastic.

"No, sir," said Rose, "I am a businessman."

There was the nut of the matter. He knew what Congressional reformers failed to acknowledge, at least at that early stage of the gun-control war: all federal gun laws and most of the state and local laws were shaped and enforced to satisfy the whims of businessmen:—manufacturers, dealers, restorers, arms-magazine publishers, the whole fraternity. Rose may have represented the smellier portion of the fraternity, but that didn't matter. As Rose once asked Perian, without getting an adequate reply, "What is the difference being a legitimate mail-order house or illegitimate mail-order house? How do you differentiate the difference between a pseudo-dealer and a regular dealer?"

For that marvelous question Rose deserved to be given the franchise for the sale of pornographic comic books in Pershing Square. It may have been accidentally brilliant, but it was a brilliant question nonetheless and could not have been phrased better by Jeremy Bentham himself; for practically speaking, the effect of both legitimate and illegitimate, or pseudo-dealer and regular dealer, was the same: both sold as many deadly weapons as they possibly could, and so far as anyone was able to discover, one type of dealer placed no more and no fewer guns in the hands of madmen than the other.

Though they often handled the same merchandise, by reputation and appearances all the mail-order gun dealers were not in the same class. Many operated with no more of a front than a mail drop and a desk that they rented by the week: they were in every respect fly-by-night and totally without credit or standing. Others were old, fairly reputable houses. Klein's Sporting Goods was among the latter. Yet just as Rose's house supplied the gun that killed Officer Tippit, Klein's supplied the rifle that killed John Kennedy.

Klein's had started as a modest family enterprise in the last decades of the nineteenth century; by the time it supplied the assassination weapon, Klein's was operating six very successful retail outlets, a mail-order distribution of sporting and athletic merchandise, and a publishing business for sports books. Mail-order firearms made up about 15 percent of their total sales volume; military surplus firearms accounted for about 25 percent of the mail-order gun sales. Klein's sales pitch was made through the usual channels: *The American Rifleman* (where Oswald saw it), *Field and Stream, Outdoor Life, Sports Afield, Guns, Guns & Ammo,* and *Guns and Hunting.*

As business enterprises go, Klein's was not without social conscience. Two years after the assassination they discontinued the sale of handguns by mail order and began to be much more cautious about the sale of long guns. Some of their reform efforts were pathetically weak—such as their attempt to spot the "possible mental incompetence or immaturity of the orderer" by the "manner in which the order is completed." Klein's good intentions were demonstrated in 1965 when the store's management supported Dodd's proposed legislation to curtail mail-order gun sales even though they anticipated that a sharp drop in all their sporting goods mail sales would be an attendant result.

Nevertheless, though it was plain that Klein's management was trying to run an aboveboard business, the facts remained that their files—subpoenaed by Dodd's subcommittee—showed the store had sent mail-order rifles and shotguns to people with criminal records in Chicago, Dallas, Philadelphia, and Los Angeles, as well as in unspecified locations in New Jersey and New York. The harmful impact of an established outfit like Klein's was, obviously, sometimes no different from that of the shoddy merchants. A Rose by any other name. . . .

FREE ENTERPRISE IS A DEADLY WEAPON

For the contempt of Congress to be focused on the shady mail-order dealers, while ignoring the root bureaucratic and Congressional causes of the gun traffic anarchy, was something like convicting Lieutenant Calley of the My-Lai massacre while letting Robert McNamara get away.

The government's attitude from the beginning—as seen in the operations of the Treasury and State Departments—has been one of excessive laissez-faire. The bureaucrats have consciously ignored or slighted every gun-control duty assigned to them. The enormous traffic in guns, both legal and illegal, has seemed neither to disturb nor even to interest the agencies at all. Moreover, corrupted by the industry which they are supposed to be controlling, the Treasury Department withholds most of its information even from Congress. Congressman John Murphy of New York, one of the more active gun-control advocates, wrote to the Treasury Department several times and telephoned once for a list of the brand names, types, and calibers of the Saturday Night Specials manufactured in this country. IRS Commissioner Harold Schwartz replied that "it is not necessary to maintain the data you desire," so bug off. Later Treasury Secretary John Connally said they did have the data and would send it; it never arrived. When Senator Birch Bayh asked for the names of the Saturday Night Special manufacturers, the Treasury sent him a list of *all* handgun manufacturers and said he would probably find the ones he wanted on the list—presumably if he was a good guesser. Bayh then asked Treasury for a count of how many Saturday Night Specials were produced by each company. The response, from Acting Assistant Treasury Secretary William Dickey, was that "there is no requirement" for his office to collect such information and he didn't intend to do so.

It is hardly excessive to say that for more than thirty years the bureaucrats have been even more neglectful of their duties than the gun merchants have been abusive of the loopholes in the law. The dominant concern seemed to be to preserve the free market, and so successful had the bureaucracy been at achieving this that by the early 1960s it would have to be considered chiefly responsible for letting the gun business get out of control. This can be easily seen by breaking the mess into two parts: first let's look at the manner in which the dealers were supervised and then at the State Department's attitude toward freewheeling imports.

The miserable failure to enforce domestic buying and selling was best seen a couple of years later in the appearance on Capitol Hill of that amusing team of incompetents, Attorney General Nicholas deB. Katzenbach and Sheldon Cohen, Commissioner of the Treasury Department's Internal Revenue Service.

There in all their splendid array, with sleek attaché cases and gleaming flunkies by their side, were the chief potentates of federal gun controls. But if their responses on this occasion were any true measure, then they revealed themselves to be very possibly the most ill-informed and lightheaded and pretentious brace of bureaucrats ever to have been flushed before a Congressional committee. They had come to Capitol Hill complaining because they didn't have enough laws to do all the things they wanted to do. They asked for more power. But then it turned out, under the questioning of some cynical Congressmen, that they wanted new laws without knowing anything about the laws that were already on the books and that they were supposed to be enforcing.

They called the gun-control situation "desperate," but then had to admit that the Alcohol, Tobacco and Firearms Division (ATFD), which was supposed to be in charge of the situation, had assigned only *five* people full time to the firearms problem—including the supervision of more than a hundred thousand gun dealers. Cohen could not even name the five people who were supposed to be doing this; in fact, he didn't even know the number until he went back to his office and looked at the job chart. Asked to describe how the ATFD worked, he replied, "I'm not sure exactly how it is." Asked what specific job was assigned to each of the five bureaucrats, Cohen answered: "We will have to give you a breakdown [later]. I don't have it in hand." These charming bureaucrats admitted they did not know how many guns were sold in the country each year.* They didn't know which states required

---

* It's curious how difficult the federal government has found this little chore of counting gun sales. It used to lag by several years. In 1968 the Stanford

gun dealers to have state licenses. ("I mislaid the list somewhere," said Cohen.) They couldn't name the leading gun-manufacturing states. They didn't know how many guns were imported. Their data on gun-law prosecutions were two years old.

Cohen acknowledged that fewer than half the hundred thousand persons carrying dealers' licenses weren't dealers at all and that the percentage of legitimate dealers might even be as low as one-third. The truth was that neither he nor anybody else in the Treasury Department had the vaguest idea how many were legit and how many weren't. Cohen conceded that his agents kept almost no watch over the dealers it licensed. The only firearms dealers they could recall ever investigating—a recollection they had

---

Research Institute asked federal officials for their latest gun-sales count and discovered that the latest was the Bureau of the Census figure for 1963. SRI's comment: "It is quite surprising that no actual count of the total firearms sold in the United States is kept by any government agency or industry group on an annual basis. *The Wall Street Journal* reports with precision the number of automobiles manufactured by brands, such as Chevrolet, Ford, or Chrysler, and how many are sold quarterly. The same is reported in terms of steel tonnage produced, airplane passenger miles and the like, but when it comes to firearms, a product lethal in nature and potentially dangerous, no such data collection exists."

Not until 1973 did the federal bureaucracy wake up to its duty. Now the Treasury Department is using powers available to it since the 1930s (but ignored until now) to make gun manufacturers file a quarterly report of their production. The authority to do this was reaffirmed by the 1968 Act. The Treasury's Bureau of Alcohol, Tobacco and Firearms was four years late in putting it to use, but that's a fantastic leap forward for this segment of the bureaucracy, which had ignored its duties for forty years.

State and local bureaucrats have been just as backward. No effort is made anywhere in the country to put together a timely and comprehensive picture of gun deaths; such data, if collected at all, is sometimes many months late. And no consistent effort is made to list gun deaths by the type of gun used, although this is crucial to an understanding of the problem.

Law enforcement agencies are virtually no help in tracking the course of guns. The FBI and such outfits as the International Association of Chiefs of Police troop before Congressional committees, talking about how horrified they are at all the gun crimes and how Congress should do something about it, when they haven't compiled the slightest beginning of a statistical record to show how many criminals have guns, where they got them, or anything else about the gun traffic. As Congressman Bob Casey once said, "You know, the FBI can tell you the color of the criminal's eyes; give you all of his history; his physical makeup and one thing or another. But they fail to report where he got the gun."

to be prodded to make—were "well, these particular mail-order dealers in Los Angeles." Investigations in one city and only one city, and very limited within the one city at that.

Cohen admitted they did not check out the character of the dealers before issuing the licenses—"Sir, with a one-dollar license fee it is virtually impossible to check these things out. We can't keep up with the volume." He conceded that they licensed dangerous characters and kooks. In fact, he claimed they *had* to. There was, for instance, the young man who had once upon a time tied his mother to a chair, gagged her and stabbed her so many times in the back she looked like St. Sebastian's sister. Then he lay in wait for his father, pounced on him when he got home and whacked him in the head with a two-bladed axe.

That mixed-up kid had applied for a federal dealer's license and Cohen insisted that "by virtue of the present wording of the law [we] are apparently without any alternative but to issue him a license to deal in firearms." Pressed on the point, Cohen granted that the Treasury Department *might* try to contest it in court "but it does place us in an embarrassing position in that the act does not give us sufficient discretion on its face." Attorney General Katzenbach not only agreed that they would have to license madmen but ex-convicts, too, as the law was written. But then it turned out that they were making all these wild statements without even knowing the wording of the law under which they were supposed to be operating. It further turned out, during painful cross-examination by a number of Congressmen who were used to the stupidities of their colleagues and most bureaucrats, but nothing like this, that Katzenbach and Cohen didn't know the Secretary of the Treasury had complete power to prescribe what records the dealers are to keep, how they are to keep them, what the dealer's relationship to his customers will be, and what precautions he should take to make sure he is not selling to unsavory characters. These powers were simply being ignored. For example: the Los Angeles cops went to Hy Hunter to inquire about a gun that had been used in a series of robberies and one shooting; he said he would produce his records for them, but he never got around to it. He always had some excuse. Oh, the records were kind of old and he had stored them away in a basement, or in a garage in Burbank. He couldn't remember just where the records were. And then when Senator Dodd subpoenaed Hunter's records, the fellow showed up with several boxes filled mostly with fishing tackle and mildewed nudie magazines. Practically all his real records, he explained, had been sent to Germany, but he was sure that Dodd would understand because "I always considered that West Germany was just like a part of the United States." The Treasury's ATFD didn't get mad at him. They never got mad at any wayward dealers, although under the Federal Firearms Act any dealer violating any provision of that law—including the requirement to keep good records and make them available—could be fined up to $2,000 and be sent to jail for up to five years.

A spotcheck in the District of Columbia indicated just how sloppily the ATFD was doing its job. A survey of twenty active individual dealers showed eleven did not keep records of any kind and that three maintained poor ones. In one of its rare moments of activity, the ATFD found a store just over the line in Maryland that was selling 40 percent of its guns to residents of the District of Columbia who had criminal records. Wouldn't it appear that a dealer with such a heavy interstate underworld patronage should be closed down? No, said Cohen, with a variation on the "slightly pregnant" theme, he wouldn't want to be so harsh as to punish that as improper interstate traffic because, after all, "It was just a few blocks across the line."

THE WORLD PEACE GAMBIT

Having seen what the government's attitude was toward regulating interstate gun traffic, let us now turn to its foreign gun importation policy. If you think you know what to expect, you're wrong. A normal person cannot possibly imagine the spirit that guided the State Department's gun policy prior to 1968, a spirit nicely caught in the comments of John W. Sipes, director of the Office of Munitions Control (OMC) of the State Department, in 1967. Admitting that his agency had the power to keep out any arms it felt to be detrimental to the security of the United States, Sipes responded with bland innocence, "We do not feel, in spite of that statutory delegation, that we have authority to deny importation of firearms for which there is a legitimate commercial market merely because some of these guns at some point get in the hands of juveniles or incompetents."

"As I recall," said Dodd, "the Mutual Security Act of 1954, as amended, authorized the President or anyone whom he might delegate, to control the importation of weapons in furtherance of world peace, and the security and foreign policy of the United States. I think this is exactly the language."

"Yes, sir."

"Well, how do we further world peace and the security of the United States by allowing Hy Hunter to import surplus military material from abroad?"

"Well, I do not know that we further it."

"I do not either," said Dodd.

"I am having a little difficulty," Sipes continued, "drawing the relationship between world peace and such importations."

Sipes was being neither callous nor obtuse. He was simply a bureaucrat who knew that Congress had passed the Mutual Security Act and the State Department was administering it without the slightest interest in or regard for anything but the problem of *how best to unload many millions of dollars' worth of U.S. arms and munitions on other countries.* No, that may be an exaggeration. Sipes did concede that his bureau gave possibly 5 percent of its time to worrying about the flood of arms washing over this country from abroad. But after all, the imports were

almost entirely small arms—revolvers and pistols and rifles, with
only a smattering of the antitank guns and machine guns and
bazookas thrown in.

This import traffic in foreign handguns and long guns was
piddling stuff to the State Department men who licensed the gun
hucksters—an economic drop in the bucket, which they did not
view in terms of people being shot down in Detroit with German
P-38s or Brooklyn gang wars with used Walthers. Indeed, they did
not even think of the imports in terms of a President who was
assassinated with a surplus Italian Army rifle. They thought of the
imports strictly in terms of balance of trade and of dollar exchange.
Every bit of testimony given by State Department officials over the
decade indicates this. So indifferent was the Office of Munitions
Control in the 1950s to what went on in the importation of guns
that it did not even keep a record of how many were brought in
from which countries; it kept no statistical breakdown of gun
imports. From 1961 to 1967 its statistical unit was disbanded
altogether. Only the prodding by gun-control advocates in Congress got it revved up again, in a minor way, after 1967, but most
inquiries at the OMC are still parried with the response, "Those
records are in our warehouse in St. Louis," meaning that for all
practical purposes they do not exist.

Sipes said that 95 percent of his concern—dictated by
Congressional and bureaucratic policy as well as by the pressures
of defense lobbyists and his immediate superiors—was with the
export sale of the really big stuff, planes and tanks, as well as
army-size quantities of rifles and machine guns.

If the OMC sometimes seemed a bit shifty, perhaps it was
because it had learned bad habits from some bad companions.
Sipes admitted quite readily that some of the hundred and fifty or
so companies his office had licensed as importers were *not* reliable,
substantial, commercial enterprises. Indeed, he just as readily
admitted that some of the companies his office had licensed
were—to use the language of the occasion—"shady ones." But the

State Department did not attempt to put the shady ones out of business because they, like the less shady companies, were considered necessary allies. They are scavengers, and scavengers keep the field clean. They bought the arms being discarded by Country X and sold them to Country Y. This gave Country X some funds to shop for updated weapons, preferably in the United States arms market.

Say, for example, that at some hypothetical moment in the mid-1960s the Pentagon's International Logistics Negotiations agency, which since 1957 had been peddling U.S. arms all over the globe, decided it was necessary to unload another batch of updated tanks on some of the two dozen countries who were its best customers. This would have been done in the name of national and international security, of course, but practical men recognized that it also was done in the name of offsetting the balance-of-payments deficit created by our military expenditures around the world, and also to improve the employment and profit conditions among defense industries at home. In any event, let us say that the ILN was successful in persuading the NATO nations that the American M-41 tanks then employed by our European allies were obsolete and should be replaced (as in fact happened). Actually the tanks were still in pristine condition and perfectly capable of being used in a first-class war. Obviously the NATO nations did not want to load their M-41s aboard barges and haul them out to sea and dump them. They wanted to sell them to get money to buy new tanks.

It's the same with small arms as with large arms. When the NATO countries standardized their ammunition, many thousands of handguns and rifles were suddenly declared surplus and put on the international market. Because of the scavenging service they perform, some of the biggest import firms seemed almost to be treated as adjuncts to the State Department. Sipes once said that "this office has made considerable use of a cooperative working arrangement." Century Arms in Vermont and International Armament Corp. of Alexandria, Virginia, were two that fell into that category because they helped our foreign allies dispose of their surplus weapons and thereby helped keep the market fluid. Fluidity is necessary for the continuation of the Pentagon's arms traffic.

BIG SHOT

Interarmco was the biggest private dealer in surplus military arms in this country. Its list of eager purchasers included South American dictators, Greek generals, and in fact every small hot-seat government in the world (except those with a Communist bent). Interarmco's myriad deals over the years included more than half a million British Enfields sold to Kenya Frontier Police for killing Mau Mau; thousands of Sten submachine guns to the Finnish Army; thousands of Enfields to Pakistan's border patrols; a couple of dozen Vampire jets (from Sweden) to Trujillo. When it had the opportunity, Interarmco would sell to both sides—for example, Thompson submachine guns and Browning heavy machine guns were sold to Batista's troops who were hunting Castro, at the same time that AR-10 rifles were sold to Castro—on the grounds, as Interarmco's owner said, "Any supplier of basic commodities sells to both sides. Coca-Cola sells to both Arabs and Israelis." He added, "We have government approval of every deal." (When Sipes was queried about the two-sided sales, he said his files which might throw light on the situation had been "destroyed.")

But Interarmco was not merely busy supplying foreign armies. For a number of years, until new laws in 1968 put an end to its almost unrestricted importation of surplus military weapons, half of Interarmco's business was with sportsmen in the United States. It still does a good business with them, having laid in a bountiful warehouse supply before the embargo.

The founder of Interarmco was Samuel Cummings, a young man with an upper-crust Philadelphia background who had become enamored of guns at the age of five when an American Legion post gave him a World War I Maxim machine gun. The gun was rusted, but he put it in good order and before long was able to take it apart and put it together blindfolded. By the time he went into the army in 1945 he was an expert in light arms. After the war and after a brief stint with the CIA during the Korean War, he hired himself out to Western Arms, a small West Coast firm, for $5,600 a year plus a commission on transactions.

When he had saved $25,000, he launched his International Armament Corporation. According to Sanche de Gramont, writing for *The New York Times Magazine*, Cummings innovated the marketing technique of buying huge stores of surplus light arms in Europe to dump on America at bargain prices. Gramont says, "Cummings knew that the basis for every fine bolt-action sporting rifle is the German Mauser. He also knew that several European countries were overstocked with Mausers. They were the wrong caliber for NATO standardization, and cost money to maintain and store. They even cost money to throw away. Finally, Cummings had faith in the United States gun market" with its millions of gun nuts and hunters, so he "bought out the entire stock of surplus light arms from several European countries, including hundreds of thousands of what he calls 'arsenal-fresh Mausers, with Hitler's fingerprints still on them.'" For a while he was selling a quarter of a million firearms in this country each year.

This was the gun import traffic that made our domestic manufacturers very unhappy. While Cummings was gaining many friends among the gun fraternity that liked bargains, he was also developing some potent enemies, especially among outfits like Colt (Cummings' British surplus Colt .45 automatics, in brand-new condition, sold for half the price asked for new Colts in this country) and Winchester and Remington (whose rifles suffered the same competitive price problem with his imported German Mausers and British Enfields).

Any firm that processed as many weapons as Interarmco did in its heyday (when millions of rifles and pistols and machine guns were stacked in Cummings' warehouses in Virginia and England and he had two hundred employees) was just naturally going to get into an embarrassing situation occasionally. And just as naturally Dodd, hounding Cummings on behalf of the American arms manufacturers, was going to make capital of Interarmco's errors. So it would have been much better for Interarmco (as its officers later admitted) if it had passed up the trivial profits from the resale of the imported Lahti antitank guns and mortars and bazookas. For these weapons unearthed a rich lode of the very worst kind of publicity. It took only one foolish advertisement for the Lahti antitank gun—"This is the ultimate in autoloading rifles. Fires a gigantic rimless, belted cartridge with a 2-ounce steel armor-piercing bullet. Ideal for long-range shots at deer and bear or at cars and trucks and even a tank if you happen to see one. We offer this fabulous tool at the price of only $99.70. Ammunition is $1 each or $84 a case of 100!"—it took only that kind of advertisement plus the use of the gun by a couple of kids to shell a vacant building in New Jersey, plus the use of antitank guns to blast open a couple of safes, and Interarmco had indirectly (it had brought in the guns but it didn't write the ad) supplied the gun-control advocates with several million dollars' worth of propaganda. It had also put its officials in a position of having to answer several hours of dreary questioning by Dodd as to why the heavy guns were imported—a process that Interarmco's officials publicly conceded they would just as soon stop.

And what was the reaction of the Munitions Control Office, which had granted the license for their importation? It wasn't excited. "Well," said Sipes, "the importers said that there were some people who collected these guns and did, in fact, shoot them for sport; or did, in fact, put them over the mantel. Yes, we were told that there were a few gun nuts who actually went out on the mountainside somewhere and fired these things for kicks."

To be sure, the Munitions Control Office found that these epresentations "were not very accurate," as Sipes put it. "This we ound did not really turn out that way. We found that some of them [that is, those that weren't being used to blast open safes in this country] turned up mounted on the decks of small craft headed down to Cuba. They were on a little safari on the beaches of Cuba, and there were other cases of illegal re-exportation of the weapon."

THE COMMON ENEMY

But none of this seemed especially to embarrass officials in the State Department, because as they saw it they had taken the only kind of safeguard that was really important before licensing the importation of the anti-tank guns: namely, they had made sure that the sale of the guns in this country did not put money in Communist pockets.

The question arose when Senator Dodd told Sipes he had heard that some antitank guns of Finnish manufacture, but captured by the Russians, had been imported from Russia. Heaven forbid! said Sipes. The law would not allow him to license imports from Communist countries because that would *"afford them a hard-currency benefit."* These guns came straight from Finland.

And when Dodd wanted to know how and why the Munitions Control office allowed the importation of 4,500 Russian-made Tokarjev 7.62-caliber rifles, once again Sipes seemed to feel no obligation to explain why his department had licensed importers who would allow the guns to fall into the wrong hands—at least a dozen of the Tokarjevs, plus thousands of rounds of ammunition, eventually were sold to members of the Ku Klux Klan—but only to assure Congress that money from sales of the guns had not fallen into the hands of Russia. He said the Finns had captured the guns "and no benefit would accrue to the Russians."

Knowing the State Department's obsession with the theme of "dollar exchange" and "hard currency" and "balance of payment," the officials at Interarmco sang right along in the same patriotic key. In fact, next to whatever physical damage Interarmco's guns did to the residents of this country, the worst thing about the importers was that they took such an infuriatingly pious position. Not for mere profit did they import the surplus weapons; oh no, they were importing foreign arms to sell here or to export to other Western countries because of a deep desire to aid world peace.

The argument put forward by Interarmco's Cummings was that the openheartedness of buyers in this country had made the rest of the Western world safe from gunrunners. Or, in his words, "The importation of such weapons to the United States contributes actually to the overall world peace and security, inasmuch as these weapons are thus taken off the world market, and instead of providing a possible source for the illegal arms trade, they are channeled into the legitimate trade circles of the United States, winding up in the hands of hunters, shooters and collectors."

But wait—there's more. Indeed, the peaceful influence of the gun dealers is many-faceted. "In addition," said patriot Cummings, "the obsolete weapons imported serve as payment for new, modern small arms needed by the various countries for defense against the East. Inasmuch as all such transactions take place in Western countries (South America and Europe), it is one more contribution to the common defense effort without costing anything to the American taxpayer. . . . [Or, to repeat] By purchasing these weapons and importing them to the United States, we have, in a small way, contributed to the strengthening of the defense against the Eastern bloc, and we have done so at no cost whatsoever to the taxpayer—strictly by private initiative."

In this flummery Cummings was merely taking a page from the State Department's dogma. They spoke as one. To see this, let us go back again to 1958, when Senator John Kennedy threw in his bill to help the New England gun manufacturers. Kennedy's bill would have outlawed importation of foreign surplus arms. The State Department opposed the bill. R. L. O'Connor, administrator of State's Bureau of Security and Consular Affairs, clearly implied that it would be better for Americans to shoot each other with surplus arms than to let the Commies have them. He testified before the House Foreign Affairs Committee: "I am frank to say that when there are questions of surplus arms cropping up abroad, which another area [Communist] is bidding for, it may very often be the better part of valor and indeed the best part of our foreign relations to have them imported into this country rather than float around."

Stressing the point, he said that when the choice was between losing lives at home or losing propaganda points overseas, "it is quite clear that to have these arms come in here [the United States] was highly beneficial."

LEGISLATION BY ASSASSINATION

Just when it seemed that Dodd's mail-order-guns show was going to die from lack of notoriety, President John Kennedy's death came along and revived it. More than reviving it, his death gave it its first really national audience. Whether he wanted to or not, Dodd now had to get in there and orate like he meant it, for he was caught by the wave of history.

Most people assumed that the Congressional gun debate after November 22, 1963, was largely motivated by a feeling of national guilt because of the murder of an important man and the desire to prevent a recurrence. This myth was perpetrated by Dodd and his allies in and out of the federal legislature, especially by his allies in the press. As a matter of fact, that was not the motivation, nor should it have been.

In the first place, one should never feel guilty about insanity. As a nation that is clearly unbalanced, the United States should not be surprised when some of its citizens reflect this unbalance to an excessive degree. Actually, America's children play by the rules far more than one might expect, considering how unmercifully they are provoked by their politicians. It's said that some of those who wrote the Constitution, and especially Benjamin Franklin, favored adding the procedure for impeachment so that the citizens would have some method other than assassination—which had traditionally been about the only route open for discarding kings—for disposing of intolerable Presidents. Whether that Constitutional provision has succeeded as a safety valve is something that can never be proved, since it has been brought into play, and then unsuccessfully, only once. On the other hand, it is plain that Americans have seldom cheated by resorting to *political* assassinations. For the most part, their politicians have fallen to kook assassins, though sometimes they have wrapped their kookiness in a flimsy veil of authentic politics. The fellow who tried to shoot Andrew Jackson saw himself as Richard III of England. John Wilkes Booth got his kicks shooting dogs and cats when he was a kid, and for anybody that nutty it is a relatively short step to shooting Presidents. Booth's explanation that he shot Abraham Lincoln to help the South was just the kind of pompous hokum that hangers-on pick up and imitate if they linger around Washington too long, as he had. Charles J. Guiteau had been several kinds of swindler—lawyer, evangelist, insurance salesman—before heeding what he later called "direct inspiration from the Deity" (at the conclusion of two weeks of prayer) and gunning down James Garfield. Oh yes, Guiteau also complained that Garfield had failed to give him an ambassadorship, but that hardly qualifies it as a political assassination. Leon F. Czolgosz has gone into the history books as an anarchist who claimed he shot William McKinley

"because he was the enemy of the people, the good working
people," but that was claptrap Czolgosz had picked up in his
psychotically lonely readings after he had had a mental breakdown
and couldn't hold a job. He was quite mad: when he wasn't
muttering the anarchistic clichés of his day, he was worrying about
people poisoning his food. John Nepomuk Schrank, a native of
Bavaria, had a screen in his head on which was periodically flashed
the message—a message, by the way, straight from McKinley in
heaven—that read: "Theodore Roosevelt is a murderer." Teddy
was out of office at the time, but he was running again, which saved
his life; for candidates are always windbags, of course, and in the
inside breast pocket of his coat was a fifty-page speech, folded
double; although Roosevelt was standing only six feet from
Schrank when he pulled the trigger, the bullet was brought almost
to a halt on its passage through the speech. Teddy went on to
deliver his speech and Schrank spent the next thirty-one years in a
madhouse.*

And so it goes. *Most* of the men who have made the forty-one
recorded assassination attempts on Presidents, Governors, Senators, and Representatives in this country since the attempt on
Jackson in 1835 have been certifiably crazy, not political activists;
and if you consider all the Hardings and Talmadges and Lodges
and Eastlands and Tammanys and Crumps and McCarthys who
plagued the nation during that period, you will have to admit that
even if all forty-one assassinations were politically motivated, the
number shows a remarkable degree of restraint on the part of our
fellow citizens. Just what Oswald's game was for sure, nobody
knows; one would have to see who signed his paycheck to know if
there was political intrigue behind it. But it's almost certain that
Kennedy's death was not political in the same way that most of the
eleven Middle Eastern and eleven Latin American and seven
Southern and Eastern European and four Far Eastern assassina-

---

* For more details, see Robert Elman's delightful book, *Fired in Anger: The
Personal Handguns of American Heroes and Villains* (Doubleday, 1968).

tions of heads of state in the fifty-year period from 1919 to 1968 were political. So "national guilt" was certainly not in order in 1963 on that account.

A much better reason for outlawing all guns—or at least for puttering around with some inadequate controls program—would have been the argument (the question of the justice of the assassination aside) that the gentility and aesthetics of Kennedy's life did not deserve such an uncouth and ugly end. To perform the post-mortem examination, they had to scrape him up: fragments of Kennedy's skull had to be picked up from Elm Street and from inside the Presidential limousine. Not pretty at all. But the appeal to aesthetics has never worked worth a damn. The public enjoys reading about their murdered Presidents, in detail. The .44-caliber bullet that hit Lincoln passed from the rear of his skull clear through his brain and lodged against the orbital plate of the left eye socket. Or was it the right eye socket? The attending doctors could never agree. But being doctors, they set out to satisfy their curiosity even while he still lived, first sticking their fingers as deep as they could into the hole and then sticking an ordinary silver probe through the bullet channel, meeting bone fragments along the way that had been broken off and pushed ahead by the bullet. As they jabbed with their fingers, brain tissue oozed from the hole. Once again, it doesn't sound very pretty, but that's the kind of hole a .44-caliber bullet makes, especially one of soft lead that spreads on impact—a hole easily admitting a finger into the head and guaranteeing that the doctors' professional play will probably not prove any more fatal than the damage already done. The public of Lincoln's day loved to read and hear about all this probing and fingering, loved to read later, too, the account of Dr. Edward Curtis' examination of Lincoln's brain after it was taken from the skull:

> There is laid bare what a few short hours ago was the fountainhead of a wit and wisdom that could save a nation. The part [brain] is lifted from its seat, when suddenly from out

a cruel vent that traverses it from end to end through these very fingers there slips a something hard—slips and falls with a metal's mocking clatter into a basin set beneath. The search is satisfied: a little pellet of lead.*

Yep. That's exactly what comes out of the hole at the end of the barrel, and let Dr. Curtis describe it ever so poetically, with all sorts of clinking, plinking, sinking tintinnabulations of the lead, lead, lead, that is still ultimately all it comes down to. Lincoln's contemporaries were delighted to read about it all.

Similar pleasures awaited Americans of Garfield's day, after Guiteau, standing only six feet away, sent a .44-caliber slug between the tenth and eleventh ribs on the President's right side, about four inches from the spine. Just where the bullet went beyond that point remained a mystery until the President was cut up in autopsy. For eighty days—during which time Garfield was in constant and deep pain, and lost eighty of his two hundred pounds—the nation thought and read about the bullet's effect. "By the everyday miracles of the telegraph and the printing press working together," the New York *Tribune* boasted, "the whole mass of the people have been admitted to his bedside." And what an entertaining sight was there. Even Alexander Graham Bell got into the show, bringing along his new "electromagnetic device" for hunting the location of the bullet from the surface. But that sort of bloodless search wasn't nearly as appealing to the doctors, who were always ready with their fingers stiff and looking for a bullet hole to insert them into. The fingering actually had begun right on the assassination spot, the floor of a Washington railroad depot. On that preliminary inspection Dr. Smith Townsend, Health Officer of the District of Columbia, later wrote, "I found that the last bullet had entered his back about two and one-half inches to the right of the vertebrae. I introduced my finger into the bullet wound." After they had got Garfield into bed, a Dr. D. Willard Bliss, among the

---

* Quoted in Stewart M. Brooks, *Our Murdered Presidents: The Medical Story* (Frederick Fell, 1966), p. 40. This book is a must for assassination buffs with a ghoulish side.

dozens who poked and prodded the President, took over briefly
and later wrote, "A slight discharge of blood was oozing from the
orifice and had soiled the clothing. I then passed the little finger of
my left hand to its full extent into the wound. . . ." Considering
the treatment, it will come as no surprise to learn that Garfield died
from infection, his body full of pus and pain, not at all the kind of
end deserved by a gentleman who could simultaneously, they say,
write Greek with one hand and Latin with the other and who, on
his deathbed, had still enough intellectual curiosity to inquire,
"What was probably the central velocity of the bullet?" Still, for
eighty days it did keep the public's mind off their other troubles,
and it gave surgeons many months of happy speculation on the
path and effect of the bullet, as they hauled corpse after corpse out
of the morgue and strung them up and took potshots at them in an
effort to duplicate the assassination.

Czolgosz used only a low-velocity .32-short cartridge to put a
hole in McKinley's midsection, the bullet passing through the
stomach and lodging somewhere in the neighborhood of the
pancreas, but that—coupled with the usual doctoring—was enough
to do the job in eight days, during which time the nation followed
breathlessly the accounts of how the President improved for a few
days, then, after doctors had cut a big enough hole that they could
get their hands inside, not just those probing fingers, he began to
sink fast, finally developed a fine case of gangrene and went out
pluckily singing "Nearer My God to Thee." The public was
reading the medical chart all the way, and wallowing in the details.

Which was one reason the mere slaughter of a President in
1963 was not enough to peg the gun-reform movement to. To most
people, it really wasn't that revolting. Oh, maybe revolting in a
way, but revoltingness has its own appeal. There was a mesmeriz-
ing enchantment in the inventory of a skull's missing parts. Seldom
in modern times had the public been given such an intimate look at
high-level gore, with the newspapers and magazines reviewing in
precise detail the bullets' impact and the probable flesh route.

One read with fascination, for example, that the Western

Cartridge Co. bullet fired from the Mannlicher-Carcano hit the back of President Kennedy's head at an estimated velocity of 1,904 feet per second, exploding most of the right hemisphere of the skull into dozens of bone fragments, leaving a hole that at its widest was five inches across and through which most of the brain on that side protruded, and then emerged still traveling at 1,780 feet a second. There's something very American about such precise measurements. And wasn't it just something that another Western Cartridge Co. bullet hit the President's neck at a velocity of roughly 1,775 feet a second, passing thereafter through 13.5 to 14.5 centimeters of tissue?

One did not have to appreciate it at the very moment of the happening. The show ran for months—in fact, it's still running—with federal investigators reconstructing everything with just the right mixture of science and paganism. The President was long in his grave, but America could relive his last moments with the experts, using gelatin and animal flesh and animal skin and what the Warren Commission delicately identified as "an inert skull." They packed the skull with gelatin and draped it with the animal skin and hair. It didn't look at all like JFK, to be sure, but what happened when the test bullet was fired from a distance of 270 feet, the distance from Oswald to Kennedy, was just the same, or almost the same, for the "bullet blew out the right side of the reconstructed skull" as everyone knew it would, and simulated hair and inert skull and gelatin went flying about, just as though it were a simulated President.

Not much can be said for a jacketed bullet that removes the back of a forty-six-year-old man's head and deposits some of his brain on his wife's hand, but the Commission did note, as if this were somehow mitigating, that "the President's head wound was not caused by a dumdum bullet." The same could not be said five years later of the bullet that caused Robert Kennedy's head wound, but it should also be noted that RFK was not more dead from the .22-caliber dumdum than JFK had been from the "clean" Western cartridge.

The meaning and purpose of all the investigations and re-creations should not be forgotten. They had nothing to do with the tragedy of a bright, handsome, popular young man being murdered. They had nothing to do with the tragic demolition of a political engine that had taken years to assemble. Their only concern was with the nation's intense preoccupation with the question of intrigue. Was Oswald really the guilty one? Did he have connections with, say, the CIA? Was there only one Oswald? Did all shots come from the same direction? This is what all the flying gelatin was about. It had nothing to do with tragedy, only with mystery; it had much less to do with the evils of assassination than with the evils of conspiracy. Which is another way of saying that if there had been no doubts about the perpetrator, there wouldn't have been nearly as much interest. Which is also another way of saying that people weren't worried so much that a gun had been used as by the uncertainty about the user. That is not the stuff from which gun reforms are made.

THE SENATOR WHO COULDN'T SHOOT STRAIGHT

The basic motivation behind the post-assassination gun debate—as with the pre-assassination gun debate—had to do with the marketplace, which is only to be expected, for while the Goddess of Freedom holds down the top of the Capitol dome, the legislative chambers and the committee rooms are ruled by that lady once designated by Ruskin as the Goddess of Getting-On, and to her the federal heart is given with passion.

A few years ago a federal employees' union reenacted on a New York street the shooting of President Garfield. The employees were commemorating the Civil Service Act; it seems that Garfield's murder by a disappointed office-seeker (Guiteau, you will recall, had wanted to be appointed an ambassador) brought about major reforms of the civil service—meaning, more security and more money, whether deserved or not—so our federal employees just naturally considered the bygone bullet in Garfield's gut to be worth celebrating. It was also quite in keeping with the tradition of assassination cum profit that Mrs. Oswald protested the federal government's failure to return her husband's rifle to her so that she could take advantage of some of the extremely handsome offers for its purchase. Hundreds of similar Mannlicher-Carcano rifles were immediately bought by souvenir-seekers who wanted to get the feel of the weapon that had brought down the President. One should also mention, by the way, the appropriateness of the legislative arena in which the gun-control laws were handled; they were intitially processed through the Senate Commerce Committee and the House Ways and Means Committee—these groups studying the problem not from the perspective of community peace and personal safety but from the perspective of business competition and treasury income. Dodd's Juvenile Delinquency Subcommittee was permitted to investigate, but for several years its parent, the Senate Judiciary Committee, was not permitted to legislate on the subject. In the Senate the legislative powers were left to Commerce.

Within the context of the marketplace, Kennedy's assassination came to the assistance of Dodd and the New England gun manufacturers. Lee Harvey Oswald had played into their hands by the manner in which he did business, and at the same time he had delivered a stiff blow to the Sports and Hucksters who dealt in used guns. If Oswald had gone to his friendly hardware store and bought a new Remington or Winchester, the subsequent course of the gun debate might have been considerably different in temper and direction. But instead, Oswald spotted an ad in the *American Rifleman* magazine which sounded attractive. It read:

LATE ISSUE!   6.5 ITALIAN CARBINE

Only 36″ overall, weighs only 5½ pounds. Shows only slight use, lightly oiled, test fired and head spaced, ready for shooting. Turned down bolt, thumb safety, 6-shot, clip fed. Rear down sight. Fast loading and fast firing.

C20-T1196.   Specially priced $12.78

C20-T750.   Carbine with Brand New Good Quality 4X
             Scope—¼″ diameter, as illustrated $19.95

C20-T751.   6.5mm Italian military ammo with free 6-shot
             clip.—108 rds. $7.50

On March 12, 1963, Oswald tore out the coupon and sent along a postal money order for $21.45 to Klein's Sporting Goods Co. in Chicago. The extra $1.50 was for postage and handling. Klein's was just one of many outlets for the Italian surplus military rifles, distributed by the wholesale dealer Crescent Firearms, Inc., of New York City. There was a brisk turnover of the weapons: no sooner in than out. Klein's had received the gun from Crescent on February 21; on March 13 Klein's cashed the money order, and seven days later the rifle, fully assembled, was on its way by parcel post to the address on the order: "A. Hidell, P.O. Box 2915, Dallas, Texas." This was Oswald's box.

When Oswald was arrested, he was allegedly carrying a Smith & Wesson .38 revolver, which he had ordered under the name A. J. Hidell from Seaport Traders, Inc., one of Rose's outfits in Los Angeles. The revolver had also started on its way to Dallas on March 20, the same day the rifle was leaving Chicago. While Rose had already figured very prominently in Senator Dodd's earlier investigative hearings in 1963, and would come in for further drubbing by Senate investigators, the .38 revolver itself never got much emphasis, possibly because it bore the hallowed trade name Smith & Wesson.

In seeking a cheap gun for the job, Oswald was sticking strictly to an old American tradition. Political murder in the United States has always been inexpensive. Our Presidential assassins have done their work for a total of less than $75. Booth shot Lincoln with a .44 derringer that could not have cost over $15. Guiteau paid $10 for the .44-caliber five-shot double-action British Bulldog revolver (with a box of cartridges and a small penknife thrown into the bargain) that he used to shoot President Garfield in the back.

Czolgosz killed President McKinley with a $4.50 five-shot double-action Iver Johnson .32 revolver. Even if Giuseppe Zangara's unsuccessful attempt on the life of Franklin D. Roosevelt is counted, that still leaves the total well below $75, for Zangara paid only $8 for the five-shot .32 revolver manufactured by U.S. Revolver Co., a subsidiary of Iver Johnson Arms & Cycle Works. (Stepping down the political scale: Dr. Carl Austin Weiss, Jr., paid only $8 for the 7.65 "FN" pistol, made in France, with which he murdered Huey Long.)

The political assassins of our nation's history can be forgiven their cheapness, however, because they were obviously equipping themselves with weapons for only one job, not with weapons that they intended to subject to a great deal of wear. Guiteau, for example, fired only ten practice rounds at trees and posts and planks before using it on Garfield. Czolgosz could not have practiced much with his Iver Johnson because he had bought it only the week before he shot McKinley. Zangara told his captors that he had never fired his revolver before spraying five bullets in the general direction of FDR; he had purchased the gun at a Miami pawnshop only forty-eight hours before the assassination effort.

It was in this same ad-hoc tradition that Lee Harvey Oswald bought and used the 6.5-mm Mannlicher-Carcano.* Even when in the best condition, the Mannlicher-Carcano had a poor reputation. Designed in the nineteenth century (it was first produced in 1891), the last new Mannlicher-Carcanos came off the assembly line a quarter-century before Kennedy reached Dallas. In *The Rifle Book*, Jack O'Connor describes the M-C's action as "terrible" and further points out with disgust that the rifle has "a coy habit of blowing the firing pin out in the shooter's face." A *Mechanix Illustrated* article in October 1964 described the rifle as "crudely made, poorly

---

* For the sake of simplicity, we are accepting the Warren Commission's highly dubious conclusions as to the guilt of Oswald. It has also been much disputed among JFK assassination bugs whether the Mannlicher-Carcano was indeed the murder weapon.

designed, dangerous and inaccurate . . . unhandy, crude, unreliable on repeat shots, has safety design fault." During World War II it is said to have earned the reputation "the humanitarian rifle" because it was so inefficient at the job of killing.

Oswald got no more than he paid for.* The firing pin was so rusty that the Warren Commission marksmen did not practice with the weapon before test-firing it because they were afraid of breaking the firing pin. The mount for the telescopic sight was frail and rickety; so much so, in fact, that the FBI reported its experts were unable to align the scope sights properly with the target at the assassination distance. In light of this fault and of the fact that at the speed at which President Kennedy's car was traveling (about twelve miles an hour) he would move about two feet during the tenth of a second that the 6.5-mm bullet needed to travel the distance from Oswald to Kennedy, it means Oswald would have had to "lead" his target but also mentally adjust that lead to an inaccurate scope. It's little wonder that there were so many skeptics about the Mannlicher-Carcano's actually having been the murder weapon. As one of the more scholarly skeptics, Sylvia Meagher, wrote in *Accessories After the Fact: The Warren Commission, The Authorities & The Report*, there is scant evidence "for concluding

---

* Carl Perian, former staff director of the Juvenile Delinquency Subcommittee, gives this version of the "loading" of the Oswald weapon: "When the Communists were trying to take over Greece, our government was looking for a supply of weapons to give to the anti-Communists in Greece. We had captured from the Italians this massive number of the Mannlicher-Carcanos which were in a basement in a castle somewhere in Italy. Our troops jokingly referred to the weapon as the gun that lost the war for Italy because it was so ineffective and inaccurate. The main problem with it was the ammunition—no quality control. So government officials brought some Mannlichers here; the National Rifle Association and Army took them to Aberdeen Proving Grounds, tested them, and worked together in the perfecting of a bullet that was fairly accurate in the gun. We gave the Greek partisans twenty-five thousand Mannlicher-Carcanos and plenty of U.S.-produced ammunition that would make the gun usable in battle. Subsequent to that, some of the ammunition that we produced to make the gun accurate got into the U.S. domestic market and Oswald got ahold of a box of that ammunition. Franklin Orth [former Executive Vice-President of the NRA] told us this story and said, 'Please don't tell anybody because we don't want to be hung with having been involved in producing the ammunition that killed the President.' "

that Oswald had practiced shooting the Carcano or that he performed an unparalleled feat of marksmanship with that decrepit weapon [prior to the assassination]. Indeed, common sense suggests that if he *had* practiced with that rifle, he would have lost no time dumping it for a bow and arrow." *

This was the most pronounced immediate reaction to the disreputable condition of the Mannlicher-Carcano: it was an unlikely weapon for accurate killing from a sixth-floor window, with the target moving away at a sloping angle. These suspicions helped develop the "two assassins" theory as well as the theory that the Mannlicher-Carcano was simply an instrument in the scheme to frame Oswald.

A more subtle but more pervasive and long-range reaction was one of resentment that a President of the United States had been done in with such a shoddy piece of merchandise in a shoddy city. Dallas is not only a place where it seemed quite normal for its district attorney to explain without obvious embarrassment to a *Wall Street Journal* reporter, "Murder in Texas often involves the frontier type of spirit in which a person has a right to kill under certain circumstances, whether or not there's a legal defense. People believe that if a man calls you a liar you have a right to kill him." It is also a place of grass-roots hypocrisy, where just about everybody goes to church but is unusually prone to mischief. The president of the Dallas Crime Commission at that time was eventually indicted for embezzlement. The year Kennedy was killed, Dallas had a per-100,000-population homicide rate of 13.4, compared to 8.1 for Phoenix, 7.6 for Chicago, 6 for Los Angeles, 5.5 for Detroit, 5.4 for New York, and 4.9 for Philadelphia. Offensive as Dallas was to many non-Texans, it seemed more so because it was the place where the gates of Camelot were permanently slammed shut by a cheap and unreliable shooting iron: a mail-order job, a job that violated the most basic tenet of patriotism: Buy American.

---

* (Bobbs-Merrill, 1967), p. 133. No book has better shown the sloppiness of the Warren Commission's investigation.

If Dodd was on the spot, it was a spot he enjoyed, for it was prominently headlined. But if he was to use this moment of national despair to capitalize on his role as the number-one gun-control spokesman in Congress, he knew he would have to have a bill that applied to the circumstances. Considering the weapon with which Kennedy had been shot, Dodd had to offer a bill controlling mail-order rifles. Public relations demanded it. And it wouldn't make the New England manufacturers unhappy either, of course.

Prior to the assassination Dodd's mail-order gun-control bill had included only handguns. The legislation had been painfully assembled during dozens of conferences between representatives of the Sports and the Hucksters over a two-year period. Always the great powerhouse lobbies for the hunters and collectors and dealers and manufacturers were in on the negotiations: the National Shooting Sports Foundation, the National Wildlife Federation, the Wildlife Management Institute, the Sporting Arms and Ammunition Manufacturers Institute, and above all, omnipresent and omnipotent, the National Rifle Association.

As a result of these negotiations a timid bill had been stitched together that would have restricted the interstate sale of pistols and revolvers to everybody except those who were willing to swear before a notary public that they were nice people. It was, everyone admitted, a rather low hurdle for the criminal to jump. Since the bill provided no safeguards against liars, it was virtually useless. Nevertheless, even that bill would probably have never emerged from Dodd's timorous hands if civil rights leader Medgar Evers had not been assassinated in Mississippi in June 1963. President Kennedy was promptly on the phone to Dodd, chewing him out and demanding that he come up with some legislation. Dodd went back to the gun lobby and said he had to make a showing. In August the handgun bill emerged (though Evers had been slain with a rifle). It had the seal of approval of the NRA—its outward approval, at least. The feeling within the crankier and more stubborn membership of the NRA was something else. In any event the NRA—which has the schizophrenic job of representing both the gun industry and the hunters—gave Dodd permission to go that far. He made no bones about operating under the NRA's authority: "Any bill which is disapproved of by sportsmen," Dodd said at the time, "has no chance of passage." So he accepted handguns as his limit.

Even so, Dodd had no great hopes that the bill would go anywhere. The gun lobby had said he could bring the bill *out,* but it did not say it would let the bill pass. Then came Dallas, and Dodd suddenly felt a giddy independence from the lobby. If nothing else, he could use Dallas as an emotional wedge to drive between the industry and the hunters, destroying the lobby's unity and leaving him in a better position to swap off on behalf of the New England manufacturers as well as produce the kind of publicity that would do his career considerable good. "There was little expectation of action on the bill," he wrote later, "until that dark day in Dallas . . .," etc.

Aside from everything else, his staff on the Juvenile Delinquency Subcommittee was urging him to press for the ultimate, to be content no longer with the handgun bill.

So he added long guns—rifles and shotguns—to his legislation's interstate-sale prohibition, insisting at the same time that it wasn't just his idea, that he had talked with the New England manufacturers "and we have their support for this measure." Perhaps he had, but it is unlikely that he or they could have anticipated the reaction from other elements within the gun lobby, who viewed the expanded bill as an unspeakable betrayal. Pressures were exerted, and the bill went nowhere. On June 24, 1964—seven months and two days after Kennedy died—it was announced that Senator Warren G. Magnuson, chairman of the Commerce Committee and the man who held in his hands the fate of the gun-control bill, had been cited by an NRA convention in Los Angeles for "displaying leadership and calm judgment" in his handling of the reform efforts. More exactly, he had done nothing, which no doubt met the approval of all those hunters back home in

Washington State. Six weeks later the committee declared the bill dead. Once again Congress had waited out the public's gusty passion, knowing it wouldn't last. Dodd, of course, was overbrimming with loud recriminations. In an interview with *Newsweek* he declared, "I intend to identify and expose the activities of the powerful lobbyists who have successfully stopped gun legislation from being passed in every Congress." But he didn't. If he had exposed only one lobby, the National Rifle Association, he would no doubt have had some pretty stories to tell. But he feared the NRA too much for that. And besides, every major gun-manufacturing company had an official on the NRA's Board of Directors. For Dodd to squeal on the NRA under those conditions would have been like squealing on his own folks.

Anyway, bombastic threats of that kind were typical diversionary tactics for Dodd. He never meant them. Rage was not something that afflicted Dodd, except toward his staff when they got in the way of one of his quiet deals on the side, or toward somebody who had promised to pay and didn't. He wasn't even a good flunky for the gun industry; he was too busy wheeling to follow instructions. He didn't have time to work for gun legislation in 1964. Aside from running for re-election that year, he was also busy dashing off to Europe to help his friend Julius Klein, the foreign agent for German munitions-makers.

In March 1965 Dodd popped up again, fluttering around the Capitol with a revived gun-control bill, but when the Big Berthas of the gun lobby turned on him, he backed off with only a brief gentlemanly struggle. He didn't get his bill out of committee.

The next year he went on trial in the Senate for misappropriating campaign funds, and he was far too busy ducking these charges to be at all interested in his mock drama with the gun bill. The result of the trial—Dodd's censure—virtually destroyed whatever effectiveness he might have had as the sponsor of the gun reform. He had lost most of his power as a cloakroom negotiator, and this meant that as long as he insisted on being the sponsor of the gun-reform legislation its chances of passage were very poor indeed. This was acknowledged by just about everyone around Congress, including some members of Dodd's staff. It was obviously acknowledged by the White House, which began sending its gun amendments to the Hill through the office of Congressman Emanuel Celler of New York, not through Dodd's office; in fact, the White House stopped telling Dodd when amendments were coming up. But Dodd refused to turn loose. Though Senator Edward Kennedy (and others) wanted very much to take over management of the legislation, Dodd hung on to it, seemingly as his only real rag of respectability in a year that otherwise found him quite naked. And this was the rag he wore through 1967.

THE RUSSIANS ARE COMING . . .
OR SOMEBODY

If Dodd's service should be colored gray, forgive him. It wouldn't have mattered if a more sanguine legislative manager had tried to exploit the assassination, for one problem in trying to utilize an emotional event for wringing reform from Congress is that Congress does not have normal glands. Whether or not that is good, it is nevertheless a fact. When others weep, Congress only blows its nose. Where others rage, Congress picks its teeth and frowns.

The Sports and the Hucksters were afraid that public outrage might override their own lobby's influence with Congress. The February 1964 issue of *Gun World* ran a black-bordered Special Editorial which regretted the death of President Kennedy but then got down to the really important point of warning that "the enemies of freedom, of our right 'to keep and bear arms,' are not removed by sublime character from seizing opportunity at this time of bereavement." E. B. Mann, editor of *Guns Magazine*, added his warning that the assassination had created "a wave of national hysteria" which "convinced many politicians that any anti-gun publicity was good publicity for whoever could get it—and there were plenty of sensation seekers in the news media who were willing to give it. . . ."

It was a baseless worry. The politicians whom *Gun World* considered "the enemies of freedom" and whom *Guns Magazine* suspected of being exploiters of the antigun "hysteria" were in a position of neither seniority nor numbers to dominate Congress. Perhaps politicians of that sort controlled the city councils of Boston or Berkeley or Milwaukee. But not the federal legislature, where the hallmark is not hysteria, but what can be called active torpor. In a crisis Congress reacts like a man who frantically pumps up the tires of a car that has lost its motor. Dissociated from the event itself, this kind of flailing action can be quite entertaining, as when a number of Congressmen defended the assassination weapon by shifting attention to the farcical Lethal Hardware List.

First came Congressman John Dingell, who is also a director of the National Rifle Association, arguing with a straight face that if someone were bent on assassination and wasn't able to get hold of a gun, he would use "knives, ice picks, pliers, hammers, sockfuls of sand, or a sock with a bar of soap in it. England has very stringent laws against firearms, but I noted in the paper recently a major train robbery was perpetrated in which millions of dollars were stolen, one of the largest robberies in history, and was achieved with iron bars. It is almost impossible to deny a citizen access to iron bars." Imaginative though his contribution had been, Dingell was not content with that list of potential murder and robbery weapons: later he added "milk bottles."

Others followed. Two months and one day after the assassination, Congressman Robert Sikes showed up as the lead-off witness against gun-control legislation.* His basic argument, believe it or

---

* Of course, to understand the wherefore of this squat Floridian with the gleaming dome of a head, you have to understand first of all that he had something of a conflict of interest, for at that time he was on the Board of Directors of the National Rifle Association. Secondly, his ideas about obedience to laws and sportsmanship may not be your ideas, since he was once arrested for shooting over a baited field, which is the equivalent of clubbing fish in a barrel or hunting deer at night by blinding them with lights.

not, was, yes, inasmuch as 44 percent of aggravated assaults are committed via stabbings, 24 percent by blunt objects, 12.7 percent by shooting, 12.3 percent by hands, fists, or feet, and 1.2 percent by use of poison, then if guns are licensed and their owners registered (something, by the way, which was not at the time even being suggested; but you must understand that much of the Congressional debate in the past decade has been over points not at issue), "naturally all knives, ice picks, scissors, et cetera, should be registered and rocks, hammers, baseball bats, rolling pins, sticks, et cetera, should be serialized and registered." As for shooting devices, he recommended that if Congress demanded the registration of guns, it should also require the registration of rubber bands.* Ten years later Sikes and the others were still using the very same arguments.

The repetition in these orations is worth mentioning. If you look through every Congressional gun-control hearing since Kennedy's death you will see something rather striking: they have the quality of the most stylized of ancient dramas in which actors appeared with masks depicting various emotions—and each actor recited lines long familiar to the audience but no less appreciated. This is true of both sides, those who want controls and those who do not. The allusions to commerce, to patriotism, to the Constitution, to manliness never vary; the horror stories change in detail but never in kind.

---

* The inmates of Attica State Prison who seized guards and rebelled in 1971 would no doubt be interested in these Congressmen's equating other weapons with guns. After the battle was over at Attica, fourteen hundred weapons were recovered from the prison yard, including two tear-gas guns, spears, Molotov cocktails, baseball bats, scissors, knives, razors and clubs—but no firearms. None of the assaulting police force was hurt, but twenty-nine of the twelve hundred prisoners were killed and scores were wounded. Could the reason possibly be that although the police were deprived of baseball bats, scissors, razors, clubs, etc., they did happen to have shotguns loaded with the heaviest buckshot and rifles and pistols loaded with dumdum bullets?

Pope Paul VI also might have something to say about the difference. A would-be assassin tried to get him with a knife during the Papal visit to the Philippines in 1970. The assassin later explained apologetically that he would have used a gun "but I couldn't get a permit."

No hearing would have been complete, for example, without the appearance of a witness to claim that England has one of the toughest gun laws in the world and one of the lowest murder rates, and therefore we should outlaw guns. No hearing would have been complete without the appearance of a witness to claim that in Switzerland every adult male is issued a rifle and ammunition to keep at home and Switzerland has an extremely low crime rate, and therefore every American male should be issued a gun. (Both sides conveniently overlook a whole range of differences between England or Switzerland and the United States that would affect law enforcement, beginning with the most obvious: both countries would fit in Arizona alone with room to spare.) No hearing would have been complete without some righteous witness showing up to quote the Bible to justify arming, yea, verily, as the gentleman from the Florida Sportsmen's Association shouted, "The Old Testament says: 'Teach the children of Judah in the use of the bow' (II Samuel i:18), and the New Testament says: 'When a strong man armed keepeth his palace, his goods are in peace' (Luke xi:21)."

Nor would the hearing have been complete without the appearance of an American Legion official to declare that any gun controls, even the weakest, were only the first step down the path toward the registration of firearms and the licensing of owners that would make us extremely vulnerable to The Invaders, whoever they may be; that when They come, They will head straight for the police station or the courthouse or wherever the records on registration are held, and They will then go around knocking on the identified doors and gather in the firearms, and we will then have to live under Their yoke forever. (What this ubiquitous witness never has explained is why The Invaders would bother making thousands of stopovers at minor bureaucratic file cabinets when in one quick trip to 1600 Rhode Island Avenue, Washington, D.C.—headquarters of the NRA—they could get their hands on the membership list representing most of the hard-line gun owners in the country. Could it be that the NRA is our weakest security link?)

Usually, of course, gun lobbyists are not so coy as to allude to a nameless enemy; usually they come right out and say Communists. And they are deadly serious about gun registration's being a Communist plot. A 1949 editorial of *The American Rifleman* warned:

> Lenin has indicated that the Communist strategy is deeply concerned with two objectives: (1) the arming of the "right" people, and (2) the disarming of those "reactionaries" who might meet violence with violence. Communists, like holdup men, have no overweening desire to be shot. Both the Communist and the thug prefer to deal with a disarmed citizenry. . . . Only when the loyal majority has been legally disarmed do we need fear the violence of the illegally armed, disloyal minority. This is not ideology. It is simple arithmetic. . . .

That editorial was reprinted and amended—on the second go-round it had added, " 'Make mass searches and hold executions for found arms.' (from Lenin's *Collected Works*, Vol. 35, 4th edition, p. 286)"—in the August 1970 *American Rifleman*. Still enamored of their argument, the NRA decided to run it through the mill again, and the 1970 editorial was reprinted in the January 1973 *American Rifleman*.

Soiled and stained with age, the last time around it was freshened up a bit by an accompanying article that the NRA staff hoped would authenticate one of the oldest yarns in the gun debate, a yarn that has been cropping up for years. It is the legend of what are known sometimes as the "Rules for Revolution" and sometimes as the "Düsseldorf Rules."

According to those who believe in the rules, they were discovered by Allied Intelligence officers in a 1919 raid on the headquarters of the Spartacist League, a German Communist organization. The believers say the rules had been written in Moscow and distributed to Communist organizations around the world. The first of the rules is "Corrupt the young. Get them away from religion. Encourage their interest in sex. Make them superficial. Destroy their ruggedness" by, presumably, draining their precious bodily fluids, as General Jack D. Ripper used to say.

Well, that gives a fair idea of the profundity of Moscow's alleged advice, so there is no use reciting any other rule except the last one, which is the one that for decades has kept the gun lobby in a state of intense excitement. Rule 10 is, "Cause the registration of all firearms on some pretext, with a view to confiscating them and leaving the population helpless."

It is hard to understand why either side in the gun debate takes this legend seriously, but in fact both sides have treated it as though it mattered. J. Edgar Hoover, no friend of Communism, testified on April 17, 1969, before a House subcommittee that his agents couldn't discover any verification for the rules and "therefore, we can logically speculate that the document is spurious." Researchers in the Library of Congress hunted high and low for authenticating evidence but failed to find any. But still the gun lobby, as well as a number of right-wing magazines, kept reprinting the "rules" and insisting that they are accurate and born of man. Sometimes, though, those who went to Congressional hearings to talk of the rules did have the grace to seem mildly embarrassed. One Legion official told Congressmen he hoped "you don't think I look under my bed at night."

Equally baffling was why the antigun side bothered to rebut; but it did. On July 10, 1970, *The New York Times* published an article whose contents were summed in the headline "Communist 'Rules' for Revolt Viewed as Durable Fraud." And the Washington *Post* followed close behind with an article headlined "Rightwing Hoax Survives Exposure." Perhaps the last voice that will be heard in this argument—though a termination is probably too much to hope for—came from the *Rifleman*'s editor, Ashley Halsey, Jr., in the January 1973 issue when he claimed to have, miracle of miracles, found the fellow who found the rules: Thomas H. Barber, a captain of Army Intelligence who had been on the Düsseldorf raid in 1919 and had come upon the document hidden in the

Communists' safe. Like so many other "proofs" that the National Rifle Association has come up with over the years, however, this one also had to be taken on faith, for at the time Halsey announced his discovery of the discoverer, Barber had been dead for ten years and two months.

Another battle in the seemingly eternal war over gun registration was fought in the Library of Congress in 1968 when Lois Buchan, reference assistant in the Library's Foreign Affairs Division, was put to work to determine how much substantiation could be found for the NRA's claim, "No dictatorship has ever been imposed on a nation of free men who have not been first required to register their privately owned weapons." She reported:

> First, four countries were examined which are democracies now, but in recent history came under Nazi dictatorship (Germany, Italy, France, and Austria). One may reasonably assume that if gun registration laws constituted a primary factor in the rise of dictatorships, these countries would have since revised their laws to prevent future dictatorships. This has not been the case. The four countries today have substantially the same gun laws as those in force prior to the advent of dictatorship. In fact, in Italy, where gun laws were relaxed by Mussolini, they have recently been restrengthened approximately to their pre-Mussolini level.
>
> Secondly, two democracies were examined which have not suffered dictatorships in their recent history (England and Switzerland). Switzerland has had gun registration laws since 1874, England since 1831. As an illustration of the strictness of the British law, a British citizen's ability to buy a gun is left to the discretion of the local police chief, whose decision is law unless overruled following an appeal to the court.
>
> Finally, two formerly democratic countries were examined which have had extended periods of dictatorships (Poland and Czechoslovakia). It might be expected that gun laws in these countries should be stricter now than before the rise of dictators. This is not the case. Though the wording of the statutes has been changed, and Communist Party loyalty has become the criterion for fitness of character, the laws are substantially the same in strictness and comprehensiveness. . . .

This brings us to our second possibility, that the registration of firearms would facilitate the German occupation of [Belgium, France, etc.]. After investigating a number of histories of this period, we were unable to locate references to any German use of registration lists to collect firearms. The German technique was to issue decrees and proclamations ordering the submission of firearms. . . . However, the possibility cannot be denied that the Germans may have used these registration lists (or indeed hunting-licenses registration), after issuing their proclamations. . . . We were, however, unable to find reference to this occurrence.

Perhaps a pertinent factor concerning firearm regulations (including firearm registrations) in Belgium, Czechoslovakia, France, and Norway, and their relationship to the German invasions is the following: Presumably, if the citizens of these countries felt that their firearm regulations greatly affected their ability to resist when their survival as a nation was at stake, the firearm regulations at the present time would be less restrictive, reflecting their World War II experience.

We therefore surveyed the current firearm regulations of the above countries and compared them to the pre-German invasion regulations. We found that the firearm regulations are at the present time essentially the same.*

All very interesting, but such arguments do not matter in the slightest. Logic and evidence have absolutely nothing to do with the gun debate in or out of Congress; only instinct and emotions and gut reactions count for anything. But that does not discourage either side, who every session send troops marching smartly before Congressional committees to recite the same statistics and anecdotes and histories and conclusions.

To say that the arguments in the gun debate are stylized in content does not mean they are stylized in delivery, which varies from witness to witness, but never reaching as colorful a pitch as on that day in 1963 when Senator Carl Hayden drove everyone to

---

* Juvenile Delinquency Subcommittee, Judiciary Committee, Senate, Hearings on Amendments to 1968 Gun Control Act to Prohibit the Sale of Saturday Night Special Handguns (U.S. Government Printing Office, 1971), pp. 480–483.

cover by waving a six-shooter and pointing it all over the committee chamber. A shriveled, baldheaded old coot with a turkey neck and glittering eyes, he looked and acted as batty as the Ancient Mariner, but he was just playing around, folks; relax. So what was Hayden doing at the hearing? Well, the old man, who as chairman of the Senate Finance Committee should have had some better way to spend his time, had trotted over to boast how, by cracky, "at nine hundred yards I hit the bull's eye fifteen consecutive times" fifty years ago and—oh yes, now he remembered why he was there—to introduce a crowd of his bleary-eyed Arizonan constituents who had driven 2,500 miles in fifty-four hours so that they could stand and cheer as their spokesman went for the committee's patriotic jugular:

> Have we forgotten Pearl Harbor? Have we forgotten that American chaplain who stood on a pitching destroyer's deck and shouted "Praise the Lord and pass the ammunition," as he braved the withering fire of Japanese Zeros? I don't think President Kennedy would want us to forget, and start down the path that disarmed the British people, merely because one enemy bullet finally found him. What a ridiculous monument to his memory.

Demagogic though that might be, it was a rare and singularly touching outburst in one respect: it did mention Kennedy's death. Look through the hundreds of pages of testimony on this topic in the first year after the assassination and you will be struck by one fact above all others: hardly anyone mentioned it. A sense of guilt, as already suggested, was not the dominant emotion in Congress.

RIFLEMEN
ON THE RIGHT

Behind the tumult and the shouting on that occasion, and behind
the baroque reasoning of the Arizona spokesman, there stood
foursquare that marvelous organization of which he was a director
—the National Rifle Association, largest sportsman's organization
in the world. I carry an NRA membership pin in my lapel with
much the same feeling I had when wearing the red garter that
marked me as a guide at the 1936 Boy Scouts National Jamboree—
that feeling that comes from being a part of the wave of the past.

If one wants to indulge in easy symbolism, it can be said that
the fight over gun controls during the past decade has been

between the three Kennedy brothers—through their active advocacy or because they have stood as the paramount lesson of why
more controls were needed—and the National Rifle Association.

The NRA and its allies are, obviously, winning. There is only
one Kennedy left while the NRA's membership has doubled during
the decade. The NRA now has one million members, most of
whom are energized by mild-to-extreme paranoia on the question
of gun controls. A typical demonstration occurred in 1957 when a
conference was called by Treasury officials: hundreds of riflemen
showed up attired in their lumberjack shirts and hunting boots, and
when John Sullivan, then chief counsel for the Juvenile Delinquency Subcommittee said something they didn't like, they began
stomping and shouting *"Sieg Heil! Sieg Heil! Sieg Heil!"* Sullivan
thought they were saying, "Speak louder," and so he did. That
brought an even more tumultuous torrent of German, and the
confusion and anger mounted until the meeting broke up and some
of the Treasury officials slipped out the back door for fear of being
attacked.

Some of the NRA's officials are quite excitable. This goes not
only for its real leaders but its spiritual leaders. Congressman
Dingell, a member of the NRA's board of directors, would be high
among the latter. When Dodd's aide, Carl Perian, talked back to
Dingell after the 1957 shout-in, the Congressman, says Perian,
"threatened to throttle me. I mean, he threatened to actually choke
me." It's possible. On another occasion a high official in the NRA
became spastic, threw a real fit, while addressing Dodd's subcommittee on the subject of the Sullivan Act, New York State's stiff
gun-control law. Oh, how he hated that law. He began babbling
and frothing. Dodd supported him and helped him through his
presentation and got him off the stand. As he stepped down and
walked away he was still trembling. On a previous occasion this
same official had appeared before a subcommittee to orate for half
an hour on the Sullivan law. When the chairman interrupted to
remind him that the bill up for discussion had nothing to do with

the Sullivan law, he shouted, "Of course it doesn't! I know that! But I just don't like the Sullivan law!"

Except for a fanatical zeal that sometimes scares even the NRA's officials, the riflemen are not oddities—that is, they are only as odd as Americans are generally. They cannot all be pigeonholed as right-wingers; voting for the NRA position on any gun-control bill can be such "liberals" as Senators George McGovern, Frank Church, Mike Mansfield, and Lee Metcalf. When Wayne Morse and Ernest Gruening were still in the Senate, playing the role of international pacifists, they were routinely voting in favor of the NRA's domestic fire-at-will policy. "Liberal" ecologists, who have a hard time recruiting establishment support for their opposition to the trans-Alaska oil pipeline, get considerable support from big-game hunters in the NRA, who fear the pipeline will kill the caribou before the riflemen have a chance. And for a similar reason no group gives liberal Supreme Court Justice William O. Douglas so much support in his fights to keep the Army Corps of Engineers from bulldozing all the remaining wetlands and forests into oblivion.

Nor is the NRA homogeneous. Former NRA President Harlon B. Carter is quite correct in saying it would be silly "to pretend that an organization of a million members in America will have a monolithic structure and a Soviet type of philosophical uniformity." The NRA is the usual big-group snakepit of ideological schisms; but Carter can afford to view them with tolerance because he is almost always on the winning side. The splinter groups within the NRA that stand for something resembling moderation are insipid, disorganized, and ignored at the policy level. Whatever satisfaction they get is to be found in writing gossipy notes to each other and to the press, such as this one to me in early 1973 from an oldtime NRA moderate:

> The NRA legislative policy is getting more hard-line due almost solely to the pressure of former NRA President Carter. He is retired as Regional Commissioner of U.S. Immigration

and Naturalization Service and has lots of time to pursue his goal of being the power behind the NRA. In recent months he has secured the close support of William Loeb, publisher of the right-wing Manchester (N.H.) *Union Leader* and also an NRA Executive Committee man. These two plus several lesser lights among directors are keeping constant pressure on the Executive Vice-President, General Rich, a not very strong guy. Rich was forced to cut short his stay at the Olympics in 1972 to get home and hire a General Fridge (USAF, ret.) because Loeb and Carter started a campaign to convince the Executive Committee that Rich was not carrying out their wishes to employ a man who could give more time to Capitol Hill lobbying than could Rich, and had more Hill presence than Rich.

Carter has been an NRA power for years and when he was President he put pressure on the late Frank Orth to fire the then editor of *The American Rifleman* and hire a man who would really raise hell with anyone who even suggested there could be anything good about any kind of gun control. The present editor (a former *Saturday Evening Post*er) is virtually independent of any control and does not even talk to the current President (retired Hercules Powder Executive F. M. Hakenjos).

By NRA tradition, the VP becomes President after the President serves a couple of terms. Currently that puts C. R. Gutermuth in line as President. However, he has been pressing for NRA to adopt a more realistic legislative stand. Because of his soft line, the hard liners (Carter, Loeb, *et al.*) are working to have him step aside and let Merrill Wright (2nd VP, a new office) move up. Wright is easy putty. There are also rumors that Rich would like to get out and to get back to Utah where he was somebody in Salt Lake City affairs—C of C, State Guard, etc. Some even suggest that Carter would realize his life dream to be NRA Exec VP, the top staff position and a powerful one IF the Exec VP was a zealot of Carter's inclinations. . . .

This is passed along not for the details, which are the transitory bureaucratic kind, but for the tone: early Borgia. Beneath the hearty fraternal exterior of NRA's officialdom, there's bilious intrigue.

Asked about the accuracy of this internecine sketch, an NRA spokesman refused to speak. Naturally. If you should enter the NRA boardroom and find every member of the Executive Committee dripping custard from his chin, one and all would refuse to admit there had been a pie-throwing fight. But confirmation of New Hampshire publisher Loeb's hard-line activities—which, by the way, are also a fine example of the kind of personal lobbying NRA executives do so well—did come from another source, Clare Crawford of the Washington *Star-News*, who obtained copies of letters Loeb had written to White House advisers Herbert Klein and Pat Buchanan and Attorney General Richard Kleindienst, reminding them that "in 1968 I persuaded the NRA to do what they had never done before, namely to endorse a presidential candidate." He also reminded them that the NRA had given Nixon a gun at a special NRA presentation banquet, urged "dear Herb" to invite "some of the stuffed-shirt type of publishers—you know who I am talking about" to meals at the White House because they would be "really flattered"—and in other ways leaned on Klein, Buchanan, and Kleindienst to help the NRA defeat Senator Birch Bayh's gun-control bill then up for consideration.

Loeb sent copies of his letters to other NRA directors with an accompanying note boasting of his intimate Nixon Administration contacts. Of Kleindienst he said, "Dick and I have been friends since we were the only newspaper supporting Goldwater back in the 1964 Presidential primary. I lunched with him alone at the Justice Department the other day and, of course, brought this matter [the Bayh bill] up along with other things." Loeb's chummy letters went out on July 17, 1972, and, as reporter Crawford points out, on August 9 "Administration lobbyists and Justice Department lawyers worked at the Capitol to weaken the Bayh bill."

The Administration obviously believes the hard-liners are the mainstream of the NRA and it is absolutely correct to think so. Having made my slight bow to the element of moderation and heterogeneity within the NRA, I hasten to add that I am convinced the conglomerate leadership of the NRA could be described as

Mencken once described William Jennings Bryan ("He was born with a roaring voice, and it had the trick of inflaming half-wits") and that the great majority of the membership is not only rabidly hard-line but slightly dotty—a classic tennis-shoe dottiness that allows the riflemen to read with murky absorption and black seriousness the kind of editorial that appeared in *The American Rifleman* of February 1973, warning that

> while leaders and their henchmen or unwitting tools continue to demand that U.S. citizens give up their guns, a Communist organization that favors shooting its way to power has expanded and quietly armed its members. The FBI's annual report, released this winter, reveals that the "Revolutionary Union (RU) has now spread to 10 states. . . . RU members have been accumulating weapons while engaging in firearms and guerrilla warfare training."

Americans of normal perspective, having long ago learned not to take too seriously the FBI's rationale for higher budgets, chuckle and nudge each other when the FBI trots out this kind of spooky stuff; but most NRA members insist on accepting the bureaucratic propaganda as the purest and most frightening dogma.

In response to my inquiry about the mental condition of NRA members, the riflemen's amiable Secretary, Frank C. Daniel, Jr., who appropriately came to the NRA from the industry (Secretary of the National Target & Supply Company), allowed as how, yes, there are some wild ones within the ranks. "There are some kooks*—well, I won't call them that—some radicals in our organization who would like everyone to own a machine gun if they want to," he said, but he insists that the NRA does not officially believe in such freedom.

---

* The ratio of kooks to non-kooks is hard to pin down, but the NRA is willing to break down its membership by other groupings: hunters, 35 percent; collectors, 20 percent; marksmen, 20 percent; and spread over the other groups as well as consisting of its own grouping, 25 percent "nonshooting constitutionalists"—which is to say, people who are dedicated to preserving full-scale private ownership of firearms.

The NRA obviously is not set up to be just another organization with a variety of interests. It has only one overriding interest and it can be as relentless with its helpers and its own officials who seem to threaten that interest as it is with outsiders. Congressman Celler bottled up a hundred and sixty-eight gun-control bills in the House Judiciary Committee for three years, but when he finally let one through, that erased all his good marks; the NRA began denouncing him as a "Nice Nelly" and a group of NRA-allied ammunition manufacturers let him know they were putting together a "killer" fund for his next election.

When Dodd appeared before Senator Magnuson's committee to change his bill to include mail-order rifles as well as mail-order pistols, lo, sitting beside him was Gen. Franklin Orth (U.S. Army, Ret.), Executive Vice-President and then chief spokesman for the NRA. But do not be misled. This was merely one of those rare occurrences in Washington when personal conscience prevailed over professional caution. Orth, now dead, was a unique fellow. He could hardly be considered a left-winger or a softie. During World War II he had toughed out a notable record for himself as a member of Merrill's Marauders in Burma. After the war he had held a number of militarist jobs, topped by an appointment to the infamous Subversive Activities Control Board.

Despite some of the flakier aspects of his background, he was, let us not retch at the word, a patriot. He was terribly upset about the Kennedy assassination and he helped Dodd rewrite the mail-order gun bill to include rifles. In fact, he would have gone farther—he would have not only cut off mail-order sales but would have required the registration of guns. Because he didn't think registration had a chance to pass, Dodd talked him out of it.

When he appeared with Dodd before the Commerce Committee, Orth stated categorically that he and the NRA favored including rifles in the bill: "Yes, sir. We do not think that any sane American, who calls himself an American, can object to placing into this bill the instrument which killed the President of the United States. That is our position."

In the history of The Great Debate, this was a remarkable moment: the foremost spokesman for the most powerful anti-gun-control lobby taking such a position. But alas for the substance of the moment, Orth was not giving an accurate description of the NRA's position. "We" did not support Dodd's bill. Only he did—or rather only he and what was shortly to be seen as a minority of the NRA's Executive Committee. He soon learned just how wide a gap there actually was between his position and that of the majority of the NRA. Photographs taken of Orth sitting next to Dodd and testifying on behalf of his bill were reproduced in many of the major gun and outdoor magazines. Accompanying articles made it sound clearly as though he had sold out to Dodd—as in fact, ideologically, perhaps he had. Out of the boondocks and the right-wing enclaves came the purists of the NRA to demand that the Executive Committee fire him. He sustained his job by only a couple of votes, but thereafter he was in fact dead as a spokesman for the riflemen. By the time the 1968 Gun Control Act was up for consideration, the NRA's Board of Directors had assigned a three-man watchdog group to review every statement he made publicly. Or at least that's what Orth told Dodd, but perhaps by that time he was suffering, understandably, from paranoia.

Trying to ease the pressure on himself by getting members of the gun industry to make their own concessions, Orth persuaded a dozen or so representatives of the industry to meet privately with Dodd. But they wouldn't give an inch. Dodd tried to get them to agree to a magic formula whereby when gun deaths reached three times—or five times, or whatever multiple they preferred—the number of deaths that were occurring at the time, then they would support gun legislation. They refused.

Orth was not the only member of NRA management who has had a hard time coping with some of the more singleminded members. In the mid-1960s, when public opinion was beginning really to lacerate the NRA's image, its Board of Directors paid out $300,000 to a Madison Avenue ad firm to "pretty up" its image.

One of the first ads distributed showed a picture of Franklin D. Roosevelt as a young man, holding a rifle, with a cutline opening "America needs more straight shooters." Well, the oldtimers in the organization were furious. *They* remembered the passage under FDR of two firearms-control measures—one licensing the users of submachine guns and the other prohibiting the sale of handguns to ex-cons or fugitives—and *they* didn't want to publicize any President who would support *any* firearms law. Not long thereafter the image crusade was ended.

In 1972, when Washington banker True Davis gave a hundred-dollar-a-plate fundraising party to help Senator Birch Bayh pay off his campaign debts, hell broke loose once more. Davis was a member of the NRA's Board of Directors, and Bayh had authored an extremely mild bill to outlaw cheap handguns—the Saturday Night Specials. How *dare* Davis assist such a rascal! Hundreds of letters from angry members poured into NRA headquarters. Some members used a picture of Davis for target practice. Shooting the picture of people they don't like is a kind of voodoo practice much participated in by the less-balanced riflemen.

The NRA benefits by its political victims' equating scurrilousness with strength. On that basis the NRA must indeed seem strong, for it is indeed scurrilous. The NRA has whispered around the federal capital that an important gun-control advocate is homosexual. It torpedoed one gun-control organization in California by publicizing the police record of the organization's publicity director. Even its dead opponents are not spared the NRA's tarbrush. In the NRA's official history, it notes that Timothy D. Sullivan, the New York politician whose name stuck with the gun-control law most hated by the NRA, was a madman struck down (or at least such an implication seems to hang in the air) by the hand of an angry God: "The law was the parting gesture of a machine politician in the final plunge of his decline from power. Only months after he introduced the bill, and hounded by charges of corruption, Sullivan was committed to an institution for the insane. He was killed by a railroad train on September 1, 1913, after escaping from custody."

As a matter of routine, the NRA's literature about pending gun-control legislation is weighted with heavy inaccuracies and sometimes outright falsehoods. When Dodd once asked his NRA buddy Orth if he thought his patriotic organization should lie so much about the items under consideration by Congress, Orth replied demurely: ". . . sometimes in the heat of battle there are regrettable excesses which are not deliberate, or are born in misunderstanding."

This "heat-of-battle" excuse sounds odd coming from an organization that pretends to bend its desires to the gentle winds of public welfare. Disavowing any taint of commercialism—no, no, it is not interested in the multibillion-dollar arms industry or the multimillion-dollar sporting-magazine industry—the NRA gets its tax-exempt status *not* under the usual Internal Revenue Code subsection that forbids "carrying on propaganda or otherwise attempting to influence legislation" but rather under the subsection that exempts "civic leagues or organizations not organized for profit but operated exclusively for the promotion of social welfare . . . and the net earnings of which are devoted exclusively to charitable, educational or recreational purposes." *

Since this puts the riflemen in the same "nice" category as such outfits as the League of Women Voters, high-pressure "educating" is not forbidden to them. The riflemen resist being described as a lobby (although some NRA officials have registered as lobbyists) but sometimes, in their more candid moments, they will reply to the question of whether or not they are a lobby as NRA Secretary Daniel did: "I guess it depends which side of the fence you are on."

From this side of the fence, one notices: after the Kennedy

---

* Would the $500,000 in the NRA budget for "executive expenses" be charity in the boardroom perhaps?

assassination and the heightening of public opposition to loose guns, the NRA's organ, *The American Rifleman*, sharply reduced the amount of space devoted to shooting and hunting articles and increased by one-third the space given to warning about firearms legislation. Between 1962 and 1964—the years bridging the assassination—the organization's total expenses rose by about 30 percent, but during the same period its expenditures for "legislative and public affairs" work (read: "lobbying") increased *more than 100 percent*.

The boys that hang out around the NRA have a hard time keeping their stories straight, because while they want to duck the designation of a lobby for tax reasons, at the same time they are proud of their lobbying accomplishments. On the one hand you'll hear Congressman Bob Sikes, a former NRA official, bragging at the annual National Rifle Association convention on March 31, 1973: "NRA also is a favorite target of the Washington *Post*—also known as the uptown edition of the *Daily Worker*. A constant advocate of leftist doctrine, it consistently brands NRA as a gun lobby and depicts us as the handmaidens of gangsters. So you bear the name lobbyist. . . . Now let me urge that you live up to the name; that you do really effective lobbying. . . . Last year there was intense pressure to bring the Bayh bill, which was just another bad antigun bill, to the floor of the House. It had passed the Senate. The same people who brought the 1968 Gun Control Act to Congress were still here and they worked day and night for the Bayh bill. They were unable to get it out of committee. This tells a very significant story. Education and personal contact with the members of Congress made the difference. NRA spearheaded this effort. NRA's leadership was the key to victory."

The riflemen cheered him for that within the confines of the convention, but a few weeks later the NRA leadership had once again decided to temper its pride with caution. When Senator Kennedy denounced them on March 6, 1973, as "a massive lobbying juggernaut against federal gun control," the NRA used the next available editorial page of *The American Rifleman* to protest that "we cannot accept the label of lobbyist. To do so would be a betrayal of free Americanism."

The NRA was much more candid and much less defensive about its lobbying role in the 1930s. When the Bureau of the Budget decided in 1934 that it couldn't go on subsidizing the NRA's rifle clubs while other citizens were on the breadline, the NRA urged its members to exert "cooperative pressure on Congress to restore funds," ending its exhortation with a Kiplingesque lockerroom rouser:

> Without organization and cooperation we would make no headway, but working together and in harmony we are able to overcome many obstacles—
>
>> "It ain't the guns nor armament,
>>   Nor funds that they can pay,
>> But the close cooperation
>>   That makes them win the day.
>>
>> It ain't the individual,
>>   Nor the army as a whole,
>> But the everlasting team-work
>>   Of every bloomin' soul."

THE MOST EFFECTIVE
LOBBY IN WASHINGTON

The fanatical cutting edge of just about "every bloomin' soul" within its ranks makes the NRA not only a powerful lobby but also one of the most hilarious and, some think, one of the most dangerous organizations in the country. And it is powerful, hilarious, and possibly dangerous for one reason: it is built on a massive foundation of obsolete notions. Which is why, no doubt, the NRA has so much influence at the Pentagon and in Congress and in our state legislatures.

Except for its $3.5-million nine-story marble-and-glass head-quarters in Washington and the weapons loved by its members, everything about the NRA reeks of obsolescence: the slogans, the trophies (the Rattlesnake Trophy, the Bronco Buster Trophy, the Daniel Boone Trophy, the Gen. George A. Custer Trophy, etc.), the tales of derring-do perpetuated in its literature, the boys-be-hind-the-barn chumminess, the blustery patriotism, the simple-minded notions of law and order. They are like things out of the attic and out of the memory of an ancient American Legionnaire: his beloved motheaten puttees; memories of "the Front" and trenchmouth in '17; the three-point antlers from deer he killed with his Model 1903 Springfield; the kewpie doll he won at the 1936 Chicago World's Fair shooting gallery. Being no more trashy than the things stuffed into most memories and attics, they are not to be ridiculed, and certainly not feared, unless the Legionnaire becomes enraptured of his experiences and gains a position from which he can impose his morality and patriotism and aesthetics on the community.

The National Rifle Association is in a rather good position to impose its philosophical memorabilia on the community. Dollar for dollar, the NRA is probably the most effective lobby in Washington. Its assets hardly put it in the same league with the oil lobby, and for a crash campaign it could not gather the kind of slush fund the American Medical Association raised to fight Medicare. But among grass-roots lobbying organizations who specialize in letter-writing campaigns, the National Rifle Association is in a class by itself. Its officials have boasted that they can get their million members to hit Congress with at least half a million letters on seventy-two-hour notice. This is probably an exaggeration; at least it has never been done. But at the height of the Vietnam War, Senator Edward Kennedy of Massachusetts said he was regularly getting more mail on the pending gun-control legislation than on the war—a response which the NRA's chief executive called "a healthy sign." During the Johnson era, when the White House sent a gun-control bill to Congress, it received only half a dozen letters of protest. That was during the first month. Then the NRA sent a newsletter to its membership, and almost immediately the White House received twelve thousand letters in opposition.*

But this shows only "shock troop" opinion, not general public opinion, and there is no reason to assume that the NRA is nearly so unified (its members have never been polled) or so potent as these letter blizzards would suggest. Nevertheless, because politicians are so prone to see great danger where only some danger exists, they have contributed to the NRA's reputation as overwhelmingly potent when aroused—and since reputation is half a lobby's strength, the NRA is strong.

It proved that, beyond doubt, in the months and first years after John Kennedy's assassination, when public feeling was highest. In his report to the NRA annual convention of 1964, Secretary Daniel noted with pride:

> Reviewed briefly, the first three months of 1964 have tried this association's defenses against unduly restrictive firearms control legislation more than they have ever been tried. They have so far successfully weathered the test, and it would appear that there is little likelihood of our being forced to accept, in 1964, any legislation at either the federal or state level which does violence to the NRA's announced policy on firearms legislation.

He was right. That year state legislatures considered a hundred and eighty-nine firearms bills—a record number for an

---

* NRA officials insist that when they stir up letter-writing campaigns they implore their membership not to be abusive; but somehow the hot blood of what the NRA calls "a shooter" just keeps breaking through. Consequently, legislators at any level who propose gun-control laws can depend on receiving letters threatening their lives, or more often the kind of friendly letters received by a Maryland Assemblyman with an Italian name, of which this one was rather typical: "You dirty wop. You should go back to your Italy and Mafia. How did you get in this country anyway? I bet you are the type who has no gun in his house to protect himself and would let any housebreaker come in and help himself to anything, even your wife, and then you would pray for a humble spirit to bear it. God help America with such as you. Were your parents ever married?"

"off" year—bills the NRA described as having been "drawn in an atmosphere of high emotion and sharp reaction not only to the assassination of the late President Kennedy but also to local tragedies." But as noted modestly in the NRA's annual report for 1964: "Members reacted promptly, firmly, and in force. No seriously restrictive proposals were enacted." And though five hundred more bills were introduced in state legislatures in 1965 and 1966, only one, in New Jersey, passed.

Every politician who has opposed the NRA comes away with tales of peril. Thinking back to the days when he was Attorney General and later Governor of California, Edmund G. ("Pat") Brown says that every time he advocated tougher gun-control laws "the walls of Jericho fell on me, and all you have to do is look at the defeat of some of our U.S. Senators where gun control became the real issue to find out why we are not getting gun laws."

This is the legend, but what are the facts? Where are the fallen bodies of the politicians who opposed the NRA? When you ask for specifics, you are asked in turn to accept assumptions. Should the NRA be given credit for the defeat of Senator Joseph Tydings of Maryland in 1970? It claims credit, and points to the half-million anti-Tydings brochures, the thirty full-page ads, the radio spots in Maryland's duck-hunting neck of the state which the rifleman paid for to oppose Tydings' reelection. The riflemen also take credit for the defeats, the same year, of Senators Albert Gore of Tennessee, Charles Goodell of New York, and Tom Dodd of Connecticut. It is highly unlikely that these scalps belong on the NRA's belt. There is no evidence that the gun lobby played a significant role in their defeats. Each of these losers had to contend with a number of emotional forces that year, not just with the gun crowd. Tydings had lost popularity with liberals because of his "no-knock" crime-control bill; and he had been grossly abused by a story planted with *Life* shortly before the election which unfairly charged him with conflict of interest. Gore was being hounded by the conservatives of Tennessee for his antiwar stand and for his civil rights moderation. As for Dodd, he was under such a heavy cloud—having just been censured by the Senate for pilfering campaign funds—that he could scarcely be seen. And if the lobby was so potent as it claims to have been, then why did it not also defeat a number of other Senators who had voted for the 1968 Act and yet who won reelection in 1970, some of them very easily, from states heavy with hunters? Such Senators, for example, as Hugh Scott of Pennsylvania, Edward Kennedy of Massachusetts, Philip Hart of Michigan, and John Pastore of Rhode Island. To be sure, the NRA buffs were perfectly aware that fellows like Scott were not by any stretch of the imagination "anti" guns and that, if it came to a showdown on a really tough bill, they would vote the NRA way. Still, these politicians were on the record as having voted against guns, so why weren't they punished? Even *Roman L. Hruska*, for god's sake, the Nebraska cornball himself, the gun lobby's closest and dearest friend in the Senate, had voted for the Gun Control Act of 1968 on final passage (as had the likes of John Tower of Texas and Herman Talmadge of Georgia, to give you some idea of the laughter in the cloakroom)! Never mind how much he had tried to cripple it before it got that far; never mind that he is a regular pixie on such occasions; never mind that he voted for it only after it was plain he could not stop it; never mind the hypocrisy—the point is he was on record as having voted for the Dodd bill, and if the NRA really had the power it claimed to have to chastize those who voted wrong, it would have felt duty-bound to teach Scott and Hruska and their mischievous playmates a lesson in sobriety at the polls. Hruska was also up for reelection in 1970, and won.

The truth is, there will always be a number of natural political deaths at the polls that the NRA can take credit for, like a voodoo practitioner who can always depend on old age and heart attacks and diarrhea to help his "spells" prove out.

As expected, the NRA took credit in 1972 for knocking off Senators Gordon Allott of Colorado, J. Caleb Boggs of Delaware, Jack Miller of Iowa, Margaret Chase Smith of Maine and William B. Spong, Jr., of Virginia because they had voted for the extremely lukewarm Bayh bill to outlaw the sale of cheap handguns.

The NRA could not, however, explain why its claimed omnipotence was unable to unseat ten other Senators, from states just as loaded with NRA members, who also voted for the Bayh bill: Senators Edward W. Brooke of Massachusetts, Clifford P. Case of New Jersey, Carl T. Curtis of Nebraska, Robert P. Griffin of Michigan, Mark Hatfield of Oregon, James B. Pearson of Kansas, Charles Percy of Illinois, Jennings Randolph of West Virginia, John Sparkman of Alabama, and Strom Thurmond of South Carolina. *Strom Thurmond.* It should be plain enough from this lineup that the Bayh bill was not seen as a threat to the gun fraternity—in fact, the gun fraternity knew very well that the bill would self-destruct in the House—and that the NRA is fudging to a hilarious degree to claim that any significant number of its members allowed action in the Senate to influence their votes in 1972.

That the lobby's power is grossly overrated was also shown in 1972 in Tydings' home state when the Maryland legislature, under the goading of Governor Marvin Mandel, passed a gun-control law not only requiring a permit to carry or transport a handgun but giving police the authority to stop and frisk suspects. NRA clubs were notably ineffective in lobbying against it, and after its passage Mandel's popularity did not decline.

Little happens at the state level, but when there is reform, the reformers usually survive. In 1966, culminating four years of tortured negotiations, redrafting, coaxing, and pleading to get it through the fearful legislature, New Jersey finally passed a rather good gun-control law, requiring a permit to buy a handgun and a "purchaser's ID card" to buy a rifle or shotgun. For both the permit and the ID card the buyer has to submit his fingerprints to a police check. Those may sound like very ordinary precautions, but New Jersey was the first state to pass a gun law in the three years after Kennedy's assassination. Fear of the lobby runs high. But, as New Jersey proved, when the lobby is challenged, its power often evaporates. Because he had taken a strong stand favoring the new law and because his political opponents had whooped up his "unpatriotic" attitude toward guns, the partisans of gubernatorial candidate Richard Hughes were afraid that he was doomed. The gun lobby even had the Boy Scouts and the Campfire Girls and all manner of hearty sportsmen's federations out beating the bushes to defeat the bill—and to defeat whoever supported it. State officials were inundated with what Attorney General Arthur Sills described as "vituperative, obscene, vile" mail. Nevertheless, not only did Hughes win the governorship; he won by the biggest plurality of any governor in New Jersey's history.

In 1972 the gun crowd really took out after Congressman John Murphy of New York. Advocating controls, he had said things about gun psychopaths that many hypersensitive gun owners for some reason thought he was applying to them. In the conservative Staten Island section of his congressional district, the angry drums in the bush were especially loud. They bought newspaper ads to denounce him as a betrayer of the American dream. Since it doesn't take much to spook a congressman, Murphy's palms were wet. As it turned out, however, he was not only returned by a comfortable margin but for the first time in his career he won the Staten Island majority, and won it handily (by 10,000 votes).

Probably the best appraisal of the NRA's real and ersatz power comes from former Congressman Abner Mikva of Chicago, who has found it effective partly because it works hard and partly because it is a spook. Mikva says:

> There's nobody even second to the National Rifle Association as being next to legislative bodies. I think I could insist from now to doomsday that Tydings was not knocked off by the lobby, but a lot of Congressmen would never believe me. When I had my gun bill ready in Congress [to outlaw all handguns except for cops and military], I talked to fifty or sixty members who said they would like to support me, to see some strong controls, but they couldn't afford to. I got no—I repeat no—rural Congressmen to sign my bill, though I could name at least two dozen rural Congressmen who said they would have liked to.

When I was in the Illinois legislature in the mid-sixties, we had a bill to register handguns. We started out with a hundred and ten cosigners. By the time the Illinois Rifle Association got through, we were down to thirty-eight. I got five thousand pieces of mail. Some of the writers even advocated repealing the Capone machine-gun law. I've learned one thing: you can't take on the gun lobby with good will.

Mikva's defeat in 1972 was reported like this by the NRA: "Mikva, the most outspoken national proponent of confiscatory handgun legislation in the House of Representatives, was turned out of office in Illinois' 10th Congressional District by a vote of 118,649 to 111,476," etc. This is typical of the NRA's proclivity for shading facts. Mikva was not turned out of office in the 10th; he was turned out of office in the 2nd District, which he had represented until the Illinois legislature redistricted him in such a way as to throw his home into an area that was 80 percent black and already represented by a black Congressman. Practically speaking, that left Mikva without a district, so he moved his home to and turned his sights on the 10th District, a highly unlikely target since it was customarily solidly conservative Republican and he was, by Congressional standards, a radical Democrat. Losing by such a narrow margin in such alien territory hardly made Mikva an example of the NRA's vaunted ability to butcher its enemies at the polls.

The primary reason for the gun lobby's success in Congress is simply that so many Congressmen have the same outlook on life as the gunmen. It isn't their ability to inspire fear but rather chumminess that puts NRA officials in solid with Congressmen: so many of both groups see themselves as "one of the boys," good drinkers, backslappers, hearty, superpatriotic, despisers of do-gooders, and—above all—tolerant of the sins of the establishment. The benefit to be derived by the NRA from this empathy was never more dramatically demonstrated than on January 14, 1966. It was a Saturday. Raul Torres of Yonkers, New York, had spent $33.13 for a 30.06 Enfield rifle and twenty rounds of armor-piercing ammuni-

tion the previous Thursday. He arrived in Washington that
Saturday afternoon with a grudge: he was angry because the only
way he was able to get out of a mental hospital was to break out. So
when he got off the bus he marched straight for the White House.
He was within one block of his destination when a cop yelled,
"Hey, where you going with that rifle?" Torres pulled back the bolt
action, slipping a bullet into the chamber, and got off one shot
before two cops tackled him. A couple of hours later, six blocks
away, the NRA opened its brand-new museum with what the
Washington *Post* called "a lively, double-barreled blast for Congressmen, weapons buffs and wives." The two hundred guests
included quite a few Congressional powerhouses.

When Congress reconvened, scarcely a word was heard about
the mad gunman. After all, they didn't want to say anything that
would embarrass those good ol' boys they'd been drinking with a
couple nights earlier.

GLORIFYING THE GAT

More than its large membership and certainly of much
more importance than its money as a source of power is
the fact that the NRA has traditionally had an almost religious
certitude of its destiny and its role in American history. If it weren't
so serious, it might almost be comical.

The officials of the NRA see themselves literally as a second
line of defense, only slightly less crucial to the security of the nation
than the Pentagon. In the authorized history of the NRA—*Americans and Their Guns*, compiled by James B. Trefethen and edited by
James E. Serven—the place of the NRA in American military
history is noted this way:

In our history books we pay tribute to the man with the gun.
He won the American Revolution and the War of 1812. He

defended democracy in 1917–18. He fought the greatest global war in history in 1941–45. The American with a gun has been a great stabilizing influence in maintaining a balance of world power. *Between the wars, the National Rifle Association has been the primary guardian of the American rifleman tradition which becomes so vital in time of war* [emphasis added].*

Although this is a remarkable bit of conceit, it is at least exaggerating in the right direction. As a quasi-civilian organization the NRA is probably a better guardian of the tradition than any purely military organization. And in a way the NRA deserves to be conceited, because the problems of gun anarchy have arisen as much from bullshit as from ballistics, as much from the glorification as from the science and production of guns; and from either approach ingenious civilians like the NRA have taken the lead. It would be both convenient and agreeable to blame the entire gun problem on the military, but we can't. Some of it, yes; after World War II the military was far too eager to declare guns outdated that weren't, and to dump them on the already glutted civilian market at prices that were hard for any lonely housekeeper to pass up. Too, many important segments of the gun industry would never have come into being, and others would not have lasted, had it not been for the military's largesse; gun designers could afford the luxury of innovation because they knew that the military purse would sooner or later pick them up and keep them going.

The remarkable part of this cooperative effort, however, was not that the military supported the gun industry but that it often did so only with great caution and sluggishness. For example, on the one hand it is quite true that Samuel H. Colt, who went bankrupt and had to close his plant at Paterson, New Jersey, would probably have passed out of the gunmaking picture and never have reopened for his celebrated continuation in Whitneyville, Connecticut, if the Army had not revived him with orders for some twenty-five-dollar .44-caliber handguns, weapons that accommo-

---

* (Stackpole Books, 1967), p. 9. This history is so biased it's almost attractive.

dated half-ounce bullets that were, according to retrospective 1972 Colt advertising, "guaranteed to empty Mexican saddles in a most satisfactory manner." (We were at war with Mexico.) But on the other hand it should be remembered that one of the main reasons Colt went out of business in the first place was that many high-ranking military officials had been hostile to his weapon.

In recent years the military seems to have adapted a policy of preferring newness to efficiency; but the military's time-honored defect was in preferring tradition to efficiency. The weapons that were used to fight the last glorious war were the preferred weapons; the weapons the generals had been trained with as cadets were the preferred weapons.

Although the advantages of rifling (the grooves within the barrel that make the bullet rotate, increasing its accuracy) had been established by both hunters and soldiers for at least half a century, and although the technique of breechloading (as opposed to muzzleloading) had been used intermittently by gunmakers for four hundred years—and had been brought to a new level of pragmatism if not yet perfection by John W. Hall at the Harpers Ferry Arsenal in the early years of the nineteenth century—nevertheless the War Department still viewed the muzzleloading smoothbore musket as the best infantry weapon, even through the Mexican War (1846).

Christian Sharps came out with his to-be-famous breechloading rifle in 1848. Colt, North & Savage, Warner, Remington, Allen & Wheelock, Hall, and others were producing not just breech rifles but *multichambered* breech rifles in the 1850s, but the Army preferred to go into the Civil War with the muzzleloading rifle, the kind that forced the soldier to stand and become a target while he rammed a new load down the barrel with a rod.

When the war ended, the U.S. Army's arsenals were overflowing with muzzleloaders; instead of throwing them away—as the Pentagon would do today—it converted them to breechloaders, and with only a few minor improvements this weapon became the stalwart .45-70 Springfield of 1873, on which the Army largely depended for fighting its Indian wars for the rest of that century, though better rifles and carbines were on the market. The U.S. Army didn't come out with its first percussion sidearms until eight years after Henry Deringer had started producing his enormously popular little percussion killer for the civilian market; percussion arms weren't standard for the Army until 1841, five years after Colt had applied the "new" idea to his revolver commercially.

All over the world there was a wonderfully leisurely cast to the military mind in those days. The British and French were stuck with so many millions of flintlock sidearms after the Napoleonic Wars (1800–14) that they didn't feel that they could afford to shift to percussion caps for another thirty-four years—and this despite the fact that in a test-firing of six flintlocks versus six percussion locks at Woolwich Arsenal in 1834, the Flintlock guns misfired one thousand times while the percussion lock guns misfired only thirty-six times.*

In the Spanish-American war, whereas our troops were still stuck mainly with the single-shot Springfield rifle, a leftover from the 1860s, the Spanish were toting the latest Mauser repeating rifles. They had the new smokeless ammunition; our men were still struggling along with black-powder ammunition that not only dispatched bullets with less power but also gave forth a billowing cloud of white smoke that tipped the enemy to the shooter's location. The Spanish could gaze at the enemy down the comforting barrel of a fine Maxim machine gun. Our men had no machine guns.

With few exceptions, the stamp of imagination that has been placed on the important gun developments in the last century and a half is definitely civilian. An artist, Joshua Shaw, developed the percussion cap. Richard Gatling was a physician. One of the important developers of percussion cartridges was Dr. Edward Maynard, a dentist. Oliver Winchester was a shirt manufacturer. It

---

* Merrill Lindsay, *One Hundred Great Guns: An Illustrated History of Firearms* (Walker & Co., 1967), p. 110. If there was ever a book beautiful enough to make you forget the dangers of firearms, this is it.

was a Scottish preacher, the Rev. Alexander John Forsyth, who perfected the use of fulminating powders for the discharge of firearms. He developed a device for pouring fulminate into a channel leading to the rifle bore; it was so tightly constructed that when the hammer struck, no flames escaped. With their usual foresight, the generals paid no attention to this great leap forward, but Reverend Forsyth didn't much care, because he was only interested in a better fowling weapon. He had begun his experiments because he noticed that the flash from the exposed powder pan had often given birds enough advance warning to let them dive and swerve away from the shot.

A list of the major advances in gun design and production in the nineteenth and twentieth centuries would show that although the inventors in Europe and England were strong competitors, the real love affair with, and the holy quest for, the faster and deadlier gun originated in the heart and mind of that rough-hewn knight, the American civilian, bent on killing Indians, killing game, or killing his neighbor.

JUST FIRE IN THAT GENERAL DIRECTION

As for the bullshit, that too has been largely civilian. Being able to work within that wider and more colorful context—and not being restricted to firing either on command or at an enemy carefully delineated by act of Congress—the civilian gunman has also outstripped the military in supplying us with the kind of perforated legends and gory lies that have kept the gun market booming. What military man of the twentieth century is seen in the public's memory as a gunslinger? Perhaps Gen. George Patton. He was a swaggering two-gun man, all right, but the gun on his left hip, which he called his "killer," a double-action Smith & Wesson .357 Magnum, was never, so far as the record shows, fired at a human being; and the gun on his right hip, a Colt Peacemaker single-action .45, had been used to shoot only three Mexican toughs and a horse, all in the same long-past engagement. For the next thirty-six years the gun was worn but apparently unused. The only other person Patton ever shot with a handgun was himself, in the leg, when he stomped too hard and a hairtrigger automatic strapped to his waist accidentally fired. That is hardly a record to match that of, say, Dion O'Banion, who responded to a car's backfire by whipping out his pistol and shooting the first Chicagoan he saw. One level below the most colorful military gunman, moreover, there is an almost total lack of color in the likes of, say, Gen. Jonathan M. Wainwright II, one of the heroes of Corregidor, who, like Patton, carried a Colt Peacemaker .45 for thirty-six years; but the only renown won by the gun was a kind of closet renown—spending three years wrapped in an oiled cloth, hidden in a tree in the Philippines while Wainwright spent those years in a Japanese prison camp. By the end of the war, it was rusty and so was he. The few authentic sharpshooting Army heroes known to the general public—men like Sgt. Alvin York of World War I fame and Audie Murphy, the most decorated soldier of World War II—were accidental soldiers, in for the emergency only, and their hearts belonged very much to civilian life.

Of all the Army engagements during the opening of the Old West, which is the only one remembered today? The embarrassing defeat of General Custer by Chief Sitting Bull and his warriors, a moment of history suitably immortalized in the old Anheuser-Busch beer ad, with the yellow-haired Custer fighting to the last with—well, what *are* those shooting irons in his hands?—some historians say a couple of Bulldog revolvers; some say a pair of Webleys, Royal Irish Constabulary revolvers; but Colt Industries' advertising department insists (though considering the outcome of the battle, one wonders why), "General Custer died with a smoking Colt in each hand."

By contrast, civilian derring-do supplied history with such moments as when Nelson Story and thirty cowpokes, driving three thousand head of cattle from Texas to Montana, were attacked by five hundred warriors under the command of Crazy Horse on October 29, 1866. The Indians presumed that the Story boys were armed only with muzzleloaders, so they spaced out their attack in waves to catch the cowboys while they were reloading. They guessed wrong, for the wily white men were carrying Remington breechloading rolling-block rifles, a type first manufactured only the year before but to become the most popular single-shot rifle of the century. Before Crazy Horse discovered his mistake, half of his braves had bitten the dust. Apparently unwilling to believe his eyes, he attacked twice more with heavy losses. The Indians were kept at such a distance that only one cowboy was killed.*

Eighty thousand Sharps carbines were used by the Union forces in the Civil War (an exception to the backward rule) and they were later the principal arm of the U.S. Cavalry in the West, but the glamor that still clings to that trade name was given by the buffalo hunters and pony express riders and Texas Rangers who for a number of years favored the product of Christian Sharps. There was, for example, the famous episode at Adobe Walls, Texas, the ruins of a trading post, when about seven hundred plains Indians— mostly Cheyenne, Comanche, and Kiowa, under the command of Lone Wolf and Quanah Parker—attacked at dawn on June 27, 1874. Twenty-eight buffalo hunters and one woman, all armed with big .44- and .50-caliber Sharps rifles, took their stand in Hanrahan's Saloon and proved such excellent marksmen that the Indians never penetrated their defense and succeeded in killing only three hunters.

As the nation became settled, it was only natural that the civilians would give birth to *organized* bullshit, and so, to help guide the military, the National Rifle Association was organized in 1871—"to promote the introduction of a system of aiming drill and target firing among the National Guard of New York and the

---

* A good little source for this and similar yarns about gun history is *Famous Guns from the Smithsonian Collection* by Hank Bowman (Arco Books, 1967).

militia of other states." In the circumstances it made good sense—the circumstances being that military training in weaponry in those days left almost everything to be desired.

Not only had the federal military establishment supplied its combat troops with less than the best available weapons; it had, much more to its shame, sent its troops into battle with grotesquely insufficient training in arms. Perhaps the U.S. Army's leaders could, until the Civil War, excuse themselves for their lack of interest in marksmanship on the ground that most of the world's military leaders were indifferent to it. George III's troops, equipped with smoothbore arms, allowed for a yard of lateral movement of their bullets at one hundred yards. Until the mid-1800s military long guns were thought of as a collective broadside of fire power, not as single weapons in the hands of individual soldiers. Fire-power was conceived in waves: a "squad" or a "company" of bullets being flung at the enemy, like a handful of pebbles flung at pigeons: throw enough often enough and you've got to hit something. The premium was on speed of loading, not on the accuracy of aim. Aiming was done in a broadside way, at the opposition ranks. One fired in the general direction, and hoped. Since the smoothbore musket could not be counted on to hit a target the size of a human body at sixty yards, except by random luck, the musketman depended on luck: if he didn't hit the enemy he aimed at, then maybe he would hit an enemy to the side or to the rear of his aim. On this point Paul Jenkins, an authority on the evolution of military tactics, has written that marksmanship in the Army was held back because

> the widespread military worship of the battle tactics of Frederick the Great of Prussia, whose use of massed fire solely at the order, followed by a desperate charge with the bayonet, had ended the Seven Years' War with victory after victory for his troops. It is hardly possible to exaggerate the supreme importance universally attributed to this tactic by the foreign

military profession throughout the nearly 150 years from 1757 to 1900.*

Except for the frontiersmen, who came equipped with their own rifles and who from long experience knew what they could accomplish with aiming, the ranks of the American military forces were filled with the smoothbore disciples of luck, not only during the Revolution and the War of 1812 but also in the Mexican War and even into the Civil War—long past the time when the military leaders should have been aware of the advances of weaponry available to their troops and certainly many years past the time when the advantages of preliminary target practice and practice in weapons handling should have been obvious to even the most muleheaded general.

Even after rationalizing, if possible, a lack of emphasis on pre-battle target practice, there was certainly no possible excuse for sending men into battle who did not know how to load or fire their weapons (as happened, for example, at Shiloh), or who had been given such elementary instructions that in the shock of combat they were capable of forgetting what to do. But such was the case, not just now and then but quite generally in the Civil War. It's said that after the battle at Gettysburg thousands of rifles were found on the battlefield that had not been fired; the men who died holding them thought they had been firing them, but the sound of battle was so loud they couldn't tell that when they had pulled the trigger, nothing had actually happened, for either they had failed to prime the rifle or they had inserted the bullet and cartridge backward— something that once done could not be undone without disassembling the rifle or using a worm screw to withdraw the charge. Some of these muzzleloading rifles were found with six or seven charges tamped down on top of one another within the barrel, the poor

* "Uncle Sam's First Regulation Army Rifle," in *The American Rifleman*, April 1934.

fellow behind the sights not having realized that none of the previous loads had been discharged.

GOLD TRIGGER FINGER

When the Civil War ended, the standing army, as usual, shrank back to only a relative handful of regulars who saw action, if at all, shooting at Indians in the far West. Rifles were once again viewed for the most part as something to hold on the shoulder during drill practices or in formal marches. Some state militiamen and National Guard troopers went for years at a time without firing their rifles.

The founders of the National Rifle Association claim it was to offset this lack of preparedness that they organized and sought a charter in New York State.

Okay, but even while giving them credit for patriotism, note that one of the NRA's principal founders published a military journal that stood to benefit from the existence of such a civilian/military lobby and that another of the principal founders wrote an arms manual from which he made a nice piece of change. His manual had gone through seven printings when the Army decided to plagiarize it and distribute it among the regular troops. At that point we find our NRA founder less interested in the promotion of weapons information among Army troops than in earning a buck, for he sued to stop publication of the competitive manual and won.

Throughout its existence, while mightily benefiting from its ties to the Pentagon, the NRA has been primarily interested in its commercial task; in reality, while claiming to be the font of citizen soldiers, this patriotism has been a front for a mammoth promotional operation for the gun, ammunition, and sporting-goods industries. The powers behind the NRA were accurately proportioned in the booths at the NRA Centennial exhibit hall: a hundred and seven commercial exhibitors, ranging from Abercrombie & Fitch (antique and modern high-grade guns), J. G. Anschutz, GmbH, c/o Savage Arms (precision target and shooting rifles and accessories), Bausch & Lomb (rifle telescope sights, spotting scopes, and sunglasses), down the alphabet to Winslow Co. of Venice, Florida, dealers in sporting rifles; fourteen booths for collectors' organizations; five booths for every branch of the military service; half a dozen booths for such outfits as the Amateur Trapshooting Association. That's a ratio of more than four to one commercial. And that is a conservative proportioning.

The NRA has always been an outfit for hucksters. During the early years of the organization's life, when the Army made clear that it didn't think too highly of the NRA's kibbitzing and it seemed for a while that the NRA might fold up, one of the most vociferous propagandists on its behalf came from the magazine *Shooting and Fishing*, which was kept alive by advertisements from gun and ammunition manufacturers; *Shooting and Fishing* later changed its name to *Arms and the Man*, and this in turn later became the NRA's monthly magazine, *The American Rifleman*. From it the NRA takes in nearly $2 million in advertising fees each year, or nearly one-fourth the organization's total income. But the *real* gold mine is exploited by *The American Rifleman*'s serving as the primary channel for propagandizing and lobbying among the country's most active gun owners. It is the most important channel of communication that the arms industry has with these people.

The NRA would doubtless have gone out of business—in fact, it did suspend operation for eight years, from 1892 to 1900—if the gun and ammunition industry hadn't seen that it was a beautiful quasi-official flag to march under. Operational expenses and expenses for conducting many of the early NRA matches were subsidized by DuPont Powder Co., U.S. Cartridge Co. of Massachusetts, Union Metallic Cartridge Co., Hercules Powder Co., Winchester, Peters Cartridge Co., and others. The industry supplied many of the trophies. And it also went to bat for the organization—which is to say, the industry went to bat for itself, for very early in the game the industry virtually became the NRA—in Washington.

Far from wanting to disguise its commercial impulses, the NRA rides this theme heavily in searching for public support; it imitates the Pentagon's argument against budget cuts on the ground that people will lose jobs. At its centennial convention in 1971 the NRA distributed to the public and press a reprint of a paper written in 1965 by Professor Alan S. Krug of the University of Pennsylvania, which pointed out that

> The firearms industry and the shooting sports have a significant impact on the American economy. In 1964, purchases of American-made firearms and ammunition (exclusive of purchases by the military) totaled $282.5 million. Sales of guns and ammunition generated 20,000 jobs and a $100 million payroll in the firearms industry. In addition, there are currently more than 100,000 retail outlets for guns and ammunition. There are more than 1,600 firms manufacturing hunting and shooting accessories, exclusive of the firearms industry itself.
>
> The sport of hunting, when taken alone, has a significant impact on the general economy. In 1963, hunters drove their automobiles 4.8 billion miles just to go hunting. According to calculations made by the economist Richard E. Snyder of the National Sporting Goods Association, this means that hunters "wore out," in one year, 47,880 new automobiles at a cost of $143 million; wore out 215,000 new tires at a cost of $5.5 million; burned up 300 million gallons of gasoline costing $101 million; used 4 million quarts of oil costing $2 million; and accounted for $9.4 million in vehicle repairs and automobile insurance pro-rated for hunting use of the vehicle only. This represents a total expenditure for transportation of $261 million.
>
> In 1963, hunters also spent a total of $675 million on food, lodging, camping equipment, duck boats, hunting apparel and other miscellaneous gear. . . .
>
> Thus, in the year 1963, hunters poured $1.2 billion into the nation's economy, not counting expenditures on firearms and

ammunition. Including the latter would raise the total to $1.5 billion.

It is not known how much is spent annually for expenses connected with shooting sports other than hunting. The investment is certainly substantial. It is known that individuals who handload their own ammunition as a hobby spend upwards of $25 million each year on tools and components.*

It's odd that the NRA would in 1971 still be pushing an essay that used statistics seven or eight years old; in the meantime, expenditures for guns and ammunition had more than doubled—it came to $581.6 million for guns and ammo in 1972, which was, next to the amounts spent on pleasure boats and photographic equipment, the biggest portion of the nation's annual $5.5 billion recreational budget—and probably expenditures for the other allied items had more than doubled too. But using either the new or the old figures, the richness of the guns and ammo racket is plain to be seen. It's obviously worth fighting for, no matter if a few innocents do bite the dust as a result. The NRA goal, of course, is not simply to hold its own but to expand massively. To increase its membership from the present million to 3 or 4 million, the NRA is driving hard to make kids hanker for firearms. As Executive Vice-President Maxwell Rich put it, "Nobody today questions the truism that you must capture youth." And to capture the mind of youth, the NRA is trying to get schools to accept precision-air-gun programs. As part of the hooker, the NRA offers membership for only a dollar. "Our training efforts," says Rich, "must be directed at those who will be our enthusiastic and active members in 1981."

Recruiting the youthful trigger finger is nothing new for the NRA, of course. In fact, its first big breakthrough on this score came in 1911, when it persuaded the Boy Scouts to establish a merit badge for marksmanship. Then, briefly, the NRA was foiled by what its official historian called "strong 'peace' organizations

* "The Socio-Economic Impact of Firearms in the Field of Conservation and Natural Resources Management." Paper No. 118 of the Pennsylvania Cooperative Wildlife Research Unit.

active throughout the land who opposed anything smacking of militarism." Inasmuch as the NRA by its own admission had been established as a paracivilian arm of the military, it smacked quite loudly of militarism, especially when applied to those of tender years. But then came World War I and, as the historian notes with relief and satisfaction, "a brighter climate prevailed in rifle training for the nation's youth." Not only was the merit badge revived, but the NRA worked out an affiliation with Scout troops. Apparently it is paying off as expected. In the pre-Christmas 1972 issue of *Boy's Life* (the favorite magazine of Boy Scouts; it has a circulation of 2.3 million) there were about eight pages of gun and ammunition advertisements out of a total of twenty-seven advertising pages. In any typical issue in any season about 10 percent of the advertising will be for guns and ammunition. To make sure that the boys knew just where *Boy's Life* stands on the subject, the magazine listed what it called "two dozen of the world's greatest gifts." One-fourth of these greatest gifts were long guns.

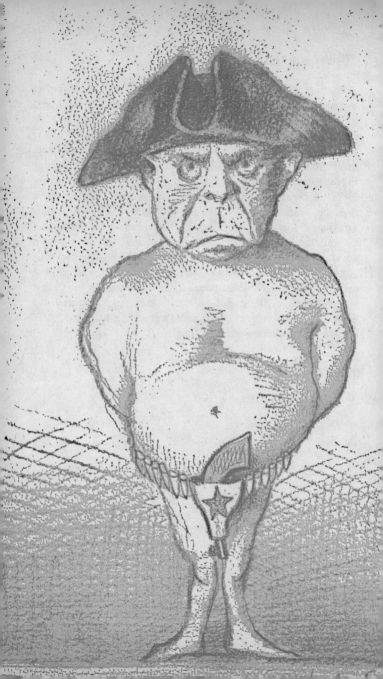

THE RIGHT
TO BEAR ARMS—
AND OTHER DUDS

If NRA propaganda simply resulted in several million Americans of all ages being persuaded to decimate flocks, herds, communities, bedchambers, and barrooms in order to provide the arms and ammo industry's executives with the kind of cigars and richly paneled boardrooms to which they have become accustomed, one could wave that aside as being of no more perverse an influence than, say, the auto industry has had on the same suckers.

But the fact is that the impact of NRA propaganda is much more insidious; it is much more difficult for a people to fight off or shrug off, because it stems from obsolete truths—truths that are still respected as a part of history but that, if literally and contemporaneously applied, as it is quite tempting to do in our lazy or sentimental moments, can do real mischief to our logic and our language. The most dangerous example of this would be the NRA's standard line on the need for, and its role in providing, the "citizen soldier." It was the line to which the NRA clung so desperately to keep from sinking during its early, perilous existence.

Its early work was not all hollow. The NRA can be credited with helping to popularize shooting sports and international shooting matches, and perhaps in some small way this popularization helped stir the consciousness of the regular Army in the need for marksman training. But this influence was so indirect and distant that it can only be speculated.

On the other hand, the NRA's influence on state militia, which was the level at which it was set up to have an influence, was less than minimal for the first thirty years of its life. Part of its problem was that this was a period in our history when state militias were considered the most stagnant backwaters of the military; they attracted few volunteers and less public respect. Putting it mildly, they were not looked upon as significant reservoirs from which the regular army could draw strength.

Consequently, the NRA—while still ritualistically claiming to be working closely with the important segments of the military—was fast deteriorating into a clubby arrangement in which only a few superannuated colonels and generals, the blowhard residue of the Civil War escapade, came together with their hangers-on periodically to bang away at some distant targets. The organization had fallen into such disrepute in the NRA's home state, New York, by 1880 that the governor decided the state's subsidy to the NRA shooting matches was a total waste, cut it to the bone, and told NRA officials that so far as he could see, the organization was of so little benefit "it would be more practical and far less expensive to arm [the militia] with clubs which require no instruction." And with that he kicked the officials out of his office.

By 1892 the NRA was so nearly defunct that it had closed

shop and put its records in storage. It would have died altogether had it not received mouth-to-mouth resuscitation from the resurgent militarism in the country around the turn of the century. The sharp upswing of militarism, coinciding with a surge toward colonialism, began with the Spanish American War in 1898—a war which the NRA's history joyously notes "set a new generation in the saddle."

In addition to the help from the arms industry mentioned earlier, President Theodore Roosevelt, who had an oddly august regard for the place of the gun in society, and Elihu Root, Secretary of War under Presidents McKinley and Roosevelt, gave the NRA the lift it needed. Especially Root. It was his idea to kill the old concept of the state militias that had existed for a hundred and eleven years under the Militia Act of 1792 and to organize instead a federalized National Guard as part of a true national military reserve. This was a keystone in the foundation of the military establishment that has plagued the civilian government ever since.

In 1903, under the heavy-handed encouragement of Secretary Root and key generals, Congress was persuaded to permit the NRA to get its hands officially into the U.S. Treasury; this came about via the establishment of the National Board for the Promotion of Rifle Practice, which, at its very first meeting, voted to turn over literally every available military shooting installation plus all available surplus weapons to the promotion of the NRA.

By 1910 the War Department began supplying the NRA with cut-rate weapons. Having adopted the Model 1903 Springfield as the official infantry arm, the department declared the Model 1898 Krag as surplus and let NRA members have them for $10 each, plus costs. NRA officials concede that this "greatly advanced" the NRA because this was the first time that the government used the riflemen as its outlet for used weapons. Thereafter the NRA could advertise that it paid to sign up. Only NRA members got the guns. Only NRA members got the free ammunition. Only NRA members got the free trips to shooting matches.

Two years later the public was exposed to an example of the

kind of chumminess that was to last forever between the federal military, the gun and ammunition industry, and the NRA. In 1912 Gen. John Bates, President of the NRA,* and other riflemen officials managed to start unloading some of their big expenses on the federal government. They wanted to hold a shooting match at Camp Perry, Ohio. So they went to Senator Henry S. DuPont of Delaware, who was conveniently chairman of the Senate Military Affairs Committee and even more conveniently a member of the powder and ammunition family, and asked him to give them a helping hand. He was only too happy to oblige, tacking a rider onto the Army Appropriations Bill that earmarked $25,000 for the NRA's matches and authorized the War Department to cooperate with the NRA in any way possible in promoting its matches and urged the State Department to do what it could to help the NRA carry America's colors around the globe. Not a bad leg up.

PRAISE THE BRASS AND
PASS THE AMMUNITION

But that was just the beginning. The momentum of the 1903 Act and the 1912 DuPont rider crested in The Big Payoff of 1916—namely, the National Defense Act of that year, authored primarily by Secretary Root, which *incorporated into government policy* all the ad-hoc favoritism of previous years:

---

* Most of the top dogs of the NRA have been military men. Most of the early presidents were generals, active or retired. They included Generals George Wingate, A. E. Burnside, Alexander Shaler, Winfield S. Hancock, E. L. Molineaux, Ulysses S. Grant, Philip H. Sheridan, et al. In recent years the important officer of NRA has been the executive vice president. The present one, Gen. Maxwell Evans Rich, is a former adjutant general of the Utah National Guard and a much-decorated colonel in World War II, during which he won the Silver Star for showing so much aggressiveness with the Ninth Army in the Ruhr that he and his jeep driver outran the rest of his outfit and wound up in a town held by the Germans—with Rich armed only with a .45 that he admits "I couldn't fire worth a damn. I did think of throwing it at somebody, however." NRA generals have a certain charm.

$300,000—an enormous sum for 1916—was set aside to promote civilian marksmanship training; the War Department was authorized to keep handing out guns and ammo to civilian rifle clubs; military instructors were made available for the NRA hobbyists; all military rifle ranges were opened to civilian gunmen; finally it created the Office of the Director of Civilian Marksmanship under the National Board for the Promotion of Rifle Practice—a bureaucratic enclave that was to swell eventually into two dozen civilian employees and three colonels, supervised by the twenty-five-member Board itself (most of whose members belong to the NRA), and operating on a budget of $5 million. The Big Shoot each year was at Camp Perry. There was considerable grousing among critics of the NRA when, at the height of the Vietnam War and the drafting of record numbers of men to fight an unpopular war, the Pentagon was assigning three thousand servicemen to provide housekeeping service at Camp Perry for the NRA devotees. The Perry matches alone cost taxpayers $2 million. During the same period Marines at Quantico, Virginia, complained that they didn't appreciate being forced to give up their weekend passes to "pull targets" (standing in pits beneath the targets and marking the spot a firer has just hit) for the NRA's shooters. Marines were told to do it or be court-martialed. For a while the riflemen were paying the Marines three dollars a day, but then the Corps hierarchy ordered the payments to cease altogether and for the Marines to work for free.

And did the federal support of this manly hobby pay off in a better-trained citizenry on which the military forces could draw? Alas, not exactly. In fact, the officially designated Civilian Marksmanship program was of insignificant value, as proved in a study conducted by Arthur D. Little, Inc., in 1965, at a cost of $100,000 to the taxpayer. In a sampling of 12,880 Army trainees it was found that only 3.1 percent had been in the National Board's program before being inducted into the Army. The study further showed that some gun club members had received no instruction at all and that some had never even shot a gun. Perhaps the most embarrassing discovery was that fewer than half of the gun club members benefiting from the government program were of draftable age.

The Congressional Acts of 1903 and 1916 were, when you think of it, rather fantastic pieces of legislation—as fantastic, say, as if Congress were to approve money to supply tennis rackets and balls in perpetuity to anybody who wanted to try out for the neighborhood team. The raid on the Treasury continued intermittently for the next three generations. By the late 1960s, when a few members of Congress began to complain rather loudly about the giveaway, the National Board for the Promotion of Rifle Practice was handing out 60 million rounds of free ammunition and selling surplus M-1 rifles for $17.50 each.

If Senator Dodd had really wanted to find out where the weaponry glut was coming from, he would have spent as much time looking at the huckstering of the Pentagon as at the import firms. Between 1959 and 1964 the Army gave away to NRA clubs 246.9 million rounds of free ammunition costing $7.2 million, plus putting on "loan"—meaning they would never be returned—$2.3 million worth of guns during the same period. Between 1960 and mid-1963, the very time when Dodd was supposedly casting about for direction in his investigation, the Army sold 268,893 .30-caliber Model 1903A3 rifles through the NRA. In March 1963, the month Dodd opened his hearings into the youth-gun problem, the Army put 150,000 M-1 .30-caliber carbine rifles on sale through the NRA and they were snapped up. Also in the Year of the Assassination the Army sold 30,000 .45-caliber pistols to NRA members. All of these weapons, of course, were sold at bargain-basement prices. And for select NRA members, the Army reserved 1,344 fine M-1 Match rifles and 309 M-1 Standard rifles, which were to be converted to Match. All in all, between 1959 and 1964, when perhaps coincidentally crime was beginning to march across the landscape with special vigor, the Army put a half-million guns indiscriminately into the hands of civilians.

Indiscriminately is putting it mildly. Oswald could have gotten a much better rifle, just as easily and even cheaper, by simply joining the NRA and buying one of the Army surplus items. The NRA did not check out its buyers; it would never have discovered that Oswald had been up to some odd things in his life. To show the NRA's laxness, a Dayton reporter joined, using the name of a man already convicted of one murder and under indictment in Ohio for three other killings. Knowing the ease with which NRA weapons and ammunition could be obtained, Robert B. dePugh, leader of the violent Minutemen organization (a typical Minuteman was arrested in Illinois with several submachine guns, a flamethrower, aerial bombs, mortars, automatic pistols, and rifles; the Minutemen once made up a list of Congressmen they wanted to kill), urged his eager extremists to join the NRA to get guns, and free ammo, and target practice. So did Malcolm X advise his followers. Nussbaum, the best-known bank robber of the 1960s, joined the NRA and got U.S. surplus guns. Between 1962 and 1966, when the civil rights crisis was developing in the South, the NRA's membership in Mississippi more than doubled—in fact, that was the highest growth rate in the country. The only check on the good character of these new members, to make sure they intended to use their free ammunition and Army-subsidized guns on cardboard targets and not on Negroes, were the Mississippi State Police—not exactly the most pro-civil rights force in the country. NRA Secretary Daniel conceded easily in an interview that the NRA might be the haven for some crazies and Ku Kluxers, but, he shrugged, "I imagine the Baptist Church has some too." Anyway, he said, the membership fee wasn't high enough to enable the NRA to check to see if new members were criminals, fugitives, drug addicts, or paramilitary extremists. When other organizations wanted to make such a check, however, they found little cooperation. For example, when Stanley Mosk, then Attorney General of California, wanted to run a check on the more than 100,000 NRA members in his state to see if among them might be some crazies getting U.S. ammunition, the National Board for the Promotion of Rifle Practice said its gun club membership lists were "not available." Daniel told me that Mosk did not ask for the NRA rolls, "but if he had, we would have refused to show them to him." *

In a nation whose hip is already heavily calloused from packing a sidearm, one may question whether the Pentagon/NRA contribution of half a million or so guns to the civilian armory (much less than 1 percent of the total holdings) is significantly damaging.

There can be no question, however, about the critical injury done by the Pentagon/NRA program to the democratic process and to that equally important commodity, the *language* of the democratic process. Lobbying the government from outside is legitimate; *lobbying that is a part of the government* destroys the process of government, and to this extent the Pentagon/NRA program has exerted a truly subversive influence for three generations. At the very time that some members of Congress were attempting to pass a gun-control measure, the Pentagon was shilling for the opposition: spending several million dollars a year

---

* The sale of Army surplus weapons has been sharply curtailed since 1968. Now the sales are limited to 300 standard M-1 rifles a year, according to Colonel Frank Lowman, director of the Office of Civilian Marksmanship, the Pentagon link to the supposedly civilian National Board for the Promotion of Rifle Practice. He says that free ammunition is also provided on a much more limited basis. Most of the ammunition, .22 caliber, goes to the 2,800 junior rifle clubs. They have 150,000 members. Whereas the Pentagon-NRA civilian marksmanship program used to accept anybody over the age of 16, now it is putting most of its money into the 12–19 age bracket. Get 'em while they're young. However, the NBPRP does still help the NRA put on 52 matches—26 rifle and 26 pistol, including the big one at Camp Perry—for persons of any age. The willingness of Congress to curtail the program seems to have been brought about when it was learned that *black* extremists were making use of their government's largesse. The first blow came when New York City cops raided a Harlem gun club and seized twelve thousand rounds of ammunition, one-third of it government issue supplied free because of the club's affiliation with the NRA. After government surplus was found in the hands of black radicals, the Pentagon announced it was going to destroy most of its used weapons and it budgeted $300,000 to build a furnace to melt down its old guns. The severe pall that black militants, and the Vietnam budget bind, put on the Pentagon NRA program now seems to be lifting. For Fiscal 1973 Congress authorized $160,000—$37,000 more than the year before—to run the National Board for the Promotion of Rifle Practice, now reduced to a staff of eleven government employees. This could be a comeback trend.

to supply guns and ammunition and shooting matches as come-ons to encourage people to join the chief lobby against the kind of gun controls that were approved by most Americans.

The Pentagon's cynical subsidies also, of course, resulted in the priming of the gun and ammunition industry in the same way that the supplying of a dozen cartons of free cigarets to anyone reaching the age of eighteen, say, would result in the subsidy of the tobacco industry. Once hooked on a cheap rifle and a few dozen rounds of free ammunition from the Pentagon, the new NRA member could be expected to spend hundreds of dollars over his lifetime keeping up the habit.

As for the Pentagon/NRA perversion of the language crucial to the gun-control debate, this can best be seen in what happened to the concept of "militia." The NRA's excuse for existence hangs solely, by its own admission, by the Second Amendment to the Constitution: "A well-regulated militia, being necessary to the security of a free State, the right of the people to keep and bear arms, shall not be infringed." In its publicity material the NRA describes itself as the "foremost guardian of the American tradition and constitutional right of citizens to 'Keep and Bear Arms'"; in other words, it sees itself as the foremost defender of the concept of the state militia, for *that* is what the Second Amendment protects, as explained by Irving Brant in his *The Bill of Rights*:

> The Second Amendment, popularly misread, comes to life chiefly on the parade floats of rifle associations and in the propaganda of mail-order houses selling pistols to teen-age gangsters. . . . As the wording [of the Amendment] reveals, this article relates entirely to the militia—a fact that was made even clearer by a clause dropped from Madison's original wording: "but no person religiously scrupulous of bearing arms should be compelled to render military service in person." It was made clearest of all in the congressional debate on the amendment. Why was a militia necessary to "the security of a free state"? Elbridge Gerry asked and answered that question: "What, sir, is the use of a militia? It is to prevent

the establishment of a standing army, the bane of liberty."
Thus the purpose of the Second Amendment was to forbid
Congress to prohibit the maintenance of a state militia. By its
nature, that amendment cannot be transformed into a personal right to bear arms, enforceable by federal compulsion
upon the states.*

This is the interpretation placed on the Second Amendment
by most Constitutional scholars and by the U.S. Supreme Court;
further argument on the point is apparently not only tiresome but
futile, as the NRA itself concedes in a pamphlet prepared by the
NRA's Legislative Information Service: "Because of judicial prece-
dent, then, the constitutional argument [that is, its own argument
that the Second Amendment applies to individuals] is of limited
practical utility." †

And yet, despite making this concession, it continues to use
the same old line in its day-to-day propaganda forays, pretending
that it has not been utterly defeated in the courts. This is the
NRA's two-part fraud—first of all, its make-believe that the
Second Amendment has anything to do with the individual, and
secondly its insistence that the organization is still working with the
Army to perpetuate the Constitutional concept of the "citizen
soldier," the oldtime militia hand. The fraud is compounded by the
fact that its officials are well aware that the National Defense Act

---

* (Bobbs-Merrill, 1965), p. 486.

† Carl Bakal, author of The Right to Bear Arms, discovered a fascinatingly
candid admission on the part of none other than Jack Basil, Jr., head of the
NRA's legislative department (chief lobbyist). It's this excerpt from Basil's
Georgetown University master's thesis:

   Certain principles may be deduced from the history of the construction,
   interpretation and administration of the right to bear arms: (1) The
   Second Amendment operates as a limitation against the National Government only; (2) The States, under their broad political powers, may
   regulate the possession and use of firearms in furtherance of the health,
   safety and general welfare of the people; (3) The prevalent assumption
   appears to be that the possession and use of firearms by an individual is
   conditional on the legislative and administrative mandate of the States;
   (4) The keeping and bearing of arms is a collective and not an individual
   right.

of 1916, the principal act which launched the NRA upon its guns and ammunition distribution program and provided funds for the shooting matches—in other words, the subsidy act that linked the militarists of the government with the arms merchants and militarists of the NRA—was the same act that *destroyed* the state militias and set up in their place a national reserve force largely free of state connections (that is, the federalized National Guard as we know it today). To say that the NRA's philosophical foundation is the Second Amendment, and that the Second Amendment's main virtue is in defending the arms of a militia that is moribund (and that, even when it was alive, did not want the NRA's help) is not only a fraud but, worse, destroys the language of legislative debate. "Citizen soldier" is a phrase that simply no longer has any meaning; the Minuteman is bronze forever.

In any event, whatever good or mediocre service the NRA gave in encouraging rifle practice in the military in its early days, that service is long past, and in their more candid moments they admit it. At the NRA's centennial convention, Executive Vice President Rich told the membership:

> Most of our competitive shooting program—consistent with the origins of the NRA—has been tied to military training. As one having a military background myself, I fully appreciate this logic. However, I must question how up-to-date we are. *Our present courses of fire are largely those of the vintage of World War I, and are based to a considerable extent on military small arms now (or in the process of being) phased out and made obsolete* [emphasis added].

And Col. Charles Askins, writing in the *Gun Digest* of 1970 with copious evidence to show that gripping the handgun with both hands significantly improves accuracy, points out that the NRA rule which governs target match-shooting requires that the gun be supported by only one hand—a rule that "is an archaic holdover from the days when the Code Duello was in flower."

DO-IT-YOURSELF LAW AND ORDER

The most attractively beguiling theme of the NRA is entitled The Armed Citizen, and it has endless variations, all of them slightly reminiscent of Beowulf's "warrior-weapons and the weeds of fight. . . ." When a rifleman talks of defending his country or shooting a household intruder, there is something of the same guttural North European tribesman in his poem of citizen wrath.

The NRA's Armed Citizen is of two types: political and private, and propping up each of them is that vague but undying spirit of anarchy that is the spirit of America. The NRA's concept of Armed Citizenry heartily endorses the old anarchist saying, "The state must never have a monopoly on the instruments of violence." One of the NRA's basic arguments against gun controls is that they would make the citizen helpless against the takeover of a tyrant: the riflemen say (without evidence) that a prerequisite of modern dictatorships in Germany and Italy and Austria was the imposition of gun registration. The NRA says flatly, "No dictatorship has ever been imposed on a nation of free men who have not been first required to register their privately owned weapons." They go farther to clearly imply that even in this country our politicians will mind their manners just so long as they know they will be forcibly resisted if they get too high-handed. Does it mean anything that the riflemen seem to be laying more stress on this theme, and doing so more wildly? On May 24, 1973, Congressman John Saylor, a prominent life member of the NRA, took the floor of the House to orate about how "two centuries of gun ownership" in this country had preserved freedom; but the clouds of treason, he warned, were gathering as an "ugly mask" to hide the effort to take some guns out of circulation. "Without the right to keep and bear arms, the American public will become defenseless against the criminal and the State. Accordingly the American system of government—that has survived on constitutional rights and guide-lines—will be disregarded and possibly disposed of for some lasting omnipotent power structure." Though others might flinch, he would not. Raising his finger, he declaimed, "I shall fight to prevent our government from falling under the control of those associated with black-shirted, goose-stepping tyrants, misfits, and hoodlums." And since Washingtonians had not seen any black-shirted, goose-stepping tyrants passing through town lately and might be confused by that remark, Saylor went on to say that the enemy's ranks also included "bleeding-heart sociologists."

In the April 1973 *American Rifleman*, the possibility of having to shoot uppity politicians was again on the minds of our patriotic gunmen:

> Now let us turn to gun owning as a deterrent to the domestic political criminal, the home-grown tyrant. . . . But the tyrant will think twice before trying to exercise tyranny over an armed populace. . . . The right to bear arms is one means of guaranteeing that governments *do* "govern well."

One might suspect that the NRA hierarchy is largely made up of Irishmen.

The NRA's hypothetical Armed Citizen of the private sort is the fellow who is ready with firearm and able to shoot your ass off if you try to interfere in his life. Deadly when aroused.

In Chicago a bus rider who became enraged because he had missed his usual stop whipped out a pistol and shouted, "I am going to get off this bus if I have to blast my way off." Not hearing an immediate screech of the brakes, he let fly with four bullets, wounding several riders. Thereupon, to continue with the description of a Chicago Police Department commander, "Another of the passengers, incensed at the audacity of the blasting rider, took out a gun and fired back, wounding several more riders. This happened in a supposedly civilized city on a bus carrying citizens to and from their work. I merely mention this because it is almost hard to believe that on a bus carrying people to and from work, out of the sixty or eighty passengers on the bus two of them would have firearms."

To loyal members of the NRA, however, the odd—and even discouraging—feature of this anecdote is that so *few* occupants of that bus were armed. The NRA's ideal, as often stated, is *the armed citizen,* and although in one of the organization's policy statements it grants that "the expression 'armed citizen' has different meanings to different people," it goes on to say that it should mean fundamentally the ability to shoot back and the gun to do it with:

> The taking of a human life is a matter of deepest concern. Nonetheless . . . in many instances, the citizen has no choice but to defend himself or his home. If he elects to use a gun, that is his privilege. The important thing is that the individual must have the opportunity to make his own decision, and obviously his decision lacks meaning in such instances if he does not have the right and the opportunity to have a gun to enforce that decision.

The riflemen aren't kidding. In the column "The Armed Citizen," appearing in every issue of *The American Rifleman,* there are a dozen or so vignettes carrying the message that the world consists of one big shootout and that the man who survives is going to be the man who has his roscoe handy and who has the ability to pop it off before the bad guy can pull the trigger on his own roscoe. It is a phantasmagoria of roscoes. It is a panorama of holdupmen beaten to the draw by crafty shopkeepers and of highwaymen come riding, riding, riding up to the old inn door, only to be met by a timely half-ounce of lead. Threading through the continuing epic of "The Armed Citizen" is the theme that gun laws hurt only the innocent, as per: "In four years of running a New York, N.Y., grocery, Persio Espinal has been held up six times. Recently three men entered the store and two drew guns. Espinal pulled a revolver from its hiding place, killed one of the robbers, and forced the others to flee. Police arrived, took Espinal to be booked for having an unregistered gun, and then began a belated search for the two fugitive robbers."

When Washington, D.C., police forced 100 or so businessmen

to surrender their special police permits allowing them to carry handguns, the NRA was outraged. "The hair-raising stories which used to be whispered about rampant vice and violence in exotic distant sink-holes of the Orient seem at times to apply with sordid reality" to the nation's capital, it editorialized in *The American Rifleman*, April 1973. Allowing for 50 percent exaggeration, the NRA still had a point when it went on to ask, "What is the police department doing about crime" besides disarming businessmen? Answer: not much; and the ironic part about it is that Washington has one cop per 153 citizens compared to one per 380 nationally— the biggest per capita police force (as it is undoubtedly also one of the lousiest) in the United States.

For many years the NRA has recognized that bad law enforcement has given it the best argument for opposing gun laws. It goes: If the cops and courts can't do anything with the laws they've got, why give them more? In 1934, fighting back the first major effort at gun-control legislation in Congress, the NRA editorialized: "Some Prosecuting Attorneys, Police Chiefs, Penologists 'view with alarm' the fact that 'known criminals can roam the streets at will with firearms.' Whose fault is it? If 'known criminals' can't be put in jail and kept there by Prosecuting Attorneys, Police Chiefs, Penologists, for such crimes as murder, burglary, holdups, kidnapping, how can they be put in jail and kept there for carrying guns? Maybe what we need is to get rid of Prosecuting Attorneys, Police Chiefs, Judges, Parole Boards who can be bought—by money or by votes!" Ever since, with only a slight adjustment to the syntax and no adjustment at all in the import, the NRA has been saying the same thing.

Anyone living within the confines of a major American city today will find this position offensive only because the riflemen excuse their advocacy of general arming on Constitutional grounds: a position that at best is fudging. What the NRA is really doing—shorn of organizational hypocrisy—is describing, and advising Americans on how to cope for themselves in, a sidewalk *anarchy*. That's fairly reasonable. The truth is that Americans aren't protected by anything at all. They are on their own. *Really* on their own, as the Trenton, New Jersey, woman learned on January 15, 1973, at eight o'clock *in the morning* when she was raped on the sidewalk a hundred and fifty yards from Trenton police headquarters while about twenty-five of her fellow citizens looked on from nearby vantage points.

Fewer than one in four persons arrested for murder is convicted; in a typical year about 3 percent of the burglary arrests result in conviction; about one out of every twelve *reported* robberies results in a conviction. If you start figuring in all the crimes that were probably committed and not reported, the ratio gets truly impressive. Former United States Attorney General Ramsey Clark estimates that an efficient burglar can count on only one chance in a hundred and fifty burglaries of being caught and convicted. It is a very wild and woolly situation, and if the NRA would admit that it is really talking about a lawless gun society rather than a lawful one, then the concept of the "armed citizen" would not seem surrealistic at all, for the citizen who supposes that the police are sweeping the streets of gun-toting criminals and that the courts are jailing these mischievous persons for suitably lengthy stays is, to put it mildly, a very trusting citizen. Let him remain unarmed if he chooses; but he should make that prayerful decision with his eyes wide open to the anarchy on every side, beginning with the anarchy of the courts and the police themselves.

Although police departments sometimes seem to have a corner on cretin servants, this is not accurate; a high percentage of prosecuting attorneys and probation officers are also of that quality, and as for judges, their part in the rape of civilization was nicely accounted for by Pat Brown, former Governor of California and former chairman of the Commission on the Reform of Federal Criminal Laws, who, when asked why gunmen so often got off so easily, acknowledged that "there are some judges that are superannuated and senile and mentally ill and alcoholics, and they should be removed." But they aren't.

During a recent three-month period the police of the District of Columbia kept tab on 361 cases in which persons were arrested for carrying concealed guns. Now, this is a crime that in Washington, D.C., has been considered worthy of packing a man off to jail for one year on first offense and for up to ten years if he is caught on the street with a gun after having been convicted of a felony. It is a pretty tough law, and it is a venerable law, dating from 1932. But in practice the law is a fraud.

Of the 361 cases, the United States prosecuting attorney simply threw out 162, either because he felt he was overworked and didn't want to be bothered with them, or because he felt that the police had fouled up on some technicality of the arrest, or because he used the charge to swap with the prisoner for a guilty plea to some lesser charge. Thus 162 potential killers who were walking the streets of the nation's capital during that three-month period never even stood before a judge with the charge hanging over them.

Of the 199 cases that did get into court, 17 were tossed out by the judge on some personal whim and 25 were acquitted. The others were convicted.

But of the 157 convictions, 103—or 66 percent—received a suspended sentence, were put on probation, or simply had to pay a fine. *Two out of three persons convicted in Washington* (if this was a solid survey) *for carrying deadly weapons never spend a day in jail.* That's those who were convicted. Of those persons who were *arrested* for carrying concealed guns in the nation's capital, five out of six can be comfortably assured that they will never serve a prison sentence.

The statistics are even more dismaying when confronted in the flesh. It is, as one Indiana police official remarked, "disconcerting to know that you have arrested a violent criminal and meet him coming down the street the next day."

If Arthur Bremer had been stuck away for a year or so when he was arrested by Milwaukee police in November 1971 for illegally carrying a concealed Charter Arms snubnosed .38, he wouldn't have been around to shoot George Wallace the next year. Instead, the charge against him was reduced to disorderly conduct, a misdemeanor, and Bremer was let go, despite a patrolman's testimony that at the time of his arrest he had been "incoherent." With that assistance from the prosecuting attorney and court, he could legally purchase the assassination pistol—another Charter Arms snubnosed .38—a few weeks later, plus a 14-shot 9-mm. Browning automatic pistol the next year, and in good conscience sign the federally required Form 4473 stating that he had never been convicted of a felony. (This form, one of the farcical "protections" of the 1968 Gun Control Act, is a Firearms Transactions Record that includes the buyer's name, height, weight, race, address, and date and place of birth; it requires the buyer to prove that he is over twenty-one and a resident of the state, and also requires him to swear—though he needn't keep a straight face while doing so—that he is not a fugitive from justice, that he is not a drug addict or "adjudicated" as a mental incompetent, that he was not dishonorably discharged from the armed forces and that he is not an illegal alien.)

There are an estimated million illegal handguns (some police officials say millions) floating around New York City, which may be enough to persuade the city's magistrates that there is simply no use in trying to get tough with the Sullivan Law. But that hardly justifies their continually surprising the public (and police officers) with such lapses of integrity as allowing a drug pusher armed with an illegal .38-caliber Smith & Wesson to pass through the court's preliminary embrace so gently that he could be back on the street, in business, and rearrested two days later with more drugs and another new .38-caliber pistol. New York Police Commissioner Patrick Murphy got to wondering whatever happened to all the armed crooks his men had run in, so he had a spot check made of every fourth person charged over a twenty-one month period with felonious possession of firearms and found—hang on now—that *not one of the hundred and thirty-six persons* had been convicted of the charge. Somehow they had got off, usually through a lazy or crooked prosecutor who preferred to swap off for a lighter charge. They have been known to do so under the inducement of a bribe—the sucker gunmen not knowing the charges would probably have been reduced anyway. A resident of Queens, arrested with a sawed-off 12-gauge shotgun and an unregistered Iver Johnson .38 revolver, swore that he paid an assistant D.A. $12,000 to get him off with misdemeanor charges; he became indignant and squealed when he found that because he wasn't carrying any ammunition at the time, a felony charge hadn't been much of a likelihood anyway.

Detroit has a fairly tough gun law: to be eligible to buy a handgun, you have to be twenty-one, a citizen, a resident of Michigan for six months, have had no felony convictions during the preceding eight years, and be free of insanity. If you're all that, then you can get a license to purchase a handgun. Then, after you've made your buy, you have to present yourself and the gun to the police chief for another checkthrough. That's what the law says. The only trouble is, most people ignore it. Detroit, which has only half the population of Chicago, has no trouble at all in scoring as many serious gun crimes as Chicago because it has the guns to do the job. Nobody really knows how many, but Detroit officials figure there must be about half a million illegal guns in town. And yet in any given year, authorities will prosecute only a thousand or so gunmen for breaking this law.

Compared to the easygoing attitude in most cities, and compared to the easygoing attitude that used to prevail in Detroit itself, the handling of these thousand arrests might almost seem granite-hard. In 1971 Wayne County (in which Detroit is situated) Prosecuting Attorney William L. Cahalan told residents of his domain that after a thirty-seven-day moratorium—during which illegal guns would be received, no questions asked—anybody caught with an unregistered gun or with a concealed weapon without a permit would be prosecuted for a felony, no exceptions. He was true to his word, and felony convictions resulted in 97 percent of the cases. There was one gaping loophole: no mandatory jail sentence was attached to the law.* Nevertheless, the first-time wrongdoer stands convicted of a felony rather than a misdemeanor (a level at which most of the local judges would rather have them prosecuted), and gun-law violators with previous criminal records have been receiving the maximum sentence, five years. Lawbreakers without previous records have been getting two years on probation. Since Cahalan's crackdown, the number of handguns being registered has nearly tripled: compared to the 2,235 permits for concealable weapons issued in 1971, there were 5,910 issued in the first eight months of 1972. This is progress of a sort, perhaps, but bear in mind that police estimate there are *at least* half a million illegal guns in the city. And judging from the way Cahalan talks the blues, he doesn't have the spirit to expand his operation. "If we put in prison every single person who violated the gun law and was arrested and brought into court, we would not have done hardly anything," he said, referring to the hundreds of thousands left untouched. "Nothing we can do in the matter of law enforcement" will amount to much, says Cahalan, who understandably feels that his conviction of .2 percent of the gun lawbreakers each year leaves the problem untouched. In other words, folks, your elected officials have given up. At best they acknowledge a state of anarchy and shrug; at worst they contribute to it.†

---

* In 1972 the Detroit city council set a mandatory $400 fine for illegally carrying a pistol and a jail term if it is loaded. But the law hasn't made much headway.

† One of the seldom-mentioned social benefits to be gained from the use of the Saturday Night Special can be deduced from the words of Detroit Police Commissioner John Nichols: "Ballistically, we have noted that the Specials are extremely inferior. Due to the low-quality steel or machining in the barrels, the rifling leaves very poor land and groove marks which makes ballistic identification most difficult. If the firearm in question has been used to any extent—fifty or sixty shots—the land and groove marks are so poor that identification by scientific means is virtually impossible." This helps maintain the decorum of the courts; since lack of bullet identification makes it more difficult for the police to put together a case, the prosecution and the judges are thereby supplied a better excuse to accept a lesser plea and they are not so easily shown to be simply disinterested, incompetent, or corrupt.

SOFT CELL

It is not so much the lawlessness of society as the *pretense* of a lawful society that breeds the kind of frustration that the NRA presents with eloquent fanaticism. Apparently a large segment of the population—convinced it should not take matters into its own hands but having suffered at the hands of armed thugs who get off with little or no punishment—dreams of a return to public gibbeting or drawing-and-quarterings. If Libya has returned to a literal rendering of the Koranic law, "And the thief, male and female, cut off the hands of both, as recompense for what they have earned," why can't we work out something of the same solution for gunmen? If Uganda has taken to the wholesale execution of armed robbers, why can't we? If President Ferdinand Marcos, that grand democrat of the Philippines, has ordered that anyone killing another with an unlicensed gun in the commission of a crime be executed by firing squad or electric chair, why can't we? Swift and awful retribution is not an ideal of recent origin, of course. In his old age, looking around with the same frustration felt by so many today, W. N. Byers, a journeyman vigilante of Denver in the 1860 era, said, "I have known a great many executions, but I don't believe one of them was ever unjust. But when they were proved guilty, they were always hanged. There was no getting out of it. No, there were no appeals in those days; no writ of errors; no attorneys' fees; no pardon in six months. Punishment was swift, sure and certain."

Wipe them out; waste them. Bitter frontier disenchantment with official justice is still common, undiminished, and unaltered over the years. The law-and-order chorus sounds the same today as when H. L. Mencken robustly demanded that the laws on the books be carried out to the last jot and tittle, indeed unto the scale of Jehovah's punishment of Sodom and Gomorrah:

What if we hanged 1,000 or 2,000 or 3,000? Would it dissuade the "psychopathic personalities" of the year following from committing other murders? Perhaps not all of them, but certainly some—and meanwhile we'd be rid of 1,000, 2,000 or 3,000 murderers. Society would be relieved of their menace once and for all time. The English, at the close of the seventeenth century, faced a wave of crime far worse than our own. All the roads of their country became so unsafe as to be almost impassable, and in London itself there were endless robberies and murders in the streets. They got rid of the nuisance during the century following by the simple process of hanging it out. When a robber or murderer was caught he was turned over to Jack Ketch. It was a brutal business, and in some of its details it was undoubtedly carried on with undue ferocity, but it worked. By the end of the eighteenth century almost every criminal strain in England had been obliterated, and the country has been notably free from crimes of violence ever since.*

In his proposed pogrom against the gunmen of America, Mencken had some, but not much mercy. For the simple possession of a gun in the conduct of a crime, he was willing to be tolerant once and to punish with nothing but a stay in "a comfortable jail or reformatory," but for the second offense of carrying a gun in the commission of a crime, whether the criminal actually used it to kill or not, Mencken urged packing him off "to the gallows or the chair instanter."

Precisely the same passions stir the breasts of gun buffs today, and is virtually the official policy of the NRA. Why discard guns, they ask, when society should be discarding criminals? Perhaps the Los Angeles Police Department gains some psychological advantage from dumping tons of small arms in the Pacific Ocean every year, but wouldn't it be more sensible to introduce several thousand California criminals to the climate of the gas chamber instead?

Some in and out of Congress suggest that the best way to keep guns out of the hands of criminals would be to sentence first offenders in gun crimes to at least a mandatory five years in prison

---

* *Liberty* magazine (July 28, 1934).

with second offenders getting at least a ten-year stretch. But where are the prisons to contain them, or the penologists with the grit to try? If each of the nine thousand or so persons caught unlawfully carrying guns in New York City each year were convicted, how could they be stuffed into New York's already bursting prisons? If the judiciary of the District of Columbia took their jobs seriously, where would they send the gun violators—to Lorton penitentiary, which already has twice as many prisoners as it was designed to contain and where the warden and his guards have in despair surrendered control to the inmates, who walk away at whim? To be exact, the AWOL rate averages about one prisoner every three days.

And even if there were space to hold our prisoners, where is the legislature or the tax-burdened citizenry willing to foot the bill? It costs $4,141 to keep a man in Lorton nine months—more than it costs at Harvard. The Attorney General of New Jersey, pounded with demands from the law-and-order crowd that all gunmen be imprisoned, sat down one day and figured it up. "If that punitive notion had been in effect in New Jersey for the past seven years," he said, "it would have cost $6 billion to keep those people in jail."

But say the money could be raised and the jails could be built, where is the government at any level who knows what jails are for? One can go to just about any state for endless examples of what prompts that question, but one can always depend on Texas for the very best yahoo example: the state which sent a rancher to prison for three years for murdering his neighbor (you can get fifty in Texas for possession of marijuana) and let him out just in time to get in a little rifle practice before murdering five wetbacks. Or Washington, D.C.: two weeks after his guards had permitted the escape of eight of the meanest fellows in the D.C. jail (a jail that, by the way, was condemned as inadequate sixty-five years ago)—all eight had been convicted of violent crimes, including rape and muggings and armed robberies; four were murderers; one was the local underworld's best-known assassin—the warden was awarded the city's highest award for service.

And then there are the likes of the eighteen-year-old who murdered a sixty-two-year-old man in 1970, was declared "criminally insane" and committed to Washington's insane asylum, but within three years had been released to renew a robbery career that, fortunately, ended when he lost a gun duel. (In the District of Columbia, between 60 to 70 percent of the armed holdups are committed by persons on parole or out on bail.) Or the twenty-one-year-old confessed murderer of a Catholic University honor student: he actually had to spend sixteen months in jail for that little trick.

So long as Kafka seems to be writing the script; so long as our screws apparently think penology has only two approaches—to let the prisoners come and go at will, as in Washington, or to bury them, as at Parchman and Tucker and Attica; so long as our senile judges and corrupt prosecutors consider the charge of carrying an unlicensed concealed weapon or manslaughter or murder to be no more than one card in a procedural poker hand—then who is to say that the riflemen are simplistic to urge each citizen to arm and to be prepared to fend for himself?

POSSE POWER

An estimated half of the 60 million households in this country are armed, according to the National Commission on the Causes and Prevention of Violence, and of these two-thirds say they have armed for protection. Can that many Americans be all wrong? In 1967, as race riots—or as some sociologists called them, "commodity riots"—whipped a number of large cities, the National Rifle Association spoke in agreement with those who are armed and in warning to those who are not, in an immediately celebrated editorial entitled "Who Guards America's Homes?" The gist of it was that the cops have failed ("New York City has increased its police force from 15,000 to 28,000—about the size of two U.S. Army divisions—in the past 22 years although its population remains the same. It now spends more than $1,000,000 a day on policing, yet its crime rate rockets") and the National Guard cannot always be depended on, so, to guard "the doors of American homes from senseless savagery and pillaging," we must look to the armed citizen either "as a civilian member of the *posse comitatus* or as one of the unorganized militia, defined as the 'whole body of able-bodied male citizens.'"

The editorial provoked anger from such now-and-then liberal journals as the Washington *Post,* which (while posting guards at its own doors and making its security increasingly tight in the years since) denounced the suggestion as a return to vigilantism. As indeed it was. Could anything be more American?

Historically at least, the NRA can point to vigilantism as a commonly adopted remedy for social disorder; and by every shred of evidence, contemporary as well as historical, the NRA is certainly wise to conclude that neither the police nor the National Guard can be counted on to protect the community.

The idea that the private citizen who feels endangered should not arm to protect himself is an idea of relatively recent origin. Certainly nineteenth-century America saw vigilantism flourishing in every region except New England and the Middle Atlantic States. Some of the vigilante associations had thousands of members. In Texas, the most hospitable soil for vigilantism, there were fifty-two organizations during the twenty years following the Civil War in which private citizens joined together to augment official police protection. California had forty-three vigilante movements. Nor were the vigilante organizations always filled with irresponsible and flighty lightweights: sometimes U.S. Senators and Congressmen, prominent judges, highly respected businessmen, governors, and churchmen belonged. When he was a young man, Leland Stanford, later Governor of California, was a member of the important San Francisco vigilante movement of 1856. Granville Stuart, one of Montana's most distinguished citizens, was the principal leader of the 1884 vigilante movement in that state which executed thirty-five horse and cattle thieves—the grimmest reaping of any vigilante movement in our history. Though frequently abused and perverted, the vigilante movement attracted many elitists in its day, especially in the West, and of course always with the same excuse: ". . . to free themselves [as Chief Justice Hosmer of Montana put it at the time] of that vile class of adventurers which infest all unorganized communities for purposes of fraud, robbery and murder." *

Vigilantism, in short, was generally the result of a feeling of that fear which in turn is the product of a feeling of helplessness—a feeling that the orthodox channels of law enforcement are not operating, that the courts and the police are corrupt and indifferent. Just like today.

And although "citizen action" has fallen into disrepute—perhaps properly so as we entertain the hope that we are about to pass over the threshold of civility—there are episodes out of our frontier history that would make an angry, besieged urban-dweller become downright nostalgic.

On September 7, 1876, Jesse James and his gang of eight ruffians, each with a carbine strapped to his saddle and two Colts hidden under long linen dusters, swooped down on Northfield, Minnesota, to rob a bank. They came, as was their normal strategy, yelling and yahooing to frighten the folks and soften them up for the heist.

But the Minnesotans didn't soften that easily.

They didn't dive under their beds; they dove for the rifle cabinets, and every bandit who came to Northfield either stayed to be buried or left seriously wounded. And by the time the pursuing posse finished the quarrel, the outlaws were even worse off. Score: Outlaws Clell Miller, Bill Chadwell, and Charlie Pitts were shot

---

* For more on this go at once to Graham and Gunn, eds., *Violence in America: Historical and Comparative Perspectives. A Staff Report to the National Commission on the Causes and Prevention of Violence,* Vol. 1 (U.S. Government Printing Office, 1969). They really develop the vigilante theme beautifully.

dead. Cole Younger was still alive, but he had been hit eleven times, one bullet shattering his shoulder and another bullet tearing off part of his face just under the eye. Jim Younger was carrying eight buckshot slugs and a rifle slug, and one of the missiles shattered his right upper jaw. Bob Younger's right elbow was shattered by a rifle bullet. Frank James was shot in the leg and so was Jesse. This does not count the birdshot that several members of the gang had been hit by. As for the citizens' marksmanship, it was clearly not accidental: Miller and Chadwell had been shot through the heart. In fact, some Northfieldians were so incensed by the invasion that—having no guns handy—they simply threw rocks at the outlaws. This was the final insulting blow, and when the first shower of rocks fell, those outlaws who could flee did so.

To be sure, the citizens of Northfield didn't escape damage. Two were killed, two wounded. The hero, if there was any one, was Henry Wheeler, son of the town druggist and himself a nineteen-year-old medical student, who, when the firing started, grabbed a Sharps 50-70 breechloading carbine and dashed to the second floor of a home on the main street. From that roost he killed Miller, destroyed Bob Younger's arm, and scared Cole into flight by shooting his hat off. (When Wheeler became a doctor and set up practice in his hometown, he would sometimes treat favored patients by opening a special closet where the outlaw Miller's skeleton hung.)

Armed citizens did an even better job at Coffeyville, Kansas, on October 5, 1892, when the Dalton gang tried to hold up two banks simultaneously. Within twelve minutes after town folks went for their guns, Bob and Grat Dalton, Dick Broadwell, and Bill Powers were dead; Emmett Dalton was so full of lead—twelve buckshot in the back, a bullet in one arm, and another somewhere in the vicinity of his hips—that the citizens of town decided it wasn't worth their trouble to lynch him. (But he lived, and after fifteen years in prison he emerged to work his vengeance by writing a book about the Daltons which was made into a movie.) Four citizens were killed in the fight and three others seriously wounded.*

In the same era an outlaw band led by the McCartys tried to hold up the Merchant's Bank in Delta, Colorado. W. Ray Simpson, a young hardware merchant, heard the shouts, grabbed his Sharps rifle and some shells, ran into the street, shot the top of Bill McCarty's head off, shot Bill's son, Fred, through the heart, and shot the horse out from under Tom McCarty, who, however, got away and sent back word that he would return to kill Simpson. When the messenger had completed his doleful forecast, Simpson smiled and asked him to take something back to McCarty; he handed the messenger a piece of cardboard about the size of a playing card on which were ten holes. The return message for McCarty was: "Made at 225 feet." McCarty never showed up for his revenge.†

The citizens of Northfield and Coffeyville and Delta did what none of the vaunted lawmen, and no group of lawmen, had been able to do: destroy three of the major outlaw bands of their time. From these examples it might be concluded that citizens today, lacking protection from police agencies and in fact endangered by existing police procedures, should arm themselves and stand ready to enforce whatever portions of the law most closely touch their personal lives. The spirit of vigilantism is spreading. In a two-month period in 1967 Detroit merchants shot nine armed robbers (six dead, three wounded; all had previous criminal records). Seeing that they could accomplish more than the cops, the city's small businessmen set up a target practice club. Of the two hundred who showed up, 70 percent had been held up at least once during the year, 40 percent of these two or more times. Vigilantism operating under the euphemism of "citizens protective organizations" now exist in Houston, in Queens, in Chicago, in New Haven,

---

* For more on such escapades as these at Northfield and Coffeyville, see Paul I. Wellman, *Dynasty of Western Outlaws* (Doubleday, 1961).
† James D. Horan, *Desperate Men: Revelations from the Sealed Pinkerton Files* (Putnam's, 1949).

in Portland, in San Jose—and new ones crop up every month. Occasionally in recent years there has been a candid racial tinge, as when the Deacons for Defense organized in several Louisiana towns to protect their communities from white nightriders. In Warren, Michigan, Fight Back was organized as an anti-Negro protective organization. But after we push back the last beer can and stop daydreaming, it's clear enough that vigilantism is a romantic and unsatisfactory answer. The criminals who afflict a city like New York do not ride into town on horses, yelling to alert the citizenry, as the bandits of the past rode into Northfield. And it somehow seems a bit farfetched to imagine the executives of Chase Manhattan and Saks and Bloomingdale's rushing into the streets with their carbines, ready to respond to the moment's peril.

Still, it seems no more flightfully imaginative than to expect protection from an unwilling and corrupt police.

PROTECT US FROM OUR PROTECTORS

Cops, in fact, are fundamental to the gun-control problem. They confuse the issue terribly. The theory of law enforcement gets all messed up with law enforcement in practice, with the result that every reasonable gun-control bill would be, if passed, an unreasonable bill in effect. Virtually every "radical" gun-control advocate in or out of Congress has proposed taking guns away from everyone but the police. In theory that's a good idea: if constables and police and state troopers and National Guardsmen were intelligent and coolheaded and honest and humane, then perhaps the general citizenry might with an easy mind lay down its arms and leave the peace of the community in the hands of its gendarmes.

But in fact these official gunmen are just the opposite of all that. Consequently, it is much more reasonable to suggest that in any gun-control movement, the police should be the *first* required to lay down their arms. When they were bucking for a pay raise in 1972, Chicago cops suggested they be paid $1 a day just for carrying a gun; better they and police everywhere be paid $10 a day to stop carrying their weapons. At least that's my suggestion, and I have reasons for it. But before sketching them out, let me admit that I have a Shanty Irish loathing for the men in blue and my reasoning tends to be somewhat warped as a result. My bumpersticker reads: "DEPORT YOUR LOCAL POLICE." However, that confession made, I still think there are Five Splendid Reasons for disarming the police before we disarm ourselves.

Splendid Reason 1: Cops are morally inferior to the rest of the community.

Look back as far as you please in American history and the story is always the same: sleazy characters running up an unbroken record of misconduct under the guise of enforcing the law. Chip through the crust of legend and the traditional rot is revealed. Wyatt Earp and Bat Masterson supposedly "cleaned up" Dodge City. Actually, when they were on the Dodge City payroll as peace officers, they spent most of their time augmenting their income as card sharks and procurers, to such an extent in fact that the Texas cowboys who ended their trail drives at that town nicknamed our two great lawmen "The Fighting Pimps." After Earp moved on to be a lawman (and again a part-time gambler, of course) at Tombstone, a stagecoach passing through the territory was robbed of $80,000; the driver and one passenger were murdered. Doc Holliday and Earp were rumored to be behind the holdup, and the gunfight at the O.K. Corral was allegedly nothing but a slaughter to quiet those who could have made a case against Earp and Holliday.

Only gossip and rumor, of course, but it fitted in with their known deportment.

Most of the famous "lawmen" of the Old West had knocked about on the wrong side of the law at one time or another, and most of the famous outlaws had at some time served as lawmen. Three members of the Dalton brothers' gang—Bob, Grat, and Emmett—served as U.S. Deputy Marshals before turning outlaw. (Another brother, Bill, prepared for outlawry by serving in the California legislature for a spell.) Between ventures into bank robbery and highwaymanship, Jim Younger earned pin money as a deputy sheriff in Dallas. John T. Morris, the Collin County, Texas, deputy sheriff who shot and killed Jim Reed (a member of the James and Younger gangs) from behind, had once been Reed's partner in stealing livestock and robbing stagecoaches.

Ed Reed, Belle Starr's bastard son (by outlaw-lawman Jim Reed), became a bootlegger at fourteen, a horse thief at fifteen, the murderer of his mother at eighteen, and a convict (for horse stealing) at the age of twenty. That's how Old West lawmen were often made. He became a Deputy Marshal of Fort Smith at the age of twenty-three, almost before he had lost his prison pallor. One of his achievements as Deputy Marshal was to shoot to death two former Deputy Marshals who had committed the heinous crime of getting drunk. At the age of twenty-four, Reed was shot and killed in a tavern brawl.

Robert Ford, Jesse James's assassin, was killed by Ed O'Kelley in Creede, Colorado. O'Kelley was a former police officer who had turned outlaw. A fellow by the name of Beckham, who rode with the outlaw Bill Doolin, had been a deputy sheriff in Texas before going bad. Bill Cook, who was such a success at holding up trains at night that the Fort Smith-Coffeyville line operated only during daylight hours, had been a faithful law enforcement posseman before his brother persuaded him to turn outlaw and organize his own band.

The notorious gunfighter Ben Thompson got his job as

marshal of Austin, Texas, after serving at least one penitentiary sentence; his pre-lawman history included fifteen indictments for murder. Although many frontier lawmen richly deserved hanging, few got it. One of the exceptions was Henry Plummer, sheriff of the Bannack mining district in Montana, who was removed from office via a lynching. At a previous law enforcement job he was convicted of murder, but pardoned. But Montana vigilantes decided they had had enough of Mr. Plummer when he was caught leading a band of road agents. In April 1884 Hendry Brown, marshal of Caldwell, Kansas, and his deputy rode over to Medicine Lodge to augment their income by robbing a bank. Brown was shot and killed; his deputy was hanged. But most of the considerable number of marshals and sheriffs who were caught in cahoots with criminals or operating rackets of their own (usually swindling and extortion) were simply dismissed from office.*

For whatever the satisfaction that can be gained from it, we can at least see that our contemporary police are following a colorful tradition. As *The New York Times*, August 29, 1971, has noted,

> The history of the New York Police Department can be read as one long story of corruption. Every 20 years or so, there is a new scandal, followed by a brief flurry of reform, followed by the long gradual slide back into what seems to be the Department's normal state of discreet but all-pervasive corruption. . . .

All-pervasive corruption. If that's the correct phrase, it simply means that New York City has not only issued free guns to its largest organized group of crooks but actually requires them to carry the guns at all times, even when off duty. Judged by headlines around the country—"Five Crime Bureau Policemen Arrested as Grafters," "Says Chief Stole 5 Times," "24 Police Indicted in Bribery Case"—the New York force seems to be no worse than average.

---

* For more on the cross-pollination of law and outlaw see Bibliography under Frantz, Horan, Lyon, O'Connor, Prassel, and Wellman.

A couple of years ago the Justice Department linked the Columbus, Ohio, vice squad to organized crime. Camden, New Jersey, police were charged with the use of narcotics and committing "natural and unnatural" sex crimes. The National Crime Commission found that one-third of the police in Washington drank or slept on the job, 20 percent broke the law, 13 percent took money from businessmen, 1 percent were into actual shakedown rackets. In Boston 26 percent broke the law and 5.5 percent were in shakedown; 30 percent of Chicago police broke the law and 4.5 percent had a shakedown racket. A followup study by Dr. Albert J. Reiss, a Yale University sociologist, pinpointed serious and pervasive corruption—everything from taking bribes from gamblers to peddling heroin to hustling for whores—in twenty-three states and the District. Reiss came away feeling that he had just uncovered the surface and that "there is extensive corruption in almost every major and many medium-sized police departments in the United States. Few of the cop-crooks, of course, are ever put in prison." Most live off their vice very well, as did the Florida sheriff—himself suspected of several murders—who bought a $50,000 home and a three-hundred-acre citrus orchard and valuable livestock on a salary that was $7,500 for quite a while and never got above $16,000.

And those who get caught often have a way of turning it to their profit. Recently in Washington, D.C., a police officer who had been implicated in a variety of criminal activities cooperated with his superiors in gathering evidence on a dozen of his brother officers who also had turned crooked; in return, the charges against him were dropped and he was allowed to retire at $7,500 a year. Now forty-two years old, if he lives twenty years, he will in effect have been paid $150,000 by the District of Columbia for having been faithful to neither the taxpayers nor his fellow criminals.

Police are extremely adept at "losing" heroin seized as evidence; some cynics believe that the sale of "lost" heroin has become one of the biggest income sources for big-city police. The New York Police Department has lost $50 million worth of drugs in recent years. Early in January 1973 the Baltimore cops, enmeshed in the worst gambling scandal in their history, announced that they had "misplaced or miscounted" about twelve hundred glassine bags of heroin (worth about $100,000) that they were supposed to be keeping locked up as evidence against pushers. Cops are also expert at helping the underground gun merchants. One of the biggest caches of illegal machine guns uncovered on the West Coast—fifty machine guns and fifty thousand rounds of ammunition—was traced to a Los Angeles reserve police officer. Police in Chicago and Kansas City were heavily involved in the illegal gun transactions of Maj. Gen. Carl C. Turner (U.S. Army, Ret.).

If the general public does not know more than a shadow of the substance of police crime and "if the struggle against the corrupt cop is less effective than it should be," says Robert Daley, former Deputy Commissioner of the New York Police Department, "there is one principal reason: Cops who are honest themselves refuse to turn in brother cops whom they know to be corrupt." The police may call that loyalty; non-police might call it collusion.

Splendid Reason 2: Cops are unnaturally fond of, one might even say queer about, guns.

"My basic training is in psychology and criminology. After seventeen years with the [Juvenile Delinquency] subcommittee, I have concluded that a great number of police officers enjoy the Wild West aspect of being a cop," says Carl Perian, and it's a conclusion only too easy to believe. "We went to the Watts riots, right in the middle of it. The cops had bushel baskets full of guns they had taken off rioters and looters. The precinct captain was very upset because we were investigating the guns. He said just because people rioted was no reason to prevent them from owning guns."

There is abundant evidence that whatever lip service police officials give to the theory of gun controls, they and especially the rank-and-file lawmen would prefer to go on living according to these simple rules of the game: the cops will support the public's freedom to arm to the teeth, and in return the public will allow the cops to buy all those armored tanks and riot guns and bulletproof paraphernalia that they have been playing with for the last four or five years. Of course, sometimes this reaches ridiculous levels, but the police seem totally incapable of seeing the hilarity of it. For example, when the U.S. Capitol chief of police (that is, the guy whose force supposedly protects the Capitol building and grounds, independent of the Washington police) appeared before a House Appropriations subcommittee in 1973 to ask for money, he portrayed his domain as being a crossroads for the underworld of the East Coast; hoodlums of every size and talent were, he suggested, likely to be found lurking in the bushes of the Capitol grounds. Asked for specifics, he admitted that in the previous year his thousand-man force had made only eight felony arrests—that's roughly one felony arrest every twelve months per hundred and ten cops. But he insisted he needed more guns, more cars, more electronic surveillance, and even a computer keyboard to keep him tied in with the FBI. That's the way the cops-and-robbers game is played in real life.

To keep it going, they must pretend that they are under constant siege, in a shootout on the hour every hour. They complain how dangerous their work is, but statistics don't support them. Either criminals are getting softer or the cops are better at ducking dangerous confrontations. In 1930 there were 5.4 policemen killed for every ten thousand members of the New York force; in 1970 only 1.9 policemen were killed per ten thousand.

Joseph Coates, a former consultant to President Johnson's Crime Commission, insists that the violent-death rate for policemen is lower than in many other occupations, including construction work, "yet police killings are nationwide news. It creates a self-reassuring image of the thin blue line stanching the tide of crime." This fabricated image is the product, he believes, of a "propaganda machine—not a conscious propaganda machine, but one nonetheless."

The headlining of crime has given police the excuse to demand wickeder firepower. One assault on a New York City police car by thugs using an automatic rifle brought immediate demands from the Patrolmen's Benevolent Association that cops be allowed routinely to carry shotguns and automatic rifles along with their .38 pistols, and that their squad cars be made bulletproof. Without official approval—in fact, against regulations—many New York cops began carrying extra sidearms; and with official approval, 750 squad cars were equipped with shotguns in 1973.

Nationwide, cops have been getting an itch to use something that doesn't just stop a suspect but splatters him all over the street. Part of their answer is the dumdum bullet—favorite of nine hundred police departments today, according to the International Association of Chiefs of Police—the flatnose or hollow-point lead bullet that spreads radically when it hits the body, driving a wide channel, pushing so much flesh ahead of it that the bullet's passage often becomes obstructed by a dam of flesh, and it stays within the body rather than passing cleanly through. The pancaking lead tends to shatter too, and fly off inside the body in many pieces. Quite messy; so much so, in fact, that most major nations agreed early in this century that they would not let their armies use expanding bullets because they were "calculated to cause unnecessary suffering." Whether the bullet stays intact or shatters, the size of the wound and the massive hemorrhaging make death rather likely. Can you count on that being the death of the suspect? Not if you know anything about police marksmanship, you can't, and as one of the more candid members of the Washington police force, Det. Sgt. George R. Wilson, a ballistics expert, put it, "There's always somebody behind him [that is, behind the target suspect, whom the cop has more than likely missed], some old lady crossing the street with her kid." The dumdum has been catching on with cops since Super Vel Co. of Shelbyville, Indiana, began pushing their flatnose and hollow-point high-velocity bullets (about 1,200 feet a second); the big outfits like Winchester and Remington, are now in the competition with their own cop-special dumdums.*

The turn to dumdums is a piece of police nostalgia. As a group they regret the loss of the kind of thundering mankilling firepower they had back in the good old days when many law enforcement agencies used .45s. The U.S. Border Patrol carried the M-1917 .45 revolvers and had all sorts of fun playing Wyatt Earp until in the 1930s a bureaucrat with rare intelligence decided the .38s were ample for hunting wetbacks. Even the Royal Canadian Mounted Police finally turned in their 455 New Service revolvers for the much daintier .38s. It is said that the Army learned in the Philippine Campaign of 1899–1901 that .38s were much too lightweight to count on as mankillers, so they returned permanently to the .45. Cops, most of whom feel that a United States fugitive is the same as a Philippine Moro, would like to move back to the big missiles too. Until the .45 or a heavy Magnum becomes officially permissible, they will try to persuade citizens to let them use the mushroom bullet in their .38s.†

Occasionally a situation arises where the cops can really use their dumdum bullets on a wholesale basis without any personal

---

* The Washington *Post*, October 8, 1972. Some more of Philip McCombs's consistently fine reporting on guns and ammunition.

† One of the more fascinating old-time arguments used by police of the past to equip themselves with heavier arms is told by David F. Musto in *The American Disease* (Yale University Press, 1973), a book about narcotics control. It seems there was a time when Southern sheriffs were convinced that cocaine not only improved the pistol marksmanship of Negroes but made them immune to damage from anything as lightweight as .32-caliber bullets. Consequently, says Musto, many lawmen who had previously carried .32 pistols moved up to the .38-caliber weapons.

If there seems to be a tinge of black magic in such thinking, perhaps that isn't unusual. Firearms have a way of lighting the brain with swampfire. It is said that in her fading years the widow of Henry Winchester, creator of the famous rifle, was consumed with the fantasy that the only way she could both stay alive and escape the crushing weight of guilt inherited from the numerous deaths attributable to her husband's rifle was to keep building onto her home in San Jose. Spend, spend, spend those Winchester rifle royalties to build, build, build: this was her mission, but at the same time it made no difference *what* was built, so she kept carpenters hammering away around the clock to produce such additions as doors opening onto walls and stairs leading nowhere.

risk at all. The Attica prison riots were just such an occasion. What a setup: there they were, 1,238 beautiful targets trapped in the prison yard—1,200 inmates and thirty-eight hostage guards. None of the prisoners had guns. So the state police took their positions safely atop the prison wall, dropped tear gas into the yard to make their targets even more helpless, and then let fly. An estimated twenty-two hundred bullets and shotgun pellets were poured into the prisoners. According to the Official Report of the New York State Special Commission on Attica, each trooper on top of the wall who was equipped with a .270-caliber rifle that day was firing bullets sold under the tradename Silvertips, which the manufacturer advertises as having a special alloy jacket that prevents "premature expansion while the bullet penetrates through thick hide and tissue in deep and vital areas. Silvertip mushrooms perfectly and releases tremendous energy that stops them cold." Twenty-nine prisoners and ten hostages were stopped cold—dead cold. One guard hostage was hit in the abdomen by a Silvertip, which ripped out a generous portion of his lower intestine and then splintered into so many pieces that, though he lived, he is thought still to be carrying about thirty shreds of lead somewhere in the bottom portion of his trunk; the surgeons gave up after removing about thirty other pieces. The cops armed with shotguns were having their own kind of fun: loaded with buckshot and fired from a distance of forty to fifty yards, each shotgun delivered a spray of deadly pellets over an area whose diameter was more than four feet. Just a bit indiscriminate. All in all, it was a great day for the state troopers, and to top it off, not one inmate wounded by gunfire was treated for four hours after the shooting stopped.

As all good Thugs will chant for you in melodious Hindi, "Kill for the love of killing!" Early in 1972 two residents of New Mexico, both Chicanos, one a well-known investigative reporter, were scheduled to appear on television to tell what they knew about police brutality and police corruption; it was said they had some scorching evidence. But they didn't make it. Shortly after midnight of the morning they were to make their exposé, the two young men were killed on top of a deserted mesa ten miles south of Albuquerque by six state and city police—who used the two men for target practice after ambushing them. To do the job right, the police had brought along not only their official weapons but also personal firearms, including sawed-off 12-gauge shotguns loaded with 00 shot, an M-1 carbine, a .243-caliber deer-hunting rifle, and an Armlaite .223-caliber AR-180 semiautomatic. The cops explained that they had caught the men acting suspiciously.

During the great Detroit and Newark riots of 1967 police excused their intemperate marksmanship by claiming that they were besieged by snipers. In retrospect it seems clear that they were exaggerating the situation so that they could "shoot niggers." In the two cities nearly nine thousand persons were arrested but not one was convicted of sniping and only two were convicted of anything relating to gun misuse—a Detroit resident was convicted of failure to register a pistol (then a misdemeanor) and a Newark resident was convicted of manslaughter by gun.

Perian was in Detroit to observe for the Juvenile Delinquency Subcommittee. He went along when the cops drove a black man—they identified him as "the last sniper"—to the station. On the way the cops were beating up the black to make him confess, and ultimately the beating got so nasty that Perian interrupted to suggest that the officers might find it just as convenient and more accurate to give the man a paraffin test to see if he had recently fired a gun. They replied, not missing a beat, "We'd rather do it our way."

In both cities the cops and National Guardsmen turned out to be the real nuts. Thirty-five Detroit civilians died of gunshot wounds but only three lawmen were gun victims and they may have been killed by other lawmen. The best summation of what happened was made by a Detroit newspaper editor:

> In our leads and headlines we used phrases like "sniper kings" and "nests of snipers," which were the wrong phrases to use and were bad mistakes. We found out when we were able

to get our people into those areas and get them out from under the cars that these sniper kings and these nests of snipers were the constituted authorities shooting at each other, most of them. There was just one confirmed sniper in the entire eight-day riot and he was drunk and he had a pistol and he was firing from a window.

In Newark, where twenty-three civilians died (all but two black), official gunmen were having an equally rousing time. Newark Police Director Dominick A. Spina admitted, "A lot of the reports of snipers was due to the—I hate to use the word—trigger-happy Guardsmen, who were firing at noises and firing indiscriminately sometimes. . . . Down in the Springfield Avenue area it was so bad that, in my opinion, Guardsmen were firing upon police and police were firing back at them."

While only 152 incidents of gunfire were documented as coming from rioters (according to the Stanford Research Institute), National Guardsmen got off 10,414 assorted rounds; state troopers fired 350 rounds of .38-caliber, 1,168 rounds of .45-caliber, 198 rounds of 00 buckshot, 1,187 rounds of .30-caliber, and 2 rounds of No. 9 birdshot.

In any gun engagement where police participate and there are several police casualties, it's safe to assume that at least some of the casualties are the result of cops shooting cops. When Mark Essex holed up in the Howard Johnson Motel in New Orleans in January 1973 and engaged in a sniper's duel with police, a number of officers were hit. Four months after the event New Orleans Superintendent of Police Clarence Giarruso admitted that Essex's marksmanship wasn't quite as accurate as his department had at first made out. "We wounded six of our own men," he told the House Crime Committee. "I'm confident they were bullets from the police helicopter."

Splendid Reason 3: Cops generally range from mentally odd to mentally unbalanced.

If, in the preceding examples of passion for armaments and

haste to execute, you seem to detect a low mentality or even just a touch of insanity, don't apologize. The vast majority of the 40,000 law enforcement bodies in this country do not subject their personnel to a rigorous screening or mental examination. In New York City, which does give its cops intelligence tests, it was discovered in 1969 that the average IQ of the 2,075 incoming officers was 98.20, with one class of 358 men averaging 93.19. That, to put it politely, is "dull normal." As for screening, New York admitted the previous year that it had sent 2,000 armed police recruits onto the streets without knowing anything for certain about their backgrounds; subsequent cursory checkups on the first 1,000 disclosed one policeman with a history of mental instability and another with a serious crime record. The effects of hasty recruitment don't often seem to bother police officials. Early in 1973 New York Police Commissioner Murphy said he wanted the Police Academy to "crank out"—hardly the word to convey high selectivism—as many new cops as it could. However, Murphy's successor in the Commissioner's post, Donald F. Cawley, a couple of months later indicated—after an especially heavy outbreak of nutty violence in the ranks—that maybe an awareness of the problem might finally be dawning on the police bureaucracy; nervously he called newsmen together and acknowledged that the New York Police Department's procedure for weeding out the psychological misfits was "clearly inadequate" and that he had set up a panel to hurriedly sift through the personnel records of the 30,000 cops to see if they couldn't identify those who had chronically shown an unnatural yen to act violent.

Police, for that matter, probably have no higher a percentage of mental cases in their ranks than does the general population—but that is indeed a frightening percentage, when one considers that the former are not only supplied arms but ordered to wear them on and off duty. The potential to the community is sufficiently clear that Harold C. Schmeck, Jr., led off his story in *The New York Times* about mysterious violence with this case:

> He was a policeman in Boston, well-liked in his community and known as a good husband and father. One night at home

he handed his wife his gun and told her to lock it up. He felt that his self-control was washing away in a surge of unreasoning rage that he could not explain and might not be able to control. He was afraid that he might shoot someone.

Then he went to his bedroom, handcuffed himself to the bed and stayed there until the rage had burned itself out. The experience was terrifying. It was followed, at intervals, by others just as bad. Then, one day, the same feeling began to sweep over him again while he was riding in a police car with two other officers. He told them what was happening and begged them to lock him in the back and take him home. They took him to a hospital instead.*

Most, of course, don't have enough sense to know they're nuts. In 1968 Ralph P. Destafano was charged with threatening the life of President Johnson, but the charge was dismissed when he was admitted to a New Jersey state mental hospital. In 1972 Destafano was arrested in Savannah, Georgia, after threatening to kill President Nixon. He was carrying a .32 pistol and forty-one rounds of ammunition. What was Destafano doing some of the time between his first threat in 1968 and his second threat in 1972? He was working as a security guard in Atlantic City. On June 21, 1972, an off-duty Pinkerton guard—who had grown up in a bad environment, being the son of one cop and the brother of another—walked into a Cherry Hill, New Jersey, employment agency carrying two .22 sawed-off rifles. Seventy bullets later, six men were dead and six others critically wounded. With his last shot, Destafano plugged himself in the head. One of his Pinkerton superiors said the guy had for some time been acting "kook-a-boo"—a radical understatement; actually he had been going around saying, "Those Jews in New York have got an electronic device wired in my head and are running me"—but other superiors thought he was a first-class guard, which gives you some idea about the others.

It's pretty scary to think how many of these armed Rent-a-Cop

---

* *The New York Times*, December 27, 1970.

cops there are roaming loose in the country. A Rand Corporation study in 1972 showed that about half the 800,000 security personnel in the United States are private cops and that their mongrel ranks are growing at the rate of about 10 to 15 percent each year. There are 40,000 private cops in New York City compared to 30,000 on the public payroll, and in Washington, D.C., it's about 50-50.

At a less dramatic, but no less troublesome, level of mental instability, there is the apparently wide affliction of paranoia and incapacitating melancholia. New York's former Deputy Police Commissioner, Robert Daley, a keen observer of the ranks, says that "cops feel alienated from the rest of society." They feel odd, cut off, singled out, abused, misunderstood. "On duty they mix only with one another, and some of them mix only with one another off duty as well." They've got troubles. Probably the execution of an unarmed suspect helps relieve the tension.

Splendid Reason 4: Cops are too quick on the trigger.

This may be just another way of saying they're crazy; as for the practical consequences, it doesn't much matter whether the cops behind the guns have lost their marbles or are just trigger-happy or mean. You can't beat New Mexico for examples. A couple of years ago New Mexico cops arrested a twenty-two-year-old man for living with a young woman out of wedlock; when they got to jail, the young man broke away and ran up the street. Now, obviously anyone charged with "lewd cohabitation" is a dangerous felon who must be stopped at all costs, so a cop got off what he later described as a "warning shot" that hit the fugitive in the back of the head and removed a sufficient amount of his brain to end the case. A couple of months later a nineteen-year-old boy broke away from an arresting officer in Santa Fe and he too was brought down by a "warning shot" in the head.

An armed guard—one of those "special officers" the country is crawling with—at the Buffalo, New York, municipal golf course shot and killed a golfer in the spring of 1972 because he didn't have his playing permit with him. (The guard had been arrested for assault and illegal impersonation before he was hired by the city as a special cop.) In Washington, D.C., that summer cops planted an unlocked bicycle to lure thieves; a sixteen-year-old boy took the bait, jumped on the bike, and rode off. A waiting cop dashed out of a nearby store, got within three feet of the boy, drew his gun, and shot him dead. Police said it was "a mistake." For professionals who are supposed to know how to handle guns, cops certainly kill a lot of people by mistake. In the District of Columbia a store security guard shot a ten-year-old girl. A policeman who had been unsuccessfully harassing a young man for a year finally cornered his pigeon in an alley and, while frisking him, "accidentally" shot him in the chest and killed him. Another policeman, later fined for a series of sex and violence episodes, stopped a motorist and "accidentally" shot him in the chest with a shotgun, with the usual results. These "accidents" all happened in just one city in one year. The same thing is happening all over.

Back to New York. Sergio and Thomas Lugo, brothers, left the Dominican Republic and went to New York in 1963, got jobs in factories, and saved enough finally to make their dream come true—opening their own grocery store in a Spanish ghetto in 1970. A few months later they were visited by two armed burglars who made off with $600. But the Lugos hadn't worked so long to see themselves wiped out like that, so they gave chase, Thomas armed only with a hammer but Sergio armed with a .38 pistol. Sergio fired a couple of times at the fleeing bandits. In a nearby tavern sat a New York cop, off duty and out of uniform but, as regulations demand, armed. He heard the shooting, rushed outside, concluded on no evidence at all that the Lugos were in the wrong, and shot and killed them both.

Three times within one year NYPD plainclothesman Thomas Shea demonstrated how close and affectionate a relationship a cop can have with his gun. On March 19, 1972, he and two other off-duty police officers interrupted their evening in a West Side bar to (according to the police department's own records) assault and shoot at neighborhood youths. Two weeks later, on April 3, 1972, to be exact, officer Thomas Shea used his gun to shoot a robbery suspect (charges against whom were later dismissed) in the neck; Shea said the guy had shot at him first but, oddly, no gun could be found. Shea managed to stay cool for a year, but then on April 28, 1973, plainclothesman Shea shot and killed a ten-year-old boy who was accompanying his stepfather to work; Shea, supported by the testimony of another cop, said that when he had tried to question the boy and his father about a taxi holdup, the boy pulled a gun. No gun was found.

On March 5, 1973, Samuel Wright, a black policeman who was off duty and out of uniform, was chasing a robbery suspect along one of Harlem's thoroughfares when two white cops, appraising the scene with their usual judiciousness, decided that any black man with a gun in his hands must be the right man to shoot, so they shot and killed Officer Wright. Black plainclothesman William F. Capers had been killed by white officers, apparently for the same reason, in April 1972.

That sort of thing happens a little too often to help race relations. In the last six weeks of 1972 Dallas cops shot six black men, killing four; in three of the shootings, including one fatal shooting, the black men were not armed. The usually conservative Negro establishment in Dallas thereupon allied itself with black militants; and relations between the races were the stickiest they had been in a decade.

In Detroit police and blacks have settled down to a permanent war status. One veteran member of that police force was involved in eight fatal shootings (in six of which he was the triggerman) of black suspects, usually unarmed or armed only with a knife, over a twenty-two-month period before his superiors slowed him down in March 1973 with a second-degree murder charge.

When Detroit police aren't shooting unarmed blacks, they are having great fun barging in on them. Cops early in 1973 raided one apartment (by mistake, they said) and chased five women, two of them dressed only in nighties, into the street. It was ten-degree weather and snowy. Later blaming a false tip, Detroit police smashed through the door of Rev. Leroy Cannon's home at four in the morning; one of the official intruders held a gun against the preacher's head and declared, "Nigger, if you breathe loud, I'm going to kill you." In another raid, without a warrant and attired in plainclothes, cops broke into the apartment of a black security guard and killed him. Apparently they had made another mistake.

But illegal raids by the cops do not occur only in Detroit, of course. In Winthrop, Massachusetts, state police, federal narcotics agents, and officers from local police departments broke down the front and back doors of the home of Mr. and Mrs. William Pine and rushed in with drawn guns; for fifteen minutes they held the Pines and their daughter at gunpoint, pushing them, shouting at them, demanding to know where the "heroin factory" was—and then the officers discovered that their warrant was for the residence next door.

In Milwaukee police have also broken into homes to terrorize families. Hunting for the man who had shot one of their buddies, cops dragged a disabled World War II veteran out of a telephone booth, kicked and beat him while shouting, "Nigger, what did you do with the gun? You're a cop-killer!" They kept him in jail overnight and released him the next day, saying they had made a mistake.

Hunting for reporter Tom Oliphant of the Boston *Globe*, whose news stories had offended the Nixon Administration, FBI agents broke into his former home near Boston (Oliphant had moved to Washington, but you can't expect the FBI to run down a tough clue like that) in the middle of the night and were giving the new occupants, still in bed, a bad time before they discovered their mistake.

In Portsmouth, New Hampshire, members of the police narcotics squad splintered the front door of Mrs. Anna Majette's apartment and came in waving guns and making threats. With a literacy problem common to cops, the Portsmouth narcs had thought the warrant said "Apartment A" when it really said "Apartment J."

The most notorious examples—not because they were much different from any of the above but because for some reason they touched the national nerve at just the right time—occurred in April 1973 in Collinsville, Illinois, when a couple dozen federal, state, and local narcotics agents and cops ripped apart two private homes. The raiders came brandishing shotguns and pistols. They caught the Herbert Giglottos in bed asleep. They handcuffed Giglotto's hands behind his back, held a cocked gun at his head ("You move, you sonofabitch, you're dead"), called his wife a "whore" and threatened to kill her; they tore the furniture apart, ripped clothing, smashed a camera and art objects. Then they discovered they were in the wrong house and departed with all the finesse that they had shown on their entry. Meanwhile, across town, brother cops and narcs were at work at the home of Donald Askew, where the Askews had just sat down to dinner. This band of officers were dressed as hippies; they did not identify themselves but, as usual, kicked the door down and entered with pistols and shotguns ready to use on the Askews if they didn't tell where the nonexistent drugs were. Once again a house was demolished and its occupants' nerves shattered (Mrs. Askew kept fainting during the raid) before the raiders realized they had broken into the wrong house.

No warrants had been issued for the Collinsville raids, so the lawmen were, of course, operating as illegally as the drug pushers they were hunting.

Splendid Reason 5: Cops don't deserve to have guns because they usually avoid dangerous situations where guns could be justifiably used.

What we are talking about in most of the preceding episodes are abuses that cops could not and would probably not attempt to get away with if they weren't armed and ready to kill. Conversely, they are usually dealing with citizens who are not armed. That imbalance makes for heavy bullying. If suffering such indignities were the price a community had to pay for the suppression of real crime along with bullying, it might be considered a bargain (and on the other hand, it might not be). But cops in many communities have given little return for their cost. If the community frequently feels a revulsion toward police conduct, the feeling is reciprocated, which probably accounts for the cops' general indifference to the safety of others, although hypersensitive to their own safety. "When a cop is killed," says Daley, "everything else stops until his murderer is caught. . . . If another cop is in trouble, everyone who is reasonably close speeds to the scene. During a recent four-month period sixty-one policemen were hurt, some seriously, in car collisions while racing to respond to a signal ten-thirteen [cop in distress]." Compare that enthusiasm for danger, for example, with police reluctance to climb the Texas University tower from which Charles Whitman was harvesting a baker's dozen of non-cops. More than a hundred Austin police, plus some thirty highway patrolmen, plus Texas Rangers and Secret Service agents (from Lyndon Johnson's Austin office) went to the campus, but for more than an hour and a half they refused to charge Whitman's position: after all, he was only knocking off people, and as Daley tells us, "cops feel alienated from the rest of society." Sullen and withdrawn, they seem to have little or no desire to uncover organized crime or to swap bullets with badmen.

They much prefer spending their time arresting winos and pinching prostitutes. In 1970 there were 113,400 arrests nationally for vagrancy and 1,825,500 arrests for public intoxication (*not* drunk driving and *not* drunk-and-disorderly—which would be arrests accompanied by some risk to the law enforcement officer— but just plain drunk), while cutthroats and footpads and narcotics dealers went about their business undisturbed by the boys in blue. "Victimless" crimes are so much safer to investigate.

It's been endemic for several generations. Of the arrests in Denver in 1873—an era in which Denver was not exactly a pantywaist town—80 percent were for either ordinary drunkenness or prostitution.

On the other hand, maybe this is interpreting those statistics the wrong way after succumbing to the cops' own propaganda line, in which the world of our time as well as the world of the Old West are portrayed as cruel and violent places, a portrayal that of course tends to augment both the policeman's salary and his reputation for bravery.

Frank Richard Prassel, something of an expert in this field, writes in *The Western Peace Officer*:

> In the main, the crimes of the Old West comprised primarily the same violations most common in modern America—drunkenness, disorderly conduct, and petty larceny. Most citizens lived peacefully and without great fear of personal attack. The cowboys' pistol, when worn, proved far more useful against snakes than rustlers. In many communities people rarely felt the need to put locks on their doors, while local saloons and gambling parlors made a sincere effort to exclude women and minors.*

But what about all those wild and woolly shootouts in the violent cowtowns? What about the showdown in the middle of the rutted main street between The Great Marshal and the black-clad, black-gloved baddy? Good questions—and one of the best answers, supplied by Prassel, is that from 1870 to 1885 (this fifteen-year stretch includes the glorious careers of Earp and Masterson and Hickok) the reputedly vice-and-violence-ridden towns of Abilene, Caldwell, Dodge City, Ellsworth, and Wichita experienced a combined total of only forty-five homicides, and of these only sixteen occurred as the result of law enforcement. That's an average of only *three* killings annually or, on a pro-rata basis, roughly one-half death per town.† No wonder our great lawmen

---

* (University of Oklahoma Press, 1972), p. 22.
† An auxiliary question would be: What about all those gun-toting cowboys? The Western historian-cowboy Homer Ayers answers that "Cowboys were really quite peaceful. Some owned six-shooters which they kept in their beds.

felt they could afford to spend most of their time whoring and gambling.

It's impossible to escape one of two conclusions: either the police of this country have always ducked the really serious crime, from New York City to Tombstone, or they have shamefully overexaggerated the amount of crime. Either they have been too blind and lazy and cowardly to give their attention to much besides alcoholism and prostitution, or such mildly antisocial behavior has been by far the preponderance of our "crime" in every era.

Whichever is the case, it adds up to our society's simply not needing the dangerous hired guns of the police departments as they now function. Regrettably, Americans have not had the same attitude toward their police as is found among the English, who, among other things, do not allow their police to carry arms except in very rare instances. As I. F. Reichert pointed out in an essay in the Washington *Post*, "The English have been vehement in reasserting a principle too often forgotten in America: The police exist solely to serve a citizenry that must determine for itself not only how it should be protected but, even more important, what it most needs protection from." * For the most part citizens everywhere police themselves by their own sense of morality. And when their personal morality and the community's intrinsic integrity do not together offer enough protection, perhaps the citizen will simply have to arm, to protect himself from his protector, if nothing else.

But a six-shooter was an unhandy thing to have hung on your body, pounding your leg all the time. If it was kept in a bed, it got rusty unless it was covered with gun oil, in which case the oil got on the bedding. Nobody I knew ever saw a two-gun man. That was for books and later for the movies. Cowboy Jim Davies had a pearl-handled single-action Colt .45 he seemed to love. He bragged about his six-full. Of course, guns did have their disadvantages: firing a pistol close to a horse's head could make it deaf; and once, in his excitement at trying to bag a big gray wolf on the dead run one morning, Flying V cowboy Bob Packer accidentally shot his mount in the head and killed it. So six-guns were rather discouraged."
* "Sticking to Their No-Guns," Washington *Post*, January 14, 1973.

SWORDS INTO PLOWSHARES, AS IT WERE

Turning from the impossibility of getting the cops to capture and the courts to properly punish gun criminals, let us now consider the equally impossible concept that we could, having come so far with them, ever get rid of our guns. One of the NRA's most infuriatingly corny bumperstickers says, "WHEN GUNS ARE OUTLAWED, ONLY OUTLAWS WILL HAVE GUNS." Unfortunately, it's probably true. Consider the size of the task. After Bermuda's governor and his aide were murdered in early 1973, Bermuda police rounded up all of the island's eight hundred registered handguns. But Bermuda's population is only fifty-three thousand; in a situation like that,

officials can cope. What hope do they have where the national
problem encompasses millions of people and millions of guns?
After all the roadblocks have been set up to confiscate dashboard
guns, after all the sidewalk stopping-and-frisking, after all the
duffel bags of returning GIs have been emptied of souvenir guns,
after all the saloons and cafés have been swept of "protective"
weaponry, after all the ghettos have been shaken down and all the
middle-class suburbs have been asked, pretty please, to turn in
their weaponry—still, there will be dozens and scores and hundreds
of pieces surfacing all over the land, like grease coming through ten
coats of paint. Who can doubt it? And most of the surviving guns,
of course, will be in mischievous hands.

Former Governor Pat Brown takes the position, increasingly
popular in officialdom,

> that handguns be made contraband, and I recognize the
> gargantuan task of trying to seize 10 million guns or making
> law violators of 10 million people that now possess guns, and
> the only answer I can give you to that question is that you
> have to begin someplace . . . I feel that we should take the
> general position that handguns should be barred except by
> police officials and other authorized people, and then try to
> find out how to seize them in the days ahead.*

Lots of luck.

Assuming that human nature is the same the world around,
why should we suppose that Americans would react any differently
to a ban on guns from the way the Filipinos reacted? When
President Ferdinand Marcos became dictator, he established
martial law and decreed that all firearms, whether registered or
unregistered, be turned in; that anyone who retained an unauthor-
ized firearm faced ten to fifteen years in prison; that anyone

* Juvenile Delinquency Subcommittee, Judiciary Committee, Senate, Hearings on S.2507, Amendment to 1968 Gun Control Act to Prohibit the Sale of
Saturday Night Special Handguns, Sept.–Nov. 1971 (U.S. Government Printing Office), p. 48.

committing a violent crime with a firearm faced the possibility of a firing squad. Very tough. Results were, by his standards, excellent: in the first seven weeks, Filipinos surrendered 450,000 firearms and violent crime dropped 80 percent. Hurrah. But officials also conceded that even in the face of terrible jail terms, Filipino citizens were withholding another 450,000—give or take a million —guns. Furthermore, they had surrendered only 1.3 million rounds of ammunition to go with the surrendered guns, about three rounds per weapon, which clearly indicated that they were holding back the key element. A homemade gun is much easier to come up with than homemade ammunition.

Collecting arms via surrender in periods of amnesty or by the government's buying up privately owned guns can work to some extent—at least psychologically it is soothing—but the recorded successes have usually been temporary and have usually been in simpler, more contained societies. During and immediately after the Spanish-American War our government set out to buy up as many of the "guerrilla" arms as possible from the citizens of Cuba, a land infested with heavily armed bandits and outlaws and homespun revolutionaries. The U.S. government first issued a proclamation forbidding the use of rifles and all other deadly weapons—an edict that was sure to be totally ignored except for the fact that somebody in the bureaucracy was smart enough to back up the order with an offer of a bounty, in gold, to anybody who would bring in firearms. So here they came by the thousands, everything from old flintlocks of the American Revolution era, to muzzleloading Remingtons of the Civil War period, to fancy new weapons. All were gathered up by our officials and dumped at sea. Historians say that the enforcement of the peace in Cuba was considerably easier to achieve for several years thereafter, but of course those Latins love guns and it was only ninety miles to the mainland's endless supply of them; so that interlude was destined to be brief.

If the effort to elicit a voluntary surrender of weapons should fail, as it most certainly would, then the government would forcibly have to recover all firearms by methods that would offend the Constitution. Stop-and-frisk would be the order of the day on every sidewalk, and every home would have to be entered and searched for weapons even though "probable cause" would be impossible to show in most cases and therefore any warrant would be bogus. We needn't pretend that this would be any radical departure from contemporary police procedures: the Constitutional rights of citizens are daily violated by the police in stop-and-frisk procedures, and our tolerance of a police-state attitude toward home privacy was amply demonstrated in 1968 when National Guardsmen, without warrants, entered and ransacked many homes inhabited by blacks in Plainfield, New Jersey, looking for firearms. Furniture was broken, clothing strewn everywhere, drawers dumped. If we can tolerate it for the blacks, we can tolerate it for the whites. But of course we won't.

The vision of Treasury agents scattering across the country to enforce a gun-seizure law is enough to make the heart fall and the hackles rise. Treasury agents have never shown any ability to handle such powers with intelligence or grace or legality. On May 12, 1934, a Negro was machine-gunned to death in St. Louis. The next month President Roosevelt signed the National Firearms Act, sometimes known as the Federal Machine Gun Act, and with that in their pocket a squad of federal gumshoes swooped down on St. Louis to clear up the machine-gun slaying of May. Apparently looking for the murder weapon, they raided the apartment of one Mrs. Desse Masterson, mother of four children, and shot and killed her, though neither she nor her husband nor anybody else in the apartment had ever been accused of the original murder or of having a machine gun or of any other federal crime. If there was a reason for that violence following so closely the passage of that 1934 Act, perhaps it can be found by turning to the most notorious "gun-control" case in recent years, which climaxed at about 8:30 P.M. on June 7, 1971, when Kenyon F. Ballew was in the bathtub and his wife was in the bedroom, dressed only in panties.

Suddenly there came a great banging and shouting and

pounding at the door of their apartment in Silver Spring, Maryland, just outside Washington. Frightened, and unable to answer the door at the moment even if they hadn't been frightened, Mr. Ballew continued to sit in the tub and Mrs. Ballew yelled repeatedly, "Who is it?"

The response to her question came in the form of an eighty-five-pound battering ram, which on the sixth ram knocked the door down; right behind came six men. The first two looked like a couple of crazies—bearded, one wearing a yellow sweatshirt and another a striped polo shirt, one wearing gray slacks and the other dungarees. Other raiders wore jackets and ties. Only one man, at the back of the group, was in uniform. All carried handguns at the ready.

Convinced that they were being attacked by either drug-crazed hippies or gangsters, Mrs. Ballew yelled for her husband to "Get a gun!" In the Ballew household it was not an empty suggestion, for Ballew collected guns and his apartment contained fourteen black-powder arms and eight cartridge arms—nine cap-and-ball replica revolvers, three flintlock replica pistols, two cap-and-ball rifles, one .22-caliber semiautomatic pistol, an M-1 carbine, two .22 rifles, a 20-gauge over-and-under shotgun, a 12-gauge double-barrel shotgun, a 12-gauge pump shotgun, and a military rifle with bayonet—most of which were loaded.

Unfortunately, Ballew reached not for one of the shotguns that—assuming they were loaded with something like 00 buckshot —would have permanently rid us of at least two or three of the mischievous trespassers. Instead, his hand went for a replica of an 1847 .44 Walker Colt black-powder cap-and-ball revolver, a replica of the famous four-pound Dragoon pistol with a nine-inch barrel that Capt. Samuel H. Walker of the Texas Rangers had helped Colt design and that was the first revolver issued by any army in the world. It was a good gun, for a replica antique, but hardly a match in Ballew's inexpert and trembling hand for the firepower that immediately overwhelmed him.

Before he could get off a shot, Ballew was hit at the top left side of the forehead, the bullet plowing through the left lobe of the brain and lodging at the back of the skull. It left him partly paralyzed and with a hospital bill large enough to be felt for the rest of his life.

As he crumpled and pitched forward, the Colt replica discharged into the wall. Fortunately he fell behind a cinder-block partition, for as he lay on the floor the intruders, standing about fifteen feet away, continued to fire at him—four more shots—and without the protection of the cinder blocks he would have been riddled.

"Murder!" Mrs. Ballew screamed, with only logic on her side. "Get the police! Police! Police!" Probably, by now, you have guessed what the reply was. "We," yelled one of the raiders, "are the police." "Then what in the hell are you shooting for?" she asked.

Instead of an answer, she was seized by the raiders, who had been joined by a swarm of other Montgomery County cops and Treasury agents, who shoved her into the hall, still dressed only in panties, while they proceeded to demolish the apartment, overturning furniture, knocking holes in the wall, smashing aquariums, pulling drawers from the dresser.

At the same time, in the same apartment house on the floor above, another weird bit of Keystone Koppery was unfolding. There another gang of cops and Treasury agents were denting in the door of an apartment where lived (or so their warrant said) a dangerous gunrunner with an arsenal of hand grenades and sawed-off shotguns. They were wrong on all counts. It was the apartment of a woman and her two daughters, one ten years old and the other a baby; and on the occasion when the cops and agents broke in, the mother was out and the girls were alone.

Aside from the fact that the Treasury agents invited county cops to come along for the sport, although the county had no jurisdiction in the matter; aside from the questionable need for violence (the U.S. Code makes it a criminal offense to execute a search warrant with unnecessary severity); aside from all the legalisms, there remained one overwhelmingly commonsense question: Why all the rush? As a Congressional critic of the occasion observed, "The normal way to get somebody to answer the door is to knock and wait. There was plenty of time. If the Ballews had had illegal hand grenades, they could not have got rid of them. You can't flush a hand grenade down the toilet like dope."

Apparently eager to make sure that everyone would be convinced that they were just as great horses' asses as they had first appeared, the authorities responded to criticism accordingly: Treasury Secretary John Connally said that his agents had conducted themselves in a manner that was "legally proper under the circumstances." He found nothing wrong with the use of the battering ram and nothing wrong with the use of plainclothes officers to conduct a raid on a private home. All Montgomery County officials said they found nothing wrong in the police procedures. U.S. District Attorney George Beall, Maryland's top federal prosecutor and brother of U.S. Senator J. Glenn Beall, said, "From our point of view, they [the raiders] did nothing extraordinary, nothing reckless, nothing culpable, nothing wrong." In fact, he added, the raid was "a letter-perfect execution of their search warrants with the exception of the unfortunate incident that occurred."

Why did the lawmen raid Ballew's apartment? Because—or so Ballew's attorney claims, and the cops have never disproved it—they had believed a seventeen-year-old boy whom they had arrested for housebreaking. Apparently in an effort to get in good with the cops, he had spun a great yarn: Ballew's apartment, he said, was full of live hand grenades. If this had been true, Ballew would have been in violation of Title 2 of the 1968 Gun Control Act. But it was not true; there were four inert, empty hand grenade casings in Ballew's apartment, all quite legal, one of which was a plastic type being used as a container for oil. Another of the casings, a heavy iron one, was used as a plaything by the couple's seven-year-old son.

If Treasury agents had run the simplest check on Ballew, they would have found he was right out of the squarest establishment's pattern book: he was a Boy Scout commissioner, a life member in good standing of the National Rifle Association, a veteran of the Army, in which he had served as a military policeman, a booster of the police force, which he had once tried to join, and a volunteer fireman.

None of those things precluded his having hand grenades in his home, of course, but the biography available to the police and the federal agents clearly showed that Ballew was a law-and-order type, a middle-America type, a he-man type—in other words, the very kind of citizen who supports his local police and, one would presume, is much admired by his local police. Even if the lawmen hadn't availed themselves of community intelligence about Ballew's life, the NRA and Boy Scout decals on his door should have given them some clue as to the kind of fellow who lived inside.

In short, if the lawmen would smash through the door and through the life of one of their own kind of people, they could hardly be expected to deal more politely with a "liberal" or "egghead" or "socialist" type. Waxing paranoid, one might wonder if indeed this were not the fear that the Treasury agents intended to arouse with their raid. Suppose the Treasury agents, who always work in collusion with the NRA, were crafty enough to *want* to make us think how awful the search-and-seizure potential of the Gun Control Act was. Suppose they were willing to victimize one of their own sort in order to impress upon all others the horror of the Act's potential as it could apply to our own homes—if, say, a gun-registration act were passed. (There is always a registration bill hanging fire in Congress.) Hadn't the NRA always warned that a registration law was the first step toward giving the bureaucrats a list by which they could come around and forceably disarm us? And didn't this Ballew raid underscore the potential of that threat a thousandfold?

Whether or not it was the result of a calculated effort, there is no doubt that the raid on the home of Kenyon Ballew had a critically depressing effect on efforts to pass any further gun-control legislation. He had become what the National Rifle Association never tired of telling its followers: "The first American citizen shot down by the enforcers of the 1968 Federal Gun Control Act." Remember the high-handed raid of 1934 mentioned earlier? The NRA used that episode in exactly the same we-told-you-so fashion. The August 1934 *American Rifleman* drew its editorial moral after recounting how a Negro had been machine-gunned to death in St. Louis the previous May, the federal Machine Gun Bill (National Firearms Act) had been signed in June, and then how Mrs. Masterson had been shot down in July by the "federal squad of snoopers" (as the NRA described the raiders): "Fortunately, there are relatively few machine guns in use around the country, so that relatively few innocent citizens may be expected to be killed by federal agents looking for machine guns. Had the original desires of the attorney general [Cummings] been carried out, however, and pistols and revolvers been included in this new federal firearms law, the Masterson incident perhaps gives a hint as to what might have happened and . . ."

Had Mrs. Masterson been set up as an object lesson on why Congress should not pass any tougher gun laws?

Following the Ballew incident, the riflemen were quickly on hand to draw another grim warning. The clear implication made by the NRA and by *Armed Citizens News* and by *Gun Week* and by all the other propaganda outlets of the gun lovers, was that this was the kind of treatment any innocent citizen might expect if further gun-control powers were given to the bureaucracy. And even granting that the gun fraternity was exploiting the episode for its own advantage, one would also have little reason not to grant the accuracy of its predictions, for the agents of the Treasury Department—while showing a strangely tolerant relationship with crooked gun dealers—in their dealings with private citizens have shown less awareness of the Constitution than any other group of law enforcement officials at any level of government, with the possible exception of Mississippi sheriffs.*

---

* I am not stubborn in this opinion, however, and readily concede that the Bureau of Narcotics and Dangerous Drugs, the Customs Bureau, the

THE WHITE FRONTLASH

The Gun Control Act of 1968 was passed not to control guns but to control blacks, and inasmuch as a majority of Congress did not want to do the former but were ashamed to show that their goal was the latter, the result was that they did neither. Indeed, this law, the first gun-control law passed by Congress in thirty years, was one of the grand jokes of our time. There are several ways to assess its character. First of all, bear in mind that it was not passed in one piece but was a combination of two laws. The original 1968 Act was passed to control *handguns* after the Rev. Martin Luther King, Jr., had been assassinated with a *rifle*. Then it was repealed and repassed to include the control of *rifles and shotguns* after the assassination of Robert F. Kennedy with a *handgun*. That's the way Congress works.

The moralists of our federal legislature as well as sentimental editorial writers insist that the Act of 1968 was a kind of memorial to King and Robert Kennedy. If so, it was certainly a weird memorial, as can be seen not merely from the handgun/long-gun shellgame, but from the inapplicability of the law to their deaths.

The 1968 Gun Control Act might have prevented Lee Harvey Oswald from obtaining his weapon in just the fashion that he did, by mail order, but being cut off from that avenue hardly deflects a would-be assassin from his purpose. Retail across-the-counter is quite as handy a method of obtaining a gun, and in fact offers a wider choice. James Earl Ray, for instance, had a fine time shopping at three gunshops in Birmingham and Bessemer, Alabama, and getting all sorts of good advice on trajectory and potency from the gun store owners before he settled finally on a

Immigration and Naturalization Service, and the Internal Revenue Service have given the Treasury's ATFB agents strong competition for the title of Most Unconstitutional In Action. Each of these agencies has come together in happy cooperation and supplied its share of thugs to the new umbrella agency, the Office for Drug Abuse Law Enforcement, which has raised warrantless door-busting to a new level of the art.

Remington .30-'06 with a 2 X 7-power Redfield variable scope and twenty rounds of ammunition. He had first bought a Remington .243, but overnight had decided that it was not sufficiently powerful to do the job he wanted, so—although the store owner assured him the .243 was "big enough to bring down any deer in Alabama"—he persuaded the owner to swap it for the .30-'06, which in the right conditions could drop a moose at five hundred yards. That sort of swapping around can't be done by mail. As it turned out, the .30-'06 and its deer ammunition did not disappoint James Earl Ray—the bullet struck Martin Luther King with enormous force, tearing off the lower right side of his jaw and leaving a hole in his face the size of a man's fist from which the blood did not spurt but instead oozed out in thick waves, like sorghum from a wide-mouthed can, and piled up in semisolid layers. He died quickly. The retail dealer had certainly helped Ray find just the right gun for the job. The 1968 Act would not interfere with that instructive store/customer relationship.

Now the Kennedy gun. During the racial violence in Watts in August 1965, Albert L. Hertz, age seventy-two, of Alhambra, California, bought a .22-caliber Iver Johnson Cadet pistol, then worth about $15, for home protection. After his fright had subsided, he passed it on to his married daughter, living in Pasadena, for her protection. She said she decided the gun was too dangerous to have in the house with two small children, so she gave it to her next-door neighbor, a boy of eighteen. He sold the gun (he later told police) to "a bushy-haired guy named Joe." Joe's real name was Munir Sirhan. Somehow, Munir says he doesn't know how, the gun fell into the hands of his brother, Sirhan Sirhan.

On the evening of June 5, as Robert Kennedy was leaving a campaign rally through the kitchen area of the Ambassador Hotel and had stopped to shake the hand of dishwasher Jesus Perez, Sirhan, who had been impatiently waiting, stepped up behind the Senator and from a distance of about three feet fired eight shots from the Iver Johnson. Three bullets struck Kennedy, the fatal one hitting the mastoid, a spongy honeycomb bone; on impact the bullet splintered, as did the bone, and a shower of metal and bone fragments spread through the right portion of his brain. The artery that supplies blood to the cerebellum was also severed. Attending physicians said that if the bullet had struck less than half an inch farther to the rear it would have encountered the thickest part of the skull and probably "that little bullet would have just bounced off," without serious damage. But it went elsewhere.

So much for the villainous instrument. Now the question is, will the 1968 Act prevent such an event's happening again? Not at all. Under the 1968 Act it would still be perfectly legal for Mr. Hertz or any other adult to buy a handgun over the counter, and it would still be perfectly legal for the gun to pass through four or five or any number of hands without a record's being made of the transfer. The only possible effect the 1968 Act would have on a similar development is that Sirhan would now have to register when he bought his .22 ammunition, but if he wanted to lie about his name and address, even that slight attention would be nullified.

Inasmuch as the assassination of John Kennedy failed to elicit any gun legislation whatsoever from Congress, and inasmuch as the legislation finally passed in 1968 had nothing to do with the guns used in the assassinations of King and Robert Kennedy, it seems reasonable to assume that the law was directed at that other threat of the 1960s, more omnipresent than the political assassin—namely, the black rioter.

In 1965 the government began winding down its decades-old practice of selling surplus U.S. military weapons through the National Rifle Association. There were two reasons for this: most of the domestic World War II surplus had already been disposed of, and second, the Establishment had been sorely rattled by the Watts riots of 1965 followed by the disclosure that black militant groups were joining the NRA for the sole purpose of getting their hands on surplus U.S. military rifles and free ammunition. True, not many were taking advantage of the NRA opportunity, but the fear of even a few militants instilled a deep chill.

With the horrendous rioting of 1967 and 1968, Congress again was panicked toward passing some law that would shut off weapons access to blacks, and since they probably associated cheap guns with ghetto blacks and thought cheapness was peculiarly the characteristic of imported military surplus and the mail-order traffic, they decided to cut off these sources while leaving over-the-counter purchases open to the affluent. It proved a totally distorted conception of where blacks were getting guns. (I should make it clear that I do not include Southern Congressmen amongst those who tried to discriminate against some guns and some gun owners; when it comes to firearms, they generally have voted equal rights. And the same goes for many Westerners.)

To appreciate the nervousness that launched Congress along the road to farcical controls, let us relive for a moment that wild-eyed period between 1967 and 1969, a period in which the white majority briefly recaptured the spirit of the U.S. Supreme Court of 1857 when it declared in the Dred Scott case decision that

> this unfortunate class [blacks] have, with the civilized and enlightened portion of the world, for more than a century, been regarded as being of an inferior order, and unfit associates for the white race, either socially or politically, having no rights which white men are bound to respect.

In this era of pro-forma rights for the black man, whites do not normally speak so frankly as the Court did in those days, nor would many of the white genteel class think of repeating publicly the honest appraisal of Tocqueville that

> we scarcely acknowledge the common features of humanity in this stranger whom slavery has brought among us. His physiognomy is to our eyes hideous, his understanding weak, his tastes low; and we are almost inclined to look upon him as being intermediate between man and the brutes. . . . It is

difficult for us, who have had the good fortune to be born among men like ourselves by nature and our equals by law, to conceive the irreconcilable differences that separate the Negro from the [white] in America.

The lower-middle-class and middle-class silent white majority was no longer silent in the 1967–1969 period, and when it expressed its opinions of blacks it frequently came out in the tones of a letter inserted into the *Congressional Record* by the Honorable John R. Rarick of Louisiana, a letter from a white Chicagoan who told of having had to move twice because his neighborhood had been ruined by blacks and then,

> Once again, the black tide came, spawning evil, filth, immorality and crime; once again, the roving gangs of black killers and vandals made the nights hideous with screams, yells, catcalls and smashing glass, and the days nearly as bad. I saw more than once blacks copulating in public, scarcely hidden behind hedges, standing in doorways, in cars parked along the curb, like animals in their indifference to public decency. . . . I found piles of human feces in the foyer of our buildings without toilet paper, and our janitor told me that this was a common occurrence wherever negroes lived in apartment buildings . . . it was a nightly occurrence to hear men [presumably, although it could well have been women] urinating from upper windows . . . Screaming sex orgies were common occurrence in the apartment across the hall. . . . Not once did I ever see black people, filthophiles, attempting to clean up their environment; all I ever saw was black people dumping their garbage out of windows. . . . Give these animals paradise, and in a month it will be a jungle fit only for animals.

The conception of blacks as animals was increasingly common among upper-class whites too, of course, although nothing so direct as that said by our unhappy Chicagoan was said openly by the opinion-shapers of America in the 1967–1969 period. Nothing that direct, no, yet there was a strange outburst of statistics and studies that pointed in the same direction. Suddenly one could hardly pick

up a newspaper or magazine without being confronted with figures
to show that while the illegitimate birth rate among white women
was 2.3 percent in 1960 and 5.5 percent in 1968, that among black
women, though showing a slower rate of increase, was consistently
much higher—21.6 percent in 1960 and 30.7 percent in 1968; that
the overall birth rate among black women is 100-percent higher
than among white women; that the crime rate among blacks was
ten times and eleven times higher than among whites for the crimes
of assault and rape, and sixteen to seventeen times higher for
robbery and homicide. Noting the birth rate and the crime rate
among blacks, Nixon Administration officials worried about a
"demographic siege" of young Negroes in the 1970s. Looking
around the central city, *The New York Times* noticed that "most of
the prostitutes are Negro." The hated welfare burden was traced
more directly to the blacks: the welfare costs rose from $6.9 billion
in 1967 to $8.8 billion in 1968, most of it in cities and attributable
to the flight of whites to the suburbs (they were leaving the city
slums at a rate of 140,000 a year in 1966 but this had increased to
nearly half a million a year by 1968) and their being supplanted by
even poorer blacks. The intelligence of the black was being openly
questioned as never before in modern times, not only by Dr.
William Shockley, the Nobel Prize-Stanford University physicist
who had been talking for so long about the mental inferiority of
blacks that some people thought he was balmy, but now the
question was being raised in fresh new quarters, spectacularly by
Dr. Arthur R. Jensen of the University of California, who had done
a study which reputedly showed that blacks tend to average fifteen
IQ points below whites on just about every intelligence test. There
were new reports of how armed forces screening tests also showed
that intelligence disqualifications for black draftees were about five
times as great as for white, and the disparity was growing. There
was a revival of interest in the 1965 study conducted by Professor
James Coleman of Johns Hopkins that showed black pupils as a
group performing significantly below whites. A noted white anthro-
pologist was even telling friends privately that "a portion of the

American problem is that the slaves were universally selected from sluggish, lazy, inferior tribes by the fact of their capture and the fact that traders wouldn't accept potential headaches. Natural selection took place of a backwards sort."

Whites, in short, were finding blacks offensive, unsavory, gritty. Far from trying to hide it, they were now often flaunting their dislike of blacks. And blacks were responding in kind. It became quite faddish to talk of "two Americas," a suggestion that Tocqueville had predicted would become a reality: ". . . there are but two chances for the future; the Negroes and the whites must either wholly part or wholly mingle. I do not believe that the white and black races will ever live in any country upon an equal footing." By 1968 the separatist movement was in full swing again. Blacks asking for their own land (one request: five Southern states) were no longer considered a joke. The Kerner Commission warned that we were moving swiftly in the direction of a black society and a white society, separate and unequal. A year later the Urban Coalition surveyed the nation and found "we are a year closer to being two societies." The National Commission on the Causes and Prevention of Violence warned that the cities seemed to be on the road to becoming "places of terror" and "fortresses," black against white, with radical groups possessing "tremendous armories of weapons." Even the director of the Justice Department's Community Relations Service, a black, said to hell with integration: he favored autonomous "black neighborhoods and black communities." Many whites said Amen to that, including such luminaries as George Kennan. In Gary, Indiana, where only 40 percent of the population was white, a part of that white minority, unhappy about having a black mayor, circulated a petition to "disannex" themselves.

There was an uglier side, easily surfacing. The Constitution sometimes seemed to be losing its status. The House Un-American Activities Committee issued ι staff report saying that detention camps should be established for the jailing, en masse, of urban "guerrillas" during race conflicts. Senator John Stennis proposed a

Constitutional amendment "to say that under certain conditions a person would forfeit their right to a trial." So much for the Fifth Amendment. Vice President Spiro Agnew proposed a legal ban on black militant literature. So much for the First Amendment. Gen. Curtis E. LeMay, American Party candidate for Vice President (under George Wallace), said he was sorry that their supporters sometimes shouted "kill them" at black hecklers, "but I am a little more in sympathy with those people than I am with the hecklers." An official of the Center for the Study of World Religions at Harvard predicted that perhaps the "problem" was so enormous that it would be solved only if "the cities were eliminated in the next world war and the percentage of Negroes in our surviving population should drop from the present 10 percent to 1 or 2."

Fueling the white population's easy fears of the loathed minority were reports from the Treasury Department that "militant groups in the United States are arming themselves with illegal .45-caliber and .50-caliber machine guns and submachine guns as well as rifles, handguns, hand grenades, dynamite and other lethal devices." A U.S. Customs commander told the House Appropriations Committee that "In World War II there were a lot of souvenir weapons sent home, but nothing of the sort that we are getting now." One day's mail from Vietnam: ninety weapons, including pistols, grenades, explosive flares, plastic explosive, and submachine guns. The Army admitted that 90 percent of the weapons reported "lost or stolen" were never recovered. Marcus Raskin, a man in touch with the radical movement, warned in *American Militarism 1970* that "more and more black people will be fighting those wars abroad and will come back to become guerrillas at home . . . to attempt 'national liberation,' in their terms, from the situation that exists for them here." One of the writers most popular among young blacks was Frantz Fanon, who preached violence as catharsis. If they wanted less elegant instruction, they could get it from the journal *Black Panther*, which advised, "The only way we can do this is to pick up the gun. We are gonna walk all across this motherfucking government and say Stick 'em up, motherfuckers—this is a hold up; we come to get everything that belongs to us."

Fear crept into the conversation of white liberals as often as it did that of white conservatives. A contributor to *The New Republic* wrote to a friend that "inaction I believe can only result in endless guerrilla warfare like that of the Irish Republican Army. Most Negroes will refrain from terrorism, but no Negroes will betray the terrorists to the American Black and Tans." W. H. Ferry, then Vice President of the deeply liberal Center for the Study of Democratic Institutions in Santa Barbara and a close student of the shifting national mood, predicted, "My own judgment is that we're going to have something that is recognizably a race war, civil war. We're going to have it within a year." *I. F. Stone's Weekly* headlined: "Second Secession and Second Civil War," apropos the riots.

Making such fears as these glow in the dark were the riots themselves, and the discovery by the National Advisory Commission on Civil Disorders that instead of there being only 1 or 2 percent of the black residents in major 1967 riot areas participating in the burning and looting, there had been about 18 percent. Other surveys showed that in some cities as many as 48 percent of the blacks thought the riots had been very beneficial. A *Time* poll found that 40 percent of non-Southern blacks thought violence necessary to attain their goals.

The whites' response was dark and moody. After the 1967 Detroit riots the *Detroit News*—as well as a number of important businesses—adopted what became known as "riot Renaissance": some windows were bricked up and metal shields were placed behind others, guards were placed on every door.

The Detroit city council voted a $1-million bond issue to outfit the cops with: seven hundred 12-gauge shotguns, one hundred Stoner machine guns (which fire a small-caliber bullet that tumbles and hits with the same results as a dumdum), one thousand M-1 carbines, twenty-five gas guns, twenty-five .30-'06-caliber rifles with 4-X scopes, twenty-five infrared snooper scopes, twelve hundred gas masks, five thousand chemical mace dispensers, fifteen hundred flak vests, nine thousand sets of fatigue clothing, half a million rounds of various kinds of ammunition, eight armored personnel carriers, four mobile support vans with radio equipment, two prisoner buses.

It was happening all over the country, both in police departments and in the general population. Blacks and whites alike were arming. Whitey wasn't going to be caught short. The number of handguns registered in Detroit in 1967—the year of the riot—was twice the number that had been registered two years earlier, and Detroiters were lining up even thicker in 1968; in the first five months they bought and registered as many handguns as in all of 1967. In Newark applications for permits to buy handguns increased 300 percent between 1965 and 1967, and the surge continued into 1968.

In the year Bobby Kennedy was killed with a pistol, Californians were buying pistols legally at the rate of twenty-six thousand a month and—if the percentage is the same out there as it is in the East—at least twice that number armed themselves via street-corner sales. Three million handguns were registered in California alone.

The 1967 riots were only a warmup for what happened within a few hours after Martin Luther King's death: in the most widespread simultaneous civil disorder in modern American history, riots swept through a hundred and twenty-five cities. Out came 21,000 regular Army troops, 34,000 members of the National Guard, an uncounted number of police and special police, and, on standby, 22,000 other Army troops—the biggest military force ever assembled, outside the Union Army during the Civil War, to deal with civil disturbances in this country. For a brief time machine guns were in place on the Federal Capitol's steps.

The fear of "armed niggers" ran deep; the flood tide rose steadily up Capitol Hill until it washed around the ankles of the great statesmen, who in addition to all their other worries could peer through the Capitol windows down the mall and imagine the sinful goings-on way off yonder in the shadows of the Lincoln

Memorial where the Poor Peoples' March had staked out a highly unwelcome and transitory encampment. They did nothing to lessen the Congressmen's fears, especially when some of the "poor" turned out to be nothing but armed thugs, like the three blacks who had come to Washington from California to participate and decided to let the city know of their presence by gunning to death two Marines and wounding two other people in a hamburger joint. The shooting didn't attract much attention in the headlines, however, because the headlines had been usurped by the assassination of Robert Kennedy on the same day.

So much for the intensity of our feelings during that period. What, as it turned out, was the reality of the threat that had us stuffing our closets and pockets with guns? We had had visions of insurrection and of ravaging armed black mobs seizing the cities, nightmares of hit-and-run warfare. But alas, Chicken Little had tricked us again. The sky had not fallen, but the top of our white gentility had blown off:

> And there, there overhead, there, hung over
> Those thousands of white faces, those dazed eyes,
> There in the starless dark, the poise, the hover,
> There with vast wings across the canceled skies,
> There in the sudden blackness, the black pall
> Of nothing, nothing, nothing—nothing at all.*

Or at least nothing compared to what Whitey had anticipated. Our material side had been slightly damaged by the riots—that's all. The damage done could be compared, say, to the accumulation of acid deposits from DuPont's smokestacks and the accumulation of inefficiency on GM's assembly lines and the accumulation of effluence from the Dow Chemical sewer lines.

As August Meier and Elliott Rudwick pointed out in their

---

* From Archibald MacLeish, "The End of the World." In *Complete Poems 1913–62* (Harcourt Brace Jovanovich, 1952).

study for the Violence Commission, "It should be emphasized that one of the remarkable things about the riots since 1964 . . . is the fact that Negro destruction was aimed at white-owned property, not white lives, even after National Guardsmen and policemen killed scores of Negroes."

But that finding was drawn in the coolness of distant hindsight. At the moment, between the convulsions of the King and Kennedy assassinations, Congress could only react instinctively. And from its instincts, never very trustworthy, came the wretched Gun Control Act of 1968.

The 1968 Act required that dealers keep a record of the names and addresses of those to whom they sold ammunition. Ammunition manufacturers (and conservationists, remember) didn't like this part of the law because they felt that it inhibited the market, squelched buyers, reduced profits. The sale of ammunition, after all, is more profitable than the sale of guns, for a man may buy a gun only once, but he will buy bullets indefinitely. Dealers and sportsmen didn't like the law either because they considered it too much of a bother. Never underestimate the irritation of an enforced pause at the ammunition counter: sportsmen do not take the matter of convenience lightly. They may be willing to slog for four hours through mud to wing one pigeon, but they do not want to spend forty seconds giving their names and addresses to the ammunition dealer. When Congressman Dingell, then on the Executive Committee of the NRA, testified against gun controls in 1967, he accused the control advocates not only of being "a group of willful men bent upon the destruction of a prosperous industry," but also, almost as bad, of attempting to "inconvenience law-abiding citizens." Oh, said Dingell, he understood that laws were okay for inconveniencing some people in some circumstances; he could be reasonable about it; in fact, "I can see no reason, for example, why a man should have a right to shoot his mother-in-law or to stab her or push her down the stairs and pour boiling water on her or feed her poison, or to put his foot on the oxygen pipe when she is in the hospital." But laws aimed at stopping crazies and criminals from buying guns and ammunition, if those same laws get in the way of hunters and plinkers, no, he wouldn't stand for it.

In 1969 the gun fraternity came back and stomped on Congress until it exempted rifle and shotgun ammunition, except for .22-caliber. Requiring that a person identify himself before he could buy bullets is not exactly what you could call "controlling" the sale of bullets, but at least the resulting records sometimes provided an interesting demography of crime. Juvenile Delinquency Subcommittee staff director Perian sent one of his secretaries to a Washington gun store to buy bullets. No sale: the staffer didn't have a gun registration for the District of Columbia, which was required. So then the girl went to two notorious gunshops in nearby Maryland and got all she wanted by using only a driver's license. While there she took down the names of ninety-three persons who had given Washington addresses when buying ammunition at the stores.

Then, says Perian, "we got out a map of Washington and found that some of these buyers were living within three to five blocks of ammunition stores in Washington. Why would they go all the way out to Maryland to buy their ammo? We ran their names through police and FBI records and found that a large percentage—more than one-third—had been convicted of felonies, including murder, assault with a dangerous weapon, rape, grand larceny, armed robbery, dope pushing, everything. We also found that some of the crimes they committed were ten to twelve days after they had purchased ammunition and the guns they used were of the same caliber as the ammo they had bought." They passed the information on to Police Chief Jerry Wilson, but he wasn't particularly interested. A typical cop, he sent out a form letter to all the people on the list telling them that it had been called to his attention that they might be in violation of the local gun law. Ex-felons can't own a gun in the District and cannot get a permit, which must be shown to buy ammunition. Therefore, with Perian spelling it out, it finally dawned on Wilson that if the ex-cons were buying bullets outside the District, well, say, that's kinda suspicious! Why, they just might have some illegal guns inside the District to use them in. But of course a good bureaucratic policeman like Wilson wouldn't want to hassle the thugs, so a form letter would have to do.

That kind of thickheadedness is fairly common. Actually it would be much more important to control ammunition than to control guns, if one wanted to affect crime rates, but most people can't see that. When the ammunition repeal bill was in the Senate, Perian cooked up a plan with Senator Edward Kennedy's staff to have him walk up to the major proponents of the repeal with a .22-caliber hollow-point and a 6.5-caliber rifle bullet in his hand and hold them out and say, "These are the bullets that killed my brothers—are you going to vote to repeal?" But he never did. He said later that, on reflection, he thought it would be too melodramatic.

As Congress was repealing record-keeping on rifle and shotgun ammunition, the ammo industry almost slipped through the decontrol of .22 ammunition. Clark MacGregor, then a Congressman from the Minnesota district in which Federal Cartridge is located (Federal Cartridge makes most of the 3 billion .22-caliber bullets produced in this country every year), had convinced many members of the House that you can't fire .22-caliber rimfire ammunition from a handgun. This was the idea brought into the conference committee session by the House's most important conferee, Congressman Emanuel Celler, chairman of the Judiciary Committee. MacGregor had hoodwinked him. "Celler was arguing with the Senate conferees about it," Perian recalls. "At that point I took a duplicate of the Iver Johnson pistol used in Robert Kennedy's assassination and a box of .22-caliber hollow-point bullets, rimfire, which is what Sirhan used, and dumped them on the table in front of Celler. Celler looked at me and said, 'You mean those bullets can be fired out of that gun?' I said, 'Congressman, those bullets can be fired out of that gun.' And Celler looked down the table at MacGregor and said, 'Well, that's it. We're for record-keeping on .22-caliber rimfire. Anybody disagree?' " That held the line for the moment. But every year the ammunition lobby comes back stronger than before, and soon they'll win freedom for the one remaining recorded handgun bullet.

The 1968 Act also presumed to weed out the unsavory and fraudulent gun dealers by increasing the fee for the federal license from one dollar to ten dollars, and by requiring dealers to prove that they really were in business by submitting a form on which they listed their place of business, their inventory, their financial means, etc., etc. Treasury officials had admitted back in the mid-1960s, you will recall, that between half and two-thirds of the 100,000 pre-1968 "dealers" weren't dealers at all but were simply individual gun owners who were paying the dollar to get special shipping privileges and to put themselves in a position where they could obtain guns faster and cheaper. How well did the new law weed out the phonies? Apparently it made the licenses more attractive, and no harder to get. "Dealerships" are flourishing as never before. Five years after the law's passage there were *155,000* federally licensed dealers, and yet Treasury agents, responding to the Nixon Administration's hearty endorsement of every aspect of gun commerce, insist with a straight face that each and every one of those 155,000 dealers has been checked out and that they are, no kidding, authentic dealers.

As for guns, the 1968 Act banned the importation of all military surplus handguns and long guns. Having waited so long, the law made little difference on that score, though it did make the New England pashas feel more comfortable; most of the surplus foreign weapons from World War II and the NATO switchover had already been imported. Officials of Interarmco estimated that 2 million foreign military weapons had been absorbed by the U.S. between 1955 and 1965. Their company alone had imported a million. There were more of the foreign military arms out there to bring in, but clearly the cream had been taken.

The 1968 Act banned virtually all interstate traffic in both handguns and long guns except to dealers. That this had been done primarily for the benefit of the old-line manufacturers and dealers —apart from Congress's riot hysteria—can fairly be deduced from something W. E. Talley, Vice President of Winchester-Western, told the Southern Wholesale Hardware Association less than a year after passage of the law: "From a dealer's viewpoint there is a bright side." Eliminating mail-order sales and requiring that "firearms must be sold only by licensed dealers increases the dealers' share of the market considerably. In addition to this, the drying up of the military surplus market will permit the local dealer to capture this market with new merchandise at better profit levels." Mail-order houses could no longer deal directly with the individual customer; now they had to use the local dealer as an intermediate marketing stopover; this, of course, meant additional cost to the customer. It hurt outfits like Interarmco very much, but it didn't hurt the gun élite like Colt because they hadn't dealt with the individual buyer anyway.*

There was a great irony in this development, for by outlawing mail-order sales, Congress was increasing the inventories of local retailers. That is, by drying up catalog sales, Congress was just expanding the retail arsenals from which rioters and the standard criminals could ultimately harvest according to their needs.

Let the gun merchants stack up their supplies—sooner or later the bad guys would come along and pick them up for free. As I pointed out earlier, the hoods of the 1920s and 1930s didn't buy their submachine guns and other heavyweight guns out of mail-order catalogs; although they bought some over the retail counter, they bought more on the black market, or they stole them from the cops or the National Guard or they broke into gunshops and pawnshops. The black rioters of Watts and Newark and Washington and all points east did the same thing. They had bought their guns on the street, not by mail, or they had stolen them. Of the 851

---

* Which may explain why, in attempting to turn back the avalanche in 1968, the International Armament Corp. listed expenditures of $9,000 for lobbying. Gunmakers like Savage, High Standard, Browning—which liked the way things were going—*together* spent only $1,047. The bigger outfits spent, or listed, nothing at all.

firearms confiscated by police at Watts, 734 had been stolen. In
Detroit, while the "nice" people were bringing home guns in record
numbers, thugs were burglarizing their homes and shops and
stealing their guns in record numbers too. The percentage increase
in stolen guns was exactly the same as the increase in legitimate
sales—100 percent between 1965 and 1967. This was one reason
Detroit Mayor Jerome Cavanaugh wailed that the "unprecedented
arms race" by just plain ordinary folks presented the most "clear
and present danger to our common future." If they didn't wind up
shooting their families by design or mistake, they would probably
lose their guns to the undesirables.

What could be said for the 1968 Act? Well, one might at least
say that it had helped the major manufacturers come considerably
closer to the goals they had set a decade earlier. In 1958, appearing
before the House Foreign Affairs Committee, E. C. Hadley,
President of the Sporting Arms and Ammunition Manufacturers
Institute, a trade group dominated by such New England firms as
Winchester and Remington, said that there were "four sources of
the industry's [financial] problem. First, the importation of American-made rifles declared surplus by our allies abroad; second, the
importation of surplus used and new foreign-made military surplus
rifles; third, the importation of foreign-made commercial arms;
fourth, the sale of surplus military firearms made by the U.S.
government within the United States."

The last of those activities was reduced considerably as of the
end of 1967; now the government sells only about 300 "surplus"
Army M-1 rifles for the bargain price of $98 each to members of
the NRA, whereas before 1968 it was selling more than 1,000 of the
weapons each year. The sale of other surplus Army rifles and
pistols has been dropped altogether. Items one and two were
outlawed by the 1968 Act. As for item three—the competition of
foreign-made commercial arms—part of that was taken care of by
the 1968 Act, but how much? Foreign-made rifles and shotguns
weren't excluded by it, and this met with the approval of some of
the largest gunmakers in this country who were, in fact, having
some of their own rifles and shotguns assembled in foreign factories

and didn't want to disturb that arrangement. As for handguns, the bigger ones could still be imported if they passed a "sporting criterion" test based primarily on size of gun and size of ammunition: the larger being equated with "sport." In 1972 the United States imported 439,883 "sporting" handguns, which was 23.4 percent more than had been imported in 1971 and, in fact, brought handgun importations back up to the level they were at before Bobby Kennedy got his head blown off and the Gun Control Act of 1968 supposedly threw up a semiwall against the foreign flood.* But what, specifically, of the smaller foreign handguns—the exotic, cheaper little items that fired .22- and .25- and .32-caliber passion bullets? Our allies' inexpensive contributions to America's Saturday Night? Yes, what of those?

Well, as a matter of fact, the Congressional effort to keep out these guns—the effort Congress was most keenly enthusiastic about—turned out to be one of the greatest flops of the 1960s. In their favor, it must be said that members of Congress seemed to sense that in mixing riot control and crime control with commerce, they were screwing up once again. In the closing days of the gun debate in the Senate, when supposedly the adrenalin was running high, only three perfunctory speeches were made on the topic during one two-day period; the average attendance was four Senators, one of whom was trapped there as presiding officer. In that sagging atmosphere the nation, grown accustomed to such things from its highest legislative body, was presented with another in the series of gun-control failures.

---

* Many of these guns imported as "sporting" weapons vary little, if any, from guns that are more honestly identified as gats. For instance, take the Astra 357 revolver made in Spain and imported by Garcia Sporting Arms Corp. The gun has a *three-inch barrel*. It is chambered for the .357 Magnum and also the .38 Special ammo, and claims to be "designed for target shooting and hunting." Oh, come on. *The American Rifleman*'s July 1973 appraisal of the gun includes this statement: "Accuracy with the .357 Magnum cartridge loaded with plain lead bullets was unsatisfactory as the bore became so badly leaded after firing 10 shots that it was difficult thereafter to keep the bullets on a standard 25-yard target." Anybody who showed up in international competition with a gun that performed like that would get laughed off the field, if he weren't bodily ejected. The import criteria are obviously being enforced by comedians.

BEATIFYING THE HANDGUN

It's only proper that as Congress's longest-running tragi-comedy goes into its final act we find once again the Saturday Night Special center stage, hissed and booed from all sides, the little villain to the last. One should also stress that it is still an *exploited* villain, deserving abuse, no doubt, but certainly not deserving it alone.

Otherwise the actors have changed somewhat. Senator Dodd is no longer around: defeated in his 1970 effort to be reelected, shortly afterward he died of a heart attack. Succeeding him as chairman of the Senate Juvenile Delinquency Subcommittee was Senator Birch Bayh of Indiana, who, before he got that chair, had often voted against major gun-control legislation; he set the tone of his takeover by firing all the staff members who knew anything about what had gone on in the past or about the gun industry, just wiped them out, and thereafter allowed the incoming staff to give the subject little attention. He also shipped all the subcommittee's gun files off to the archives, beyond the reach of prying reporters.

Still, like Dodd, Bayh recognized gun controls as a good emotional topic to parlay for headlines, and inasmuch as he wanted very much to be considered for the Democratic Presidential nomination in 1972, he plunged in—or perhaps one should say, bellyflopped in—and splashed around in the same mud puddle that Dodd had used for headlines for a decade. Bayh knew very little about the cheap handguns or any other guns, for that matter, but "Saturday Night Special" was obviously a good bouncy expression that was beginning to catch on. Congressman John Murphy of New York had had eight months of great publicity in *The New York Times*, playing the antigun line, with five cops on the New York police force getting bumped off to help promote his reform campaign. In April 1971, when Murphy held an antigun press conference in New York City, he was confronted with a spectacle to gladden any politician's heart: fifteen radio microphones and eight television cameras. The *Christian Science Monitor* had done a series on gun control featuring the Saturday Night Special and so had the *Wall Street Journal*. There was obviously a deep vein of publicity gold to be mined in them thar little guns, and so in the early fall of 1971 Bayh called for a public subcommittee probe into the problem.

The politics of the moment were very much in evidence. If you will bear in mind that at the time Bayh opened his hearings—in fact, until the second day of the hearings—he had not even introduced his bill (to ban the manufacture and sale in this country of guns failing to meet a "sporting criterion"), you will see the political plot begin to thicken. For it so happened that Senator Edward Kennedy, a member of Bayh's subcommittee and at that time also considered a possible contender for the Democratic nomination, seven months earlier had introduced his own gun-control bill, a bill that would do everything Bayh's would do and more (it would also have registered all guns and licensed all owners). Seeing Kennedy as competition, Bayh did not allow the Kennedy legislation to come up in the early hearings.

But just when Bayh thought he had outfinessed all rivals for publicity, he ran up against Mayor John V. Lindsay of New York City. Naturally, no gun-control investigation would be complete without some message from the New York cops, so Bayh asked Commissioner Murphy to testify. Murphy at first declined, and then he said he would come down and testify *if* his boss, Lindsay, were permitted to be the chief spokesman. Bayh was reportedly furious—for Lindsay, who had recently switched to the Democratic Party, was also suspected of harboring Presidential ambitions—but there was nothing Bayh could do but accept. His claque figured Lindsay wanted to come in and steal the spotlight, and they were right. Lindsay loves to talk about gun controls and he came in orating and pounding the table and showing off a bunch of Saturday Night Specials; the television cameras were all for the Mayor, an especially cruel blow, particularly when Lindsay began denouncing Bayh's proposed bill as altogether inadequate and wishywashy.

Bayh never climbed above that inauspicious beginning, which matched his Presidential effort. And although he finally got his bill through the Senate in 1972, he gave it such a weak push (while voting to kill stronger bills that were competing with it) that it rolled to a stop in the House. (Bayh decided he wouldn't bother to try again in 1973.)

Meanwhile, there were other, more important actors on the stage who should be introduced. First of all there was Senator Roman Hruska, Nebraska's harlequin, the man who could tie Dodd in knots in a debate. So long as a Democrat was in the White House and Dodd, backed by the New England gunmakers, was in the chairmanship, Hruska could hope only to wage a delaying war.

But now that Republican Richard Nixon was President, Hruska, the ranking Republican on the Senate Judiciary Committee, was the big man on its Juvenile Delinquency Subcommittee. Furthermore, he now had some highly placed pals where it counted. Richard W. Velde, associate administrator of the Law Enforcement Assistance Administration (which has spent millions of dollars equipping the cops with heavier armaments), was a protégé of Hruska's and had been on his committee staff in the Senate.* Donald E. Santarelli, who had been Velde's pro-gun counterpart on the House Judiciary Committee staff during the control battles of the 1960s, after serving as an Associate Deputy Attorney General moved over to become administrator of LEAA. Another close ally of Hruska's was Eugene Rossides, who during Nixon's first term was an Assistant Secretary of the Treasury. But best of all, Hruska had Nixon. The President was his carte blanche.

It must be great fun for Hruska to have a man in the White

---

* Velde appears to be another typical gun sport. Jack Anderson reported on October 2, 1972, that Velde "has just forfeited $50 collateral, which he posted on charges of violating federal migratory bird laws. He was accused of shooting geese and ducks on a Maryland farm, which federal agents claimed was baited."

House who is obviously obtuse about the entire problem of gun controls and willing to leave such matters in the hands of his right-wing, gun-happy supporters. At every press conference at which the gun question arose, Nixon airily waved it aside by saying that "we discussed that with Senator Hruska," etc., or (one of Nixon's classically dopey remarks about guns) "I feel that Senator Hruska will now work with the Judiciary Committee in attempting to find the formula which will get the support necessary to deal with this specific problem, without, at the same time, running afoul of the rights of those who believe they need guns for hunting and all that sort of thing." This is actually the Nixon view of gun usage: hunting *and all that sort of thing.* He has needlessly conceded that "I have no interest in guns and so forth." The day after Senator Stennis was shot with a .22 handgun (an instrument Nixon described as a "cheap gun kind of thing"—showing more than his usual amount of omniscience, since neither he nor any other member of his Administration had ever seen the gun which, for all they knew, may have been the most expensive .22 on the market)—the President said something would have to be done about those small-caliber guns although in this instance the use of a .22 was a blessing because "obviously, if they [the bandits] had had a .45, he [Stennis] would be dead." * If that's the way he felt, then logically Nixon should have asked for controls on the bigger guns instead of the smaller, but he didn't, and Stennis must have wondered whose side Nixon was on.

What the Hruska-Nixon-Santarelli-Velde gang hoped to do with their combined clout will be explained in a moment. Some background first:

The 1968 Gun Control Act prohibited all foreign military surplus weapons from entering the country, and it also prohibited the importation of guns that failed to meet what is loosely called the "sporting criterion." Those standards put an immediate end to the flood of junky little guns—some selling for only a couple of dollars—that had been coming into the country from West

---

* From transcript of news conference, January 31, 1973.

Germany and Italy and Spain and Brazil and Japan, from most of the industrial or semi-industrial nations where labor is cheap. West Germany accounted for nearly as many as all the other countries put together; Germany is *der Vaterland,* for example, of the outfit that manufactures the Rohm pistol, and Rohm is indeed a name that every police department knows how to spell. Chicago police records show one-fourth the Saturday Night Specials taken into custody in that city are Rohms. However, Eig and H & R and IMP pistols have accounted for their share of DOAs too.

Imports of pistols and revolvers—expensive, well made, cheap, poorly made, and every kind in-between—totaled 513,019 in 1966. In 1967 this jumped to 747,013. In 1968, after importers had been warned that the new embargo was imminent and that they should stock up, the number soared to a "last chance" importation fling of 1,155,368 handguns. Then in 1969, pistol and revolver imports slumped to 349,352 and have not since climbed again over the half-million level, although they are moving toward it.

An even cleaner view of the decline can be seen in U.S. Tariff Commission records that show $445,000 worth of pistols and revolvers valued over $4 and not over $8 were imported in 1968, but none was imported in 1970; $17.2 million worth of handguns valued over $8 were imported in 1968; only $5.7 million in 1970. As was the intent of the law, it obviously hit the cheaper foreign handguns the hardest. Price was not mentioned in the law, but since the cheap guns are usually the smaller, it came to the same thing.

The 1968 Act ostensibly outlawed the foreign-made Saturday Night Special by setting up what the Treasury Department calls "Factoring Criteria for Weapons," by which a handgun would be rated according to its length, frame construction, weight, caliber, safety features, and miscellaneous equipment—one point for each quarter inch over six inches total length, one point per ounce weight, three points for .22 long rifle to .38 caliber (compared to zero points for .22 short and .25 calibers), etc. The law was intended to keep out all but the larger, heavier weapons—the weapons less easily concealed for criminal purposes and more easily used for sporting purposes.

It was, needless to say, a fraudulent method for measuring a "good" gun. If the Charter Arms .38 that Arthur Bremer used to shoot George Wallace had been made in Germany, its two-inch barrel would have disqualified it from importation. But if the barrel on the same gun had been *four* inches long, it would have been importable under the factoring criteria even though it would have been no less easily concealed and would have been no more useful as a "sporting" weapon. Too, the administration of the act by the Treasury's Bureau of Alcohol, Tobacco and Firearms (BATF) was from the beginning, perhaps intentionally to develop more public antagonism to the Act, extremely arbitrary. In the first year of the Act's existence, one company was permitted to import a pistol with a four-inch barrel and one with a six-inch barrel, but not one with a five-inch barrel; one day the BATF allowed alloy casting for some guns, the next day it didn't. Many of the weapons allowed into the country were no more usable for "sporting" purposes than many of the guns that were excluded. It was all very high-handed and useless.

The uselessness was most dramatically apparent in The Loophole. What a loophole. The 1968 Act embargoed the cheap Saturday Night Specials all right, but it did *not* embargo gun *parts*. That little slip helped inspire the immediate blossoming of an enormous junk-gun industry. American gun merchants—not the stuffy old granddads like Colt and S & W, mind you, but rank upstarts—saw the opening at once and began importing parts like crazy and assembling them in this country, with the result that there was hardly any letup in the supply of Specials. For what they weren't importing as parts to reassemble, they were making right here in this country out of American parts. A third way of filling the market was to import cheap foreign handguns that had sufficient barrel length to pass the "sporting" criteria, and then to saw the barrels off. The Saturday Night Specials they turn out, in factories situated in south Florida, in New York City, on Long

Island, in Nashville, in Santa Monica, in converted garages and converted warehouses, may be a little more expensive than the foreign genre (the domestic junk guns usually sell for between $15 and $25) but they serve the same purpose and the same clientele.

About a dozen U.S. companies have dominated the cheapie gun market since 1968; seven of them using American parts while the other five relied primarily on imported parts. In 1968, when the whole SNS gun was still importable, only 18,000 parts were brought in from other countries; but the next year, with the whole gun embargoed, 568,500 parts were imported. Nowadays they are bringing in enough parts to assemble more than a million Saturday Night Specials. So between the two production lines, one all-American and the other part-foreign, perhaps as many as two million Specials are put on the market each year. That, at least, happens to be the guess most widely favored by writers who have kept watch on this market; the Treasury says it's too high, but the Treasury is no more accurate at this guessing game because neither it nor the Commerce Department keeps a record specifically of Saturday Night Special production, partly because they don't want to be bothered and partly because there is no official agreement on what a Saturday Night Special is.

When everyone was laughing at what a flop the 1968 Act was in killing the junk-gun market, Senator Bayh stepped in with his proposed remedy: give the Treasury Department the power to outlaw the manufacture and sale in this country (except to cops) of any gun that didn't meet some vague "sporting" test, just like the imports. But that would do away with the snubnosed .38—one of the most popular home-defense guns. In fact, it would do away with snubnosed everything, even those of immaculate quality. Anyway, one man's "sporting gun" is another man's "belly gun"; the criteria were too vague. So Bayh obviously did not have a winning formula.

His bill, moreover, offended the gun lobby because it was written in such a way as to endanger the market for not only the unknown trade-name guns but also for the big companies, as

pointed out in the November 1972 *American Rifleman*. With the bill
already dead in that Congress, the NRA organ apparently felt it
was safe to admit that the major gun manufacturers were peddling
Saturday Night Specials too. It commented under a photo of
twenty guns: "There isn't a single so-called 'Saturday Night
Special,' by anybody's definition, in this assortment of quality
handguns by established American manufacturers that the Bayh
Bill, S.2507, would have barred from dealer sale. Some would have
been eliminated because of small size and caliber, some because of
the hammer-drop test on single-action revolvers. Many not shown
here also would have been affected." In the photo were six guns
made by Colt, five made by Smith & Wesson, five made by Sturm,
Ruger, two by High Standard, one by Charter Arms, and one by
Dan Wesson.

Bayh's bill obviously was not the one sought by the established
old-line gunmakers. Quite the contrary. But some scheme had to be
rigged up to make them happy, for 2.5 million cheapies sop up a
considerable portion of a handgun market that Colt and Smith &
Wesson and their economic peers would like very much to have
back. The importers of SNS parts were also developing powerful
enemies among such companies as Century Arms and Interarmco;
as long as the SNS import problem persisted, Interarmco could
never hope to reestablish the wide-open importation program of
Lugers and Berretas and P-38s and other fairly costly but much
desired handguns. Also so long as the taint of the Saturday Night
Special hung over the import traffic, Interarmco *et al.* could never
hope to soften Congress into permitting once again the importation
of those fine foreign surplus military weapons—not that there were
a great many left to be purchased, but there were still a few
hundred thousand.

So for once the big manufacturers and the big importers,
though often at odds in the past, now agreed wholeheartedly:
somehow they must cook up a scheme whereby the competition
from the boilerplate handguns could be done away with (a tip of
the hat to Colt and S & W) while at the same time the quality

foreign guns of any size would be readmitted (a tip of the hat to such outfits as Interarmco and Century Arms).

Hruska, Nixon & Co. had, and still have, just the plan. The preliminaries for bringing the scheme to fruition were laid in 1972 but the legislation that went with it was not successful. Rewarmed, it was ready to be trotted out again in 1973, but the Watergate outlawry—led by pistol-packing G. Gordon Liddy, known as "the gun lobby's man in the White House"—made that a bad year for the Nixon crowd to bring up the subject of guns.* However, the scheme will doubtless be presented repeatedly to Congress in the years ahead, until that less than astute body passes some version of the bill. If the plan is successful, it will be a solution helpful to *both* sides of the gun industry as well as to the NRA and all its adjuncts. At the same time, it will leave the gun-control advocates worse off

---

* The owner of Hunter's Haven just over the Potomac later identified Liddy as the fellow who had showed up in his store a year earlier, flashing a White House card and saying he wanted to buy (illegally) a small arsenal of handguns for the White House. It's now presumed he wanted to outfit his burglary gang.

Ex-FBI agent Liddy ran unsuccessfully for Congress in 1968, using a faked photo showing him wielding a club to break up a mob of blacks. He was a law-and-order candidate. So he came to Washington and was hired by Assistant Secretary of the Treasury Eugene Rossides as a special assistant. Rossides, working quietly with Senator Hruska, was trying to pull off the delicate stunt of outlawing the Saturday Night Special while expanding the rest of the gun market. When Liddy tried to butt into this operation and take over the Bureau of Alcohol, Tobacco and Firearms, Rossides gave him the bounce. But Liddy landed on his feet, in a better job as an aide to John Ehrlichman in the White House, where he continued to be the inside lobbyist for the NRA hardliners.

Then there was John J. Caulfield, a former New York City cop who became head of the criminal investigation division of the Treasury's gun-control bureau. Aside from being accused of participating in some of the political dirtywork, Caulfield was named by convicted Watergate burglar James McCord, Jr., as the man who passed along an offer of executive clemency in return for McCord's silence on the burglary-bugging case. McCord testified that when he turned down the offer, Caulfield said something that sounded an awful lot like a threat on McCord's life. After McCord gave this testimony, Caulfield took leave from his job at the firearms bureau.

Then, too, the public was likely to remember that one of the early problems in the White House cover-up was how to sneak E. Howard Hunt's pistol out of the White House. All in all, it was not a promising year for the White House and Hruska to raise their little gun scheme in Congress.

than before, which is saying a lot. In fact, it will leave them in the ditch.

These were the three parts of the plan:

First, the reputation of the handgun as a genre would be enhanced. It had been getting too much criticism. Fellows like Commissioner Murphy of the New York Police Department were making the slogan "Handguns are only for killing people" fairly popular. If this continued, the public might force Congress to give serious consideration to outlawing the manufacture and sale of *all* handguns, except for cops. That proposal has been seriously pushed already by a few Congressmen with a reasonable amount of clout. Just before he quit Congress, Emanuel Celler had a bill to do it. The bill got nowhere, but even its presence was enough to frighten the industry. So their first effort was to boost the reputation of handguns in general before turning again to the assassination of the Saturday Night Special.

The perfect way to boost the handgun was to tout it as a *hunting* weapon, for all hunting weapons are sacred in America; it is because rifles and shotguns are used mostly for hunting—though they are used plenty in crimes too—that they have escaped the registration and licensing restraints imposed on handguns in some states. Making the public accept handguns as hunting weapons was a trick to challenge Madison Avenue, for that has truly not been their reputation. The NRA's own experts used to laugh at the idea. Writing in the January 1934 issue of *American Rifleman*, Kenneth Fuller Lee laid it on the line:

> Pistols and revolvers ought never to be considered in the light of supplanting the rifle or shotgun. No man in his right mind would think of deliberately setting out on a trip after big game armed solely with the belt gun. . . . The ancient belief that a man's pistol might save his life in case his rifle jams during a determined charge is mostly, in my opinion at least, a matter of fallacious theory. About the only North American game which is likely to do much "charging" is the Alaskan brown bear—and who wants to face a charging Brownie at close range with any pistol yet devised by Man?

Nowadays, to hear the NRA types talk about it, one might conclude that any man owning a handgun and having any pride at all would dash out forthwith and confront a Brownie. Writing in the 1973 issue of *Gun Digest*, Bill Davidson packaged the argument neatly: Handguns are accurate enough to be used for hunting.

> If the average listener to "The Advocates" debate on handgun legislation, or the average *Time-Life* or *LA Times* or *Washington Post* reader could learn that a .357 Magnum revolver will group three shots inside 3 inches at 50 yards or inside 6 at 100, we would be on the way to convincing him of the asininity of the handgun-ban bleating.

Handguns will wing fewer innocent passersby—". . . the maximum danger range of even a .44 Magnum factory round is less than a mile and a half—compared to two and a third miles for the .30-'06 class of rifle cartridge." And the handgun is effective—"Delivered by a reasonably skilled shot, a magnum-caliber handgun bullet is effective on game out to 200 or perhaps 250 yards under optimum conditions." His article was accompanied by a picture of "Arizona handgunner-guide Ollie Barney, Jr., with near-record-class mountain lion he bagged with his S & W .44 Magnum revolver. Barney guided author to hefty javelina a few years ago, specializes in 'pigs,' lion, bear." The propaganda also came through magazines of more general circulation, such as *The New York Times Magazine*, in which an official of a handgun club was quoted: "I've taken deer with a .44 Magnum handgun. Drops them like you hit it with a stick of dynamite. . . ." And *The American Rifleman* even had kind words to say of the sporting possibility to be found in a gun whose measurements are of the Saturday Night Special class; an expert who owned a .22-caliber Smith & Wesson Kit Gun with a two-inch barrel was quoted: "I've killed more small game with it than any handgun I've ever owned."

Well, it isn't all malarkey. The gun crowd does have impressive developments on its side. The power of ammunition has been stepped up in a revolutionary way in recent years, including ammunition usable in handguns. The handgun .44 Magnums can match the old deer-rifle cartridges for power; and as of 1972 a new handgun killer, the .454 Casull Magnum, could deliver *twice* as much energy as the .44 Magnum. A mild steel quarter-inch plate that is only dented by a .44 Magnum will be penetrated by a .454 Casull. The bullet has been used to bring down deer at one hundred yards.

Of course it is absurd to suggest that handguns were conceived as hunting guns, but the gun industry has alchemized absurdities before, and it is well on the way to doing so in this instance. Having started salvaging the generic reputation of handguns, it was then ready to continue the rest of its scheme.

Step Two was built on the interplay of two clever arguments: the need for fair play in international trade and the need for consumer protection.

The intent was to persuade Congress to do away with the 1968 Act's "factoring criteria"—no more points for length of barrel and weight of gun and caliber, if you please—and to replace it with criteria for *reliability* based on actual test-firings. Congress would have to be persuaded that the only rational basis for outlawing a firearm was quality: safety and efficiency. If a gun is well made—the argument goes—then it will be safe for the user; it will also, incidentally, cost considerably more than a gun that is not well made, and costing more, it might be beyond the price reach of the small-time brigand who accounts for most of the street crime. Another plus.

As for the fair-trade argument, it went like this: Under the General Agreement for Tariffs and Trade (GATT), the United States is forbidden to discriminate against foreign products. "Like" products, domestic and foreign, are supposed to have "like" treatment. Whatever criteria are used to keep out foreign products must, under GATT, be used also to keep domestic products off the market.

The Gun Control Act of 1968 prohibits the importation of any gun that fails to meet the "sporting criterion," yet American-made guns that would fail to pass this test are flooding the domestic market. If we outlaw Saturday Night Specials from, say, Germany because they have two-inch barrels, then we should outlaw the manufacture and sale of domestic SNSs with two-inch barrels—that was the Hruska argument. A "non-sporting" handgun from abroad should, under GATT, be treated no more harshly than one manufactured in Miami or Nashville. On the other hand, the Nashville or Miami smalltime gun operator should be treated just as harshly as operators in Germany. And the only fair stick for beating them both—the argument emphasized—was one with quality as the sole criterion. Throw out the sporting test and bring in the safety and reliability test, and we can once again permit the importation of any and all foreign guns of any size and weight and caliber (so long as they pass the quality test), which will give our sportsmen and collectors a wider choice while establishing a friendlier relationship with those countries whose gun factories depend heavily on the U.S. market.

To make it seem that the international fair-play part was important, Treasury officials set about to hoax-up the impression that gun-manufacturing countries that had cosigned GATT were raising hell with us. Assistant Secretary of the Treasury Rossides breathlessly informed the Senate Juvenile Delinquency Subcommittee that as a result of the GATT violations "seven nations have filed formal protests with the State Department." When I went down to the Treasury to inquire further, six high officials crowded into a small office with me and overwhelmed me with sad stories: they claimed that as a result of our banishing foreign nonsporting handguns, dozens of towns in half a dozen European countries had become ghost towns—"little poverty-stricken Appalachias," they called them. One Treasury flack said, "Italian officials are very unhappy. They put an embargo on Florida oranges, and when we complain they say, 'Well, if you won't let us send Italian guns, you can't ship us Florida oranges.' And the same economic devastation is seen in Spain and Germany and elsewhere because of the discriminatory features of the Gun Control Act." To hear the

Treasury fellows tell it, a major international crisis was at hand.

Unfortunately, the State Department wasn't cooperating with their scheme. They said they hadn't heard about any poverty and considered the gun question "a minor matter." At the Italian Embassy a cheerful official responded, "It is true that Italy was damaged a little by the gun embargo, but it is not true that Brescia and its province—the center of our gun manufacturing—is 'ghost-like.' There are too many really important things in GATT to worry about guns right now. Where did you hear that we had ghost towns? [The Treasury Department.] Oh. Well, then, you should be a gentleman and write it that way."

Officials at the Brazilian Embassy were equally ignorant of any economic slump caused by the guns embargo, and at the German Embassy an official said, "I have no knowledge of unemployment caused by the Gun Control Act. We have very vehemently opposed the law, of course, but we have no unemployment. We have so little unemployment in Germany that we even employ quite a lot of foreign labor."

Nevertheless, Treasury officials proceeded with their little farce. *They* would rescue U.S. trade from the shoals of gun discrimination; *they* would create an atmosphere of international fair play by establishing standards that would apply to domestic manufacture as well as to foreign imports. And as a fillip to their heroism, they set forth to do all this in such a way as to protect the American consumer from defective products—which in a consumer-oriented era they recognized as being a much more sensitive point than the question of whether it was intelligent to manufacture the product at all.

THE U.S. SEAL OF APPROVAL

So with $135,000 in tax money they proceeded to the third step: the Treasury hired the H. P. White Laboratory of Bel

Air, Maryland, to test a hundred and fifty guns representing fifty-eight different models of handguns (from seven foreign countries and the United States) to determine if an objective test for safety and reliability could be set up. The test was started in February 1971 and completed in late August. Significantly, although the press and the general public were refused information about what was going on at the White labs, the NRA gun lobby was kept abreast of it all, and when the tests were about half finished, NRA officials were permitted to come in and take pictures and look over the records of the experiment. One official at the White labs explained that "in order not to offend the shooting community too badly, they [Treasury officials] sort of solicited the NRA's participation in this. So they went overboard to divulge information to them."

The NRA, which speaks for the big gunmakers, immediately published in *The American Rifleman* an article suggesting that most foreign guns were flunking the H. B. White tests, as were all inexpensive domestic guns, whereas the standard U.S. big-name guns were doing very well. This premature and inaccurate appraisal irked a top official at the test lab, who told me:

> Here's a typical statement from the NRA article, "Many small imported low-grade handguns failed in some respect"—what is "some respect"?—"long before their firing tests reached five thousand rounds." The implication is that small imported low-grade handguns are either unsafe or unreliable. Well, I can cite within our test data here a small imported low-grade handgun that whistled through everything we could throw at it. And I can cite a very expensive U.S. prestige weapon that failed after fifteen to sixteen rounds. . . .
>
> To say that because most American guns made it through three thousand rounds while many European guns didn't make it to two thousand rounds and therefore it is our conclusion that American guns are better than foreign guns—that's not necessarily true. It's too gross a conclusion from a limited sample. You can't say that without exploring the nature of the failure. If the gun failed to fire at the five

thousandth round because the firing pin was peened over so badly—that constitutes a failure. If it failed to fire because the whole action just blew up—that also constitutes a failure. For our purposes, one failure is a statistic like another, although they may be vastly different failures. It is not an evaluation.

The testing would seem to say to us that *the failure cannot be related to cost, origin, type, whatever.*

Asked specifically if he thought the Saturday Night Special was necessarily a bad, unsafe gun, he replied, "No. But because of the glut of these on the market, you are much more likely to have a problem with that sort of gun if you just walk in and buy one without some standard to go by."

To look at the White Laboratory result summary, one would at first conclude that this official was being too kind to the Specials. Of the twenty-two .22-caliber handguns subjected to the test, only one passed, and that one cost $71.50, considerably above the typical SNS price. Of the five .25-caliber handguns, none passed.

But a broader look at the test shows that the SNSs didn't do too badly, or at least did no worse than most guns. Of the one hundred fifty handguns tested, nearly half, seventy, were American-made; the rest were from Germany, Brazil, Spain, Italy, Belgium, Switzerland, and France. They were of every cost level.

Of the fifty-eight models, only six completed the test; of the one hundred fifty individual handguns, only thirty-five completed the test. Failure meant that a gun was no longer able to fire at all, misfired 25 percent of the time, or had become so rickety as to be extremely hazardous to the shooter. With one hundred fifteen of one hundred fifty guns collapsing, by H. B. White standards the gun market is obviously loaded with lemons, and not all of them at the SNS cost level by any means.

But as a matter of fact, the White test was hardly the sort to interest SNS owners. Who pays $15 for a handgun and expects it to be able to stand up in a demolition derby of five thousand standard rounds plus fifty proof rounds (50 percent overloaded)? The Specials aren't bought for a lifetime of target practice; they are bought to sit in the dresser drawer until the owner wants to shoot his/her spouse; a test-firing of five shots should do. The White Laboratory test was proffered as a "consumer" test, but few customers need a $135,000 test to let them know that a $15 Rohm thrown together by superannuated Black Forest elves isn't likely to take the same beating as a $120 Colt—and most don't care, thanks just the same.

All sorts of gun-reform advocates got snookered by the consumer angle. James V. Bennett, former director of the federal prison system and president of the National Council for a Responsible Firearms Policy (a council that, except for its stationery, was virtually defunct), approved the "principle that our laws must prevent the sale of articles, tools, clothing, equipment or appliances that may be inherently dangerous to whoever owns them. We are seeking to protect the consumer from potentially dangerous articles. The Saturday Night Special is in that category. When it backfires or explodes it creates a casualty, the cost of which all of us are likely to pay in our taxes to support our health and social security programs."

The explodability of Saturday Night Specials has been vastly overplayed, a rather obvious propaganda exploitation. Testifying before the New York City Council's Public Safety Committee, which voted to outlaw the manufacture and assembly within the city of the SNS, Deputy Commissioner Luis Neco of the New York Police Department's Legal Division insisted the Special was a weapon equally dangerous to the user as well as to the target victims because of its tendency to explode in the user's hand. He offered no evidence for saying so, because there is no evidence of such a "tendency." Specials sometimes are so badly constructed that they blow up, but this is a rare occurrence. One is about as likely to get hurt in that way as to be hit by a meteorite. In all the years that the Saturday Night Special has been denounced in and out of Congress, there has been no documented case, so far as I can discover, of a person's being seriously hurt by such an accident.

A quality-control test is not gun control; it is market control.

Never was that more candidly shown than in early 1973, when, with the approval of the White House, Congressman/NRA Director Dingell, Congressman John Saylor of Pennsylvania, an NRA life member, and Congressman Bob Casey of Texas, an NRA member, introduced a preliminary, jerry-built version of what the White House intended to present later as its quality-control legislation. The Dingell bill, as the NRA explained to its members, was simply a kind of temporary holding action to be pushed only if the antigun forces began to show strength before the real NRA-White House bill could be unveiled—that is, it was simply there "to head off the worst of the antihandgun bills." Still, in principle, it followed the NRA–White House–Hruska scheme by proposing to ban any handgun from the American market, whether made overseas or in this country, that has a die-cast frame or receiver which melts at temperatures of less than 800 degrees Fahrenheit. "Hotter than a two-dollar pistol" would no longer apply to the U.S. market, if Dingell has his way. His rationale: "If manufacturers are prohibited from selling handguns with die-cast zinc-alloy receivers or frames, the increased cost of manufacture will drive Saturday Night Specials off the market." Ah, what clever deceit to make one little gun bear the whole burden of reform. Such legislation does not outlaw handguns; it does not even outlaw the very small handguns that, obviously, would be most useful for getting close to the quarry (banker, Senator, etc.). It only outlaws, or tries to outlaw, a certain size pricetag. If the NRA-Nixon-Hruska-Dingell crowd succeed in getting Congress to adapt a White Laboratory-type test under the guise of gun control, then the Special, that absurd little piece of deadly gadgetry, will indeed be standardized off the market. Many gun-control advocates will cheer, not knowing that at that point the trap will have been sprung—and they will be in it, caught, so easily brought down that they provided hardly any sport. Respectability will then have been stamped upon the handgun traffic in America; after that, all guns sold on the open market will be federally certified as being "safe" and "reliable."

If that happens, then any really significant extension of the

Gun Control Act of 1968 beyond removal of the Saturday Night Special from the new-gun market will be extremely difficult, if not impossible, to accomplish. Even under the best of conditions, Congress hesitates to oppose the gun lobby, and any reform movement within Congress would be at a tremendous extra psychological disadvantage if the lobby could argue that only "safe" and "reliable" guns were being sold.

If the performance standards are applied on imports without discrimination, it will also mean—if GATT is to be satisfied—that the floodgates will again be opened to foreign military surplus weapons. At least that is the opinion of Senator Hruska, who hopes devoutly that this will be the case. NRA's position on military surplus imports is not yet clear, but Jack Basil, NRA's legislative director, speaks kindly of them: "We would be in favor of getting rid of unsafe guns. We're for it, the gun manufacturers are for it, everybody's for it. People play on emotions too much when dealing with gun safety. At the time of President Kennedy's assassination, they were yelling about the Italian rifle Oswald used. They were being melodramatic about guns, rather than judging them from technical standpoints. Same thing is true about the way they judged foreign military surplus guns. Before the 1968 law, a lot of people were saying the U.S. was the dumping ground of castoff guns. They were using emotional phrases like that. Actually, some of the foreign military surplus stuff is excellent quality."

A resumption of military surplus imports also is favored by some key members of the Administration. Santarelli, one of the Justice Department's gun policy shapers, after stating the obvious in 1969—that "by embargoing all military surplus and firearms not generally suitable for sporting purposes . . . a new protected industry has been created in the United States" (meaning Colt, S & W, Winchester, Remington, *et al.*)—went on to tell the Senate he believed it "unfair to exclude the good with the bad" and that he thought some foreign surplus military weapons were very good.

Indeed they are. Good, and sometimes inexpensive. Often as inexpensive as Saturday Night Specials. Many of the more than one million of these goodies that were imported in the last year before the embargo are still on the market, and their bargains shine from the advertisements in any gun magazine: a British Enfield Mark 1, the kind of .38 that, as the ad says, was "designed for rapid, close-quarter, defense work," only $19.95; a .450 Webley & Scott by the famous British maker, with a two-and-a-quarter-inch barrel (fits in the pocket nicely), only $20; the same kind of Luger used by the Luftwaffe during World War II, $36; the P-38, sidearm for the German Army of the same era, only $19; a French M-35S, built much like a Browning automatic, $23.

Many of them would probably pass the performance test. Which would mean that so long as the supply of military surplus imports held out, our aspiring hoodlums could look forward to going into business with a lifetime gun for well under $40, perhaps half that amount. Of course, he will have to pay more for the heavier-caliber ammunition, but offsetting that extra expense will be the comfort of knowing that he will no longer be faced with the embarrassing misfirings that so often marred the performance of the Saturday Night Specials.

When the high-performance European guns come flooding back in, then many gun-control advocates who now scorn the Saturday Night Special as the work of the devil may sigh almost nostalgically for its return, for, say what you will about it, it does have one virtue: it falls apart fast. Fire a hundred rounds from some of the species and there's a good chance it won't be usable except as a paperweight. Not so, the elegantly crafted hundred-dollar rod. There are Colts and Smith & Wessons that have fired many thousands of rounds over many years, and though they are outwardly battered they are just as deadly efficient as ever.

Most of the 30 million or so handguns in this country are the quality jobs, and they will still be around and will still be just as dangerous fifty years from now unless they are bought up (or confiscated) and melted.

Most ironically, if the standards are changed to quality—rather than size and weight and caliber—there will be a great many new .22- and .25-caliber European automatics of good design and craftsmanship coming in again, flat, compact, pocket jobs, easily concealed, perfect for the hit man—costing $75 and up, but many thugs of pride will be only too happy to pay their, or your, money for a little extra class. "Those guns," says ballistics expert Charles Rorke of the New York Police Department, speaking of the better-grade European output, "cause us a lot of mischief. They are really popular with the underworld." Now banned under the factoring criteria of size and weight, but doubtless of sufficient quality to survive test-firing standards, is, for example, the .25-caliber Beretta Model 20, a veritable vest-pocket job, only four and seven-tenths inches long and weighing only eleven ounces empty but called by *Gun Digest 1973* a "small wonder" and an "incredible" little weapon with which, at twenty-five meters, one is able to achieve a grouping of eight shots within a four-inch diameter. That should make it almost accurate enough for a shootout with the cops.

But the foreign imports will face stiff price competition from a number of .22- and .25-caliber automatic pistols coming off the assembly lines of the *major* gun manufacturers in this country. Some of the little vest-pocket jobs have for years been standard items in the catalogs of such outfits as Colt and S & W, while others were rushed into production to fill the market vacuum created by the 1968 Act. Typical of the new wave is Plainfield Ordnance Co.'s Model 71 automatic with a two-and-a-half-inch barrel, overall length of four and seven-eights inches, coming in .22, .25, .32, and .380 calibers, with the price on the lower-caliber guns starting at about $70, and the Sterling Arms .25-caliber automatic that is four and a half inches long, weighs only ten ounces, and costs $39.95.

What we are talking about here are well-built guns that in size and weight and concealability would qualify as Saturday Night Specials; they are SNSs in everything but price and reputation, and they are even that in price for the person willing to pay a bit more to whoop it up. If GATT were satisfied by imposing a size and weight "sporting gun" standard in this country, these guns would be outlawed. But if an H. B. White Laboratory test becomes the standard for marketing, many of them will survive. The upshot of it all will be, of course, that the manufacturers of cheap guns will be driven out of business and replaced by the manufacturers of less-than-cheap guns, but the outpouring of small weapons onto the American market will not change in the slightest. It will only have the U.S. seal of approval.

The established old-line gun industry will see that as a great victory. Libertarians who believe a man should be allowed to pick his own brand of poison will see it as a defeat. And advocates of gun control, if they have any sense, will recognize it as a total disaster.

It is, however, a disaster for which they have helped clear the way by their willingness to discuss guns mostly in terms of price and caliber, in terms of "useful" guns and "killer" guns. This is a futile, confusing, and meandering route toward control.

When Pat Brown went to Washington to testify against the Saturday Night Special, he stressed what everyone already knew: "most murder in real life comes from a compound of anger, passion, intoxication and accident—mixed in varying portions. The victims are wives, husbands, girlfriends, boyfriends, prior friends or close acquaintances. . . . All the statistics show that if you choose with care the people who will share your bedroom with you or your kitchen, or the adjacent bar stool, you will improve your chances from one in 20,000 to one in 60,000." * Professor Frank Zimring's study of homicides in Chicago is frequently cited by gun-control advocates. Zimring found that half of the murders were for these reasons, in this order: general domestic, money, liquor, sex, love triangle—and that in 57 percent of the cases the offender or the victim or both had been drinking.

The prototype who emerges from such evidence is white or

* Juvenile Delinquency Subcommittee, Judiciary Committee, Senate, Hearings on S.2507, Amendment to 1968 Gun Control Act to Prohibit the Sale of Saturday Night Special Handguns, Sept.–Nov. 1971 (U.S. Government Printing Office), p. 45.

black trash: a low-class squabbling drunken ne'er-do-well. It's not hard to get agreement that guns should be kept from such people. But *nice* people should be permitted to have guns. Right? Brown must think so too, because he keeps a handgun in his home.

Congressman Murphy of New York, in pushing his bill to outlaw the Saturday Night Special, said, "These gun nuts think their weapon is an extension of their prick." By this he did not mean anything so simple as the gun's location, nothing so straightforward as the equipage of Chicago's once ebullient Dion O'Banion, who always carried three pistols, two near his left armpit and a third in a special centrally located pants pocket, hanging more like a chastity belt than a rod. No, Murphy meant nutty nut, "the deeply disturbed individual who equates a firearm with his masculinity." It's easy to work up agreement that guns should be kept from the hands of the kind of psychotic that remark conjures up. But of course no one would think it applied even remotely to the Chief Justice of the Supreme Court, Warren Burger, who answered his doorbell one night to confront two reporters with a full-size six-shooter. And of course nobody would be so sacrilegious as to suggest that Dwight David Eisenhower had thought he was extending his penis when, as he admitted later, he never went into the streets of New York, during the time he was president of Columbia, without carrying his Army six-shooter.

Gun-control advocates have been manipulated into playing the gun status game, and that is a game in which they are guaranteed to make fools of themselves, for there simply is no way to equate quality or price or size or caliber with anything of social import. Were the reformers against the snubnosed Saturday Night Special because its bullet worked within the body with especially deadly erraticism? The "nice" .22s of the highest price and the longest barrel manufactured by élite U.S. gun companies send forth bullets that operate in exactly the same fashion. Did the reformers think there was something especially evil in the combination of small size and small price? If murder's the game, cheap small handguns aren't necessary; it can be played on a U.S.-made

.22 rifle that costs no more than $25; about 10 percent of the murders are committed with rifles and the .22 is the most popular. Did they feel that the bigger calibers, for some mysterious reason, were safer or, for some even more mysterious reason, more civilized? Garfield and McKinley and George Wallace would not likely agree. And before anyone tries to assign a particularly devastating social reputation to the Saturday Night Special, let him first consider that no part of any war has ever been fought with the species.

History will not support the snooty caste-consciousness in gun traffic. All guns are terrible, no doubt, but one kind no more than the others. And if there is virtue in any gun, no gun is completely without it. "The Saturday Night Special is a useless thing," Assistant Treasury Secretary Rossides said with a Ciceronian gesture, "and therefore, it can stand a federal ban." On the contrary, it can be very useful even to people of high position and great wealth, to people of all levels who want a gun only for one occasion and a small gun at that, and especially to those who need almost an extension of the hand to wave goodbye. When he contemplated suicide after being censured by the Senate, did Senator Dodd, supposedly the enemy of the Saturday Night Special, turn to a product of his beneficiary, Colt Industries? No, he got his staff to bring him a .25-caliber foreign cheapie (it was his willpower, not the gun, that misfired).* When Dorothy, the former wife of Gen. John ("Tommy Gun") Thompson's son, Marcellus, decided to end her life because of ill health, she chose to put her mouth around the muzzle and her finger on the trigger not of one

---

* Suicide is the kindest explanation to be given for Dodd's pocketing the little gun and taking it to the Senate chambers, and it is the reason that his staff has heretofore publicly given. But Perian believes that Dodd might have taken the gun to the Senate with homicide in mind. Senator John Stennis had chaired the ethics committee that censured Dodd for misusing campaign contributions; but worse, in Dodd's mind, was the fact that Stennis had subjected him to cheap moralizing. On one occasion Stennis had said to him, "Down in my country [Mississippi] when a boy gives you a nickel for your campaign, that's what you spend it on. You don't buy candy with it." Dodd hated Stennis for his piousness.

of the historic weapons her former father-in-law had made famous, but instead spoiled the silence of her St. Regis Hotel suite with the more demure pop of a dainty automatic pistol, the strictly measured quality of which would have qualified it as a Saturday Night Special. She had chosen well. For a lady like Dorothy, who was once the favored dancing partner of the Prince of Wales, what more fitting death weapon than one commemorating Saturday, the most social night of the week?

THE TROUBLE WITH E PLURIBUS UNUM

I have no wise summation for this book, no dramatic, pithy wrapup. If the gun scene is more or less today as it was in November 1963, that's to be expected. John Kennedy's assassination, and all the assassinations that preceded and followed, and all the murders and armed robberies and suicides and bushwhackings—all this gunplay is simply part of America. It's us. We enjoy it more than we will admit. We experience the assassination of a Kennedy with all the wailing gusto that an Irish wake deserves. We are honest enough to admit, by implication at least, that gunplay involving some of our lesser celebrities doesn't always, or uniformly, make us feel nearly so depressed. When Martin Luther King was shot, John Connally of Texas as much as said it was good riddance (Connally's eulogy: "He did not deserve assassination but he contributed much to the chaos, and the strife, and the confusion, and the uncertainty in this country"), and Senator Robert Byrd, now the Senate Whip, made much the same response. From the other ideological perspective, liberals did not seem terribly broken up when George Wallace was shot (that is, they were mainly worried about how much help this would be to the reelection of Nixon), and the shooting of Senator John Stennis inspired quite a few liberal cracks, discreetly made, about the irony of this happening to the biggest gunman of them all—a reference, of course, to Stennis's chairmanship of the Armed Services Committee. Assassination is not a part of our politics, but we are such an enthusiastically political nation that we will find a place for the assassinations that are thrust upon us. We are like the old Wobbly who, shortly after Huey Long's assassination, told a colleague, "I deplore the use of murder in politics, but I wouldn't give two cents to bring the sonofabitch back to life."

Ordinary murders do not really bother us as much as we sometimes pretend because, after all, only one out of every twenty-two thousand persons will go out that way in any given year, and, as we have suggested here, we can be relatively certain that the one person will be an unclean sort. Armed robbers are much more irritating because they cannot be trusted to stay on their own side of the tracks; but even armed robbers have a place in the nation's heart because they touch, in a maverick sort of way, the theme of capitalism we love so much. Are they not, after all, simply nomadic low-overhead merchants with a kind of hard-sell? Shortly before Carl V. ("Boo Boo") Green died of an overdose of heroin, he talked with Shelby Coffey, editor of the Washington *Post*'s magazine, about the mechanics of pulling a grocery store holdup, a type of enterprise Boo Boo was very experienced at. "Everybody has a job to do and if he does it like he's supposed to, ain't no trouble at all," Boo Boo explained. "Got one man whose job is to watch the door. Got one man whose job is to hold a gun on the customers. Got one man whose job is to get the money out of the register. And *your* job [meaning Whitey, the store manager] is to shut up and hand over the money so nobody gets hurt." As forced mergers go, Boo Boo described one as neatly compatible with the business ideals of America as most of the mergers approved by the Justice Department. Some of the great family fortunes of this nation were developed out of the same strict attention to everyone's just doing his job. Such Calvinism is, after all, closely allied to crime.

In other words, all the dark deeds that are supposed to persuade us to change our ways do not really add up to much of an influence. We will never reform. We will go on being what we are; and what we are is a people who are, in fact, much nicer and more genteel and peaceful than might be expected, considering our background. At an appropriate moment Chicago's Mayor Daley once cried, "My God, we've had the killing of a President and his brother, the assassination of an outstanding religious leader, and now we have the shooting of a Presidential candidate. . . . My God, what kind of society have we?" The answer is, the kind of society that elects Mayor Daleys. We have a trashy society. Emma Lazarus's most famous lines from the poem at the base of the Statue of Liberty are words supposedly uttered by our patroness:

> "Give me your tired, your poor.
> Your huddled masses yearning to breathe free,
> The wretched refuse of your teeming shore.
> Send these, the homeless, tempest-tost to me. . . ."

And the rest of the world did just that. We became the world's greatest experiment in landfill. America is built on an awesome amount of wretched refuse. But if we are trashy, at least we are trashy in that grand and gloriously anarchistic-qua-democratic manner that no other part of the world has ever been able to develop or enjoy, and it is because of this characteristic that the gun industrialists find us such suckers for their merchandise. They know the right social nerves to touch, the right patriotic ligaments to twang, the right slogans to keep repeating. "God made man, but Colonel Colt made him equal." It's a cheap, flip, simplistic, wahoo, strutty way to view life. It's the kind of sloganeering that has made us the most violent major nation in the history of the modern world. That's what I tell myself, but those genes that came over to supply labor for Oglethorpe's debtor colony keep responding the wrong way.

Bibliography

The Annals of the American Academy of Political and Social Science, Vol. 364 (March 1966) and Vol. 391 (September 1970).

Arendt, Hannah, *On Violence* (Harcourt Brace Jovanovich, 1969, 1970).

Bakal, Carl, *The Right to Bear Arms* (McGraw-Hill, 1966).

Billroth, Theodor, M. D., *Historical Studies on the Nature and Treatment of Gunshot Wounds From the Fifteenth Century to the Present Time* (New Haven, Nathan Smith Medical Club, 1933).

Bowman, Hank W., *Famous Guns from the Smithsonian Collection* (Arco, 1967).

Brant, Irving, *The Bill of Rights* (Bobbs-Merrill, 1965).

Brooks, Stewart M., *Our Murdered Presidents: The Medical Story* (Frederick Fell, 1966).

Clark, Ramsey, *Crime in America* (Simon and Schuster, 1970).

Conant, Ralph, *The Prospects for Revolution. A Study of Riots, Civil Disobedience, and Insurrection in Contemporary America* (Harper's Magazine Press, 1971).

Cook, Fred J., *The FBI Nobody Knows* (Pyramid Books, 1965).

The Crime Commission of New York State. *Special Reports to the Commission on Firearms Legislation and Psychiatric and Expert Testimony in Criminal Cases* (Albany, 1928).

Davidson, Bill R., *To Keep and Bear Arms* (Arlington House, 1969).

Depperman, W. H., *Shooter's Choice* (World, 1952).

Elman, Robert, *Fired in Anger. The Personal Handguns of American Heroes and Villains* (Doubleday, 1968).

Estey, George F. and Doris A. Hunter, *Violence. A Reader in the Ethics of Action* (Xerox College Publishing, 1971).

Fogelson, Robert, *Violence as Protest. A Study of Riots and Ghettos* (Doubleday, 1971).

Frederick, Karl T., "Pistol Regulation," *The Journal of Criminal Law and Criminology, including the American Journal of Police Science* III: 1 (January–February 1932), III: 3 (September–October 1932).

Girard, Maj. Alfred C., "The Latest Experiments on the Effect of Small Calibre Rifles" (U.S. Army pamphlet).

Graham, Hugh Davis and Ted Robert Gurr, eds., *Violence in America: Historical and Comparative Perspectives. A Staff Report to the National Commission on the Causes and Prevention of Violence* (U.S. Government Printing Office, June 1969).

Hatcher, Maj. Julian S., *Textbook of Pistols and Revolvers. Their Ammunition, Ballistics and Use* (Small-Arms Technical Publishing Co., 1935).

Haven, Charles and Frank Belden, *A History of the Colt Revolver and Other Arms by Colt's Patent Fire Arms Manufacturing Co. from 1936 to 1940* (William Morrow, 1940. Reprinted by Bonanza Books).

Heaps, Williard A., *Riots, U.S.A., 1765–1970* (Seabury Press, 1970).

Helmer, William, *The Gun That Made the Twenties Roar* (Macmillan, 1969).

Hofstadter, Richard & Michael Wallace, eds., *American Violence: A Documentary History* (Vintage, 1971).

Horan, James D., *Desperate Men: Revelations from the Sealed Pinkerton Files* (Putnam's, 1949).

Interstate and Foreign Commerce Subcommittee, House of Representatives, Seventy-first Congress, Second Session, Hearings on several bills pending before the committee to regulate the interstate shipment of firearms, April 1930 (U.S. Government Printing Office, 1930).

Judiciary Committee, House of Representatives, Ninetieth Congress, First Session, Hearings on H.R.5037, 5038, 5384, 5385, and 5386 (Anti-crime Program). Serial No. 3, March–April 1967 (U.S. Government Printing Office).

Juvenile Delinquency Subcommittee, Judiciary Committee, Senate, Various hearings: On Interstate Traffic in Mail-Order Firearms, 1963; On Amendments to Federal Firearms Act, 1965; On Amendments to Federal Firearms Act, 1967; On bills to Register Firearms, Establish a National Firearms Registry, and Disarm Lawless Persons, 1968; On various Senate resolutions, 1969; On Amendments to 1968 Gun Control Act to Prohibit the Sale of Saturday Night Special Handguns, 1971 (U.S. Government Printing Office).

Keith, Elmer, *Shotguns by Keith* (Stackpole, 1967).

"Kerner Report," U.S. Riot Commission *Report of the National Advisory Commission on Civil Disorders* (Bantam Books, 1968).

Knudten, Richard D., *Crime in a Complex Society: An Introduction to Criminology* (The Dorsey Press, 1970).

Kobler, John, *Capone. The Life and World of Al Capone* (Putnam's, 1971).

Lindsay, Merrill, *One Hundred Great Guns: An Illustrated History of Firearms* (Walker & Co., 1967).

Lowenthal, Max, *The Federal Bureau of Investigation* (Harcourt Brace Jovanovich, 1950).

Lyon, Peter, *The Wild, Wild West* (Funk & Wagnalls, 1969).

McAdoo, William, *When the Court Takes a Recess* (Dutton, 1924).

Meagher, Sylvia, *Accessories After the Fact: The Warren Commission, The Authorities and The Report* (Bobbs-Merrill, 1967).

Nelson, Bruce, *Land of the Dacotahs* (University of Nebraska Press, 1967).

O'Connor, Richard, *Wild Bill Hickok* (Doubleday, 1959).

Peterson, Harold L., *A History of Firearms* (Scribner's, 1961).

Prassel, Frank Richard, *The Western Peace Officer. A Legacy of Law and Order* (University of Oklahoma Press, 1972).

President's Commission on Law Enforcement and Administration of Justice, *The Challenge of Crime in a Free Society* (Avon, 1968).

Radzinowicz, Leon and Marvin E. Wolfgang, eds., *Crime and Justice. Vol. 1: The Criminal in Society; Vol. 2: The Criminal in the Arms of the Law* (Basic Books, 1971).

Serven, James E., ed., *The Collecting of Guns* (Stackpole, 1964. Reprinted by Bonanza Books).

Summers, Marvin R. and Thomas E. Barth, eds., *Law and Order in a Democratic Society* (Charles E. Merrill, 1970).

Thayer, George, *The War Business. The International Trade in Armaments* (Simon and Schuster, 1969).

Toland, John, *The Dillinger Days* (Random House, 1963).

Touhy, Roger with Ray Brennan, *The Stolen Years* (Pennington Press, 1959).

Trefethen, James B., compiler, and James E. Serven, ed., *Americans and Their Guns* (Stackpole, 1967).

Ways and Means Committee, House of Representatives, Seventy-third Congress, Second Session, Hearings on H.R.9066 (National Firearms Act). April–May 1934 (U.S. Government Printing Office).

Ways and Means Committee, House of Representatives, Eighty-ninth Congress. First Session. Hearings on Proposed Amendments to Firearms Acts, Parts 1 and 2, July 1965 (U.S. Government Printing Office).

Wellman, Paul I., *Dynasty of Western Outlaws* (Doubleday, 1961).

Whitehead, Don, *The FBI Story* (Random House, 1956).

Wills, Garry, *The Second Civil War: Arming for Armageddon* (New American Library, 1968).

Winant, Lewis, *Firearms Curiosa* (Bonanza Books, 1955).

INDEX